Portugal's homegrown port-wine
MATT MUNRO / LONELY PLANET ©

Plan Your Trip
Portugal's Top 12

MATT MUNRO / LONELY PLANET ©

Lisbon

History, culture and pumping nightlife

The capital of the Portuguese world, Lisbon (p37) is a fascinating place of trundling trams, breathtaking architecture and thumping nightlife. The Alfama district, with its labyrinthine alleyways, hidden courtyards and curving, shadow-filled lanes, is a magical place in which to delve into the soul of the city. It's also where you are most likely to hear fado, the melancholy music of the city's old working-class districts.

1

Porto

Portugal's romantic second city

It would be hard to dream up a more romantic city than Portugal's second largest. Laced with narrow pedestrian laneways, Porto (p89) is blessed with baroque churches, epic theatres and sprawling plazas. Its Ribeira district – a Unesco World Heritage Site – is just a short walk from centuries-old port wineries where you can sip the world's best port. A sense of renewal – in the form of modern architecture, cosmopolitan restaurants and a vibrant arts scene – is palpable.

2

INAQUIM/GETTY IMAGES ©

Algarve

Stunning beaches, secluded islands

Sunseekers have much to celebrate when it comes to beaches. Along Portugal's south coast, the Algarve (p125) is home to a wildly varied coastline. There are sandy islands reachable only by boat, dramatic cliff-backed shores, rugged rarely visited beaches and people-packed sands near buzzing nightlife. Days are spent playing in the waves, taking long ocean-front strolls and surfing memorable breaks. Praia da Marinha (p129)

3

Évora

Queen of the Alentejo

One of Portugal's most beautifully preserved medieval towns, Évora (p151) is an enchanting place to spend several days delving into the Portuguese past. Within the chunky, 14th-century stone walls built to protect the town from invaders, Évora's narrow, winding lanes lead to striking architectural works: an elaborate medieval cathedral (pictured) and cloisters, Roman ruins and a picturesque town square. Historic and aesthetic virtues aside, Évora is also a lively university town, and its many attractive restaurants serve up excellent, hearty Alentejan cuisine.

Rio Douro Valley

Breathtaking valley wine route

The exquisite Alto Douro wine country (p165) is the oldest demarcated wine region on earth. Its steeply terraced hills, stitched together with craggy vines that have produced luscious wines for centuries, loom either side of the Rio Douro. Whether you get here by driving the impossibly scenic back roads, or by train or boat from Porto, take the time to hike, cruise and taste. Countless vintners receive guests for tours, tastings and overnight stays, and if you find one that's still family owned, you may sample something very old and very special.

ZOONAR GMBH/ALAMY ©

Braga

Portugal's lively third city

Portugal's third-largest city is blessed with terrific restaurants, a vibrant university and raucous festivals, but when it comes to historic sites it is unparalleled in Portugal. Braga (p179) has a remarkable 12th-century cathedral, a 14th-century church, and not one but two sets of Roman ruins, countless 17th-century plazas and an 18th-century palace turned museum. Then there's that splendid baroque staircase: Escadaria do Bom Jesus. Church at the top of Escadaria do Bom Jesus (p184)

SÉRGIO NOGUEIRA/ALAMY ©

Coimbra

Portugal's best-known university town

Portugal's atmospheric college town, Coimbra (p191) rises steeply
from the Rio Mondego to a medieval quarter housing one of Europe's
oldest universities. Students roam the narrow streets clad in black
capes, while strolling fado musicians give free concerts. Kids can
keep busy at Portugal dos Pequenitos, a theme park with miniature
versions of Portuguese monuments; grown-ups will appreciate the
upper town's student-driven nightlife. Porta Férrea (p195)

7

Aveiro

Portugal's answer to Venice

Every visitor to this coastal city (p205) sooner or later finds themself aboard a *moliceiro*, a traditionally fashioned boat that was once used to dredge up seaweed from the bottom of the town's canals. Retired from service many years ago, these have now been put to work as a tourist attraction. Away from the water Aveiro is a lively place of museums, great seafood restaurants and cafes selling sickly sweet *ovos moles*.

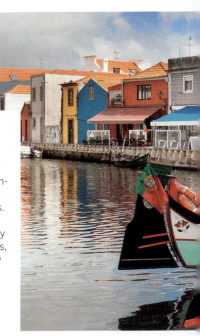

ELENA SB/SHUTTERSTOCK ©

9

Sintra

Fairy-tale palaces and castles

Less than an hour by train from the capital, Sintra (p217) feels like another world. Like an illustration from a fairy tale, Sintra is sprinkled with stone-walled taverns and has a whitewashed palace looming over it. Forested hillsides form the backdrop to the village's storybook setting, with imposing castles, mystical gardens, strange mansions and centuries-old monasteries hidden among the woodlands. The fog that sweeps in by night adds another layer of mystery, and cool evenings are best spent fireside in one of Sintra's many charming B&Bs. Far left: Palácio Nacional da Pena (p221); left: Palácio de Monserrate (p223)

JOSE ELIAS/STOCKPHOTOSART · EVENTS/ALAMY ©

Óbidos

An enchanting walled town

Wandering through the tangle of ancient streets of Óbidos (p229) is enchanting any time of year, but come during one of its festivals and you'll be in for a special treat. Whether attending a jousting match or climbing the castle walls at the medieval fair (pictured), or delving into the written world at Fólio – Portugal's newest international literature festival – you couldn't ask for a better backdrop.

TOMASZ WOZNIAK/500PX ©

Cabo do São Vicente

The edge of the ancient world

It's thrilling standing at Europe's most southwestern edge (p239), a headland of barren cliffs to which Portuguese sailors used to bid a nervous farewell as they sailed past during Portugal's golden years of exploration. The windswept cape is redolent of history – if you squint hard (really hard), you'll see the ghost of Vasco da Gama sailing past. These days, a fortress and lighthouse perch on the cape and a new museum beautifully highlights Portugal's maritime-navigation history.

ROBERTHARDING/ALAMY ©

Batalha

A marvellous monastery

This medieval Christian monument (p254) – a Unesco World Heritage site since 1983 – constitutes one of Portugal's greatest national treasures and one of Iberia's finest chunks of Gothic architecture. The monastery has a certain magic with the whimsy of Manueline adornments and the haunting roofless shell of the unfinished Capelas Imperfeitas wowing the thousands of tourists who make a pilgrimage to Batalha (p251) here every year.

Plan Your Trip
Need to Know

When to Go

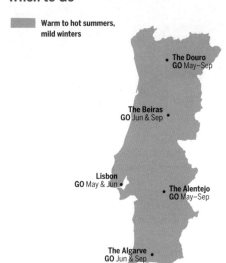

Warm to hot summers, mild winters

The Douro
GO May–Sep

The Beiras
GO Jun & Sep

Lisbon
GO May & Jun

The Alentejo
GO May–Sep

The Algarve
GO Jun & Sep

High Season (Jul & Aug)
○ Expect big crowds in the Algarve and coastal resort areas.

○ Sweltering temperatures are commonplace.

○ Warmer ocean temperatures.

Shoulder Season (Apr–Jun & Sep–Nov)
○ Wild flowers and mild days are ideal for hikes.

○ Lively festivals take place in June.

○ Crowds and prices are average.

Low Season (Dec–Mar)
○ Shorter, rainier days with freezing temperatures at higher elevations.

○ Lower prices, fewer crowds.

○ Frigid ocean temperatures.

Currency
Euro (€)

Language
Portuguese

Visas
Generally not required for stays of up to 90 days; some nationalities will need a Schengen visa.

Money
ATMs widely available, except in the smallest villages. Credit cards accepted in mid-range and high-end establishments.

Mobile Phones
Local SIM cards can be used in unlocked European, Australian and quad-band US mobiles.

Time
Portugal, like Britain, is on GMT/UTC in winter and GMT/UTC plus one hour in summer. This puts it an hour earlier than Spain year-round. Clocks are set forward by an hour on the last Sunday in March and back on the last Sunday in October.

Daily Costs

Budget: Less than €50

- Dorm bed: €15–22
- Basic hotel room for two: from €30
- Lunch special at a family-run restaurant: €7–9
- Second-class train ticket from Lisbon to Faro: from €22

Midrange: €50–120

- Double room in a midrange hotel: €50–100
- Lunch and dinner in a midrange restaurant: €22–35
- Admission to museums: €2–6

Top End: More than €120

- Boutique hotel room: from €120
- Dinner for two in a top restaurant: from €80
- Three-day surf course: €150

Useful Websites

- **Lonely Planet** (www.lonelyplanet.com/portugal) Destination information, hotel bookings, traveller forum and more.
- **Portugal Tourism** (www.visitportugal.com) Portugal's official tourism site.
- **Portugal News** (www.theportugalnews.com) The latest news and gossip in Portugal.
- **Wines of Portugal** (www.winesofportugal.info) Fine overview of Portugal's favourite beverage, covering wine regions, grape varieties and wine routes.

Opening Hours

Opening hours vary throughout the year. We provide high-season opening hours; hours will generally decrease in the shoulder and low seasons.

Banks 8.30am to 3pm Monday to Friday
Bars 7pm to 2am
Cafes 9am to 7pm
Clubs 11pm to 4am Thursday to Saturday
Restaurants noon to 3pm and 7pm to 10pm
Shopping malls 10am to 10pm
Shops 9.30am to noon and 2pm to 7pm Monday to Friday, 10am to 1pm Saturday

Arriving in Portugal

Aeroporto de Lisboa (Lisbon; p301) Metro trains allow convenient access to downtown (€1.90, 20 minutes to the centre, frequent departures from 6.30am to 1am). The AeroBus (€3.50) departs every 20 minutes from 7am to 11pm, while a taxi to the centre will cost around €15 and take around 15 minutes.

Aeroporto Francisco Sá Carneiro (Porto; p301) Metro trains run frequently to the city centre (€2.45, including €0.50 Andante card) and take about 45 minutes. A taxi will cost €20 to €25 and take around 30 to 60 minutes.

Aeroporto de Faro (Faro; p301) Buses run to the city centre (€2.20) every 30 minutes on weekdays and every two hours on weekends. A taxi will cost around €13 (20 minutes).

Getting Around

Transport in Portugal is reasonably priced, quick and efficient.

Train Extremely affordable, with a decent network between major towns from north to south. Visit Comboios de Portugal (www.cp.pt.) for schedules and prices.

Car Useful for visiting small villages, national parks and other regions with minimal public transport. Cars can be hired in major towns and cities. Drive on the right.

Bus Cheaper and slower than trains. Useful for remote villages that aren't serviced by trains. Infrequent service on weekends.

For more on **getting around**, see p302

Plan Your Trip
Hot Spots For...

Food & Drink

Though not one of the world's celebrated cuisines, no one can deny that Portugal serves up some tasty fare, especially meat, seafood, wine and desserts.

Water Fun

Portugal's coastline is all about getting out onto or under the water, whether that be on a surfboard, with flippers on your feet or in a boat.

Architecture

Portugal possesses a wealth of architectural heritage, from the fairy-tale castles and palaces of Sintra to the Manueline creations of the 16th century.

Diverse Culture

Though small, Portugal's cultural landscape is pretty diverse, from the Algarve's Islamic-era heritage, through Lisbon's melancholic fado music to Porto's wine culture.

Lisbon (p37) As the Portuguese capital, Lisbon has the greatest variety when it comes to dining, with top chefs plating up imaginative creations.

Pastel de Nata (p93) Lisbon is the birthplace of the famous egg custard tart.

Douro (p165) The Unesco-listed Douro Valley, where Portugal's finest wines are produced, can be toured by car or scenic train line.

Quinta do Vallado (p168) A wine-tasting session at this winery established in 1716.

Algarve (p125) Seafood dominates menus along the coast and this is definitely bivalve zone, with hordes of fresh clams, oysters, mussels, cockles and whelks.

Cataplana A Portuguese version of paella that always comes in servings for two.

Algarve (p125) Portugal's south coast is water sports central. And the beaches are pretty good, too.

Ilha da Barreta (p129) This island is accessed by boat through nature-filled lagoons.

Cabo do São Vicente (p239) Surfing is as big as the Atlantic's thundering waves at Portugal's southwestern-most tip.

Sagres (p243) A surfing paradise with a great après-surf scene come sundown.

Aveiro (p205) The Atlantic's chilly waters come to you in the shape of a network of canals in this coastal settlement south of Porto.

Boat Tours (p208) Take a canal trip aboard a *moliceiro*, a traditional seaweed dredging boat.

Lisbon (p37) Lisbon is one of Europe's most attractive capitals, and this despite the 1755 earthquake that almost razed it to the ground.

Mosteiro dos Jerónimos (p46) A superlative example of the Manueline style.

Porto (p89) The architectural feature most prominent in Portugal's second city is *azulejos*, the beautiful hand-painted tiles that adorn many buildings.

São Bento Train Station (p105) Beautifully adorned railway station.

Sintra (p217) A short hop from Lisbon, this area of wooded hills has some of the finest architectural monuments in the country.

Castelo dos Mouros (p220) A dramatic castle with amazing views inland and out to sea.

Lisbon (p37) Portugal has given the world a very distinct type of music – the nostalgia-induced fado, a style that emerged from its working-class districts.

Fado Nights (p83) Many bars and restaurants put on fado performances.

Algarve (p125) Across the south coast remnants and reminders of the centuries the region spent under Moorish rule remain.

Silves Castle (p131) This huge, 11th-century hilltop castle was built by the Moors.

Vila Nova de Gaia (p96) Across the river from Porto's centre, this hillside boasts some of the best wine lodges in the country.

Graham's (p96) An original British-founded wine cellar, established way back in 1820.

Plan Your Trip
Local Life

Activities

Outdoors enthusiasts will find plenty to appreciate in Portugal. With a whopping 830km of coastline, there's first-rate surfing all along the Atlantic's wild coast. There are also countless opportunities for all kinds of other water sports, particularly in the Algarve. Inland, rolling cork fields, granite peaks and precipitous river gorges form the backdrop for a host of other activities – from walking and bird-watching to horse riding and paragliding. Golf is big in Portugal, especially along the Algarve coast, and there are many exhilarating opportunities for mountain biking. Football (soccer) is a national obsession and watching a match is a great experience.

Shopping

There are many great markets throughout Portugal, where you can browse the local wares. In Portugal's north, Barcelos hosts a particularly famous Thursday market. Crafts to look for in Portugal include ceramics (painted bowls, mini wine jugs) and tapestries.

There's also great and quite affordable wine and port to be had. Weird and wonderful creations from cork are a common memento from the Algarve. Food such as salami, olive oil, cheese and myriad sweet things also make respectable souvenirs. For self-caterers and picnickers these markets also provide a source of fresh and sometimes exotic produce.

Entertainment

Fado, that mournful, uniquely Portuguese sound, is famous in the capital where it was born. Lisbon naturally has a good range of dinner clubs and small restaurants where you can catch live shows by some of the best performers. Outside of Lisbon, and to a lesser extent Coimbra, fado is not as common. You'll find concerts (indie rock, pop, folk) at bigger towns throughout the year. Portugal is a country of festivals with something going on in the big cities, and even in some smaller ones, throughout the year, but especially over the summer months. English-language theatre is rare, even in Lisbon.

Eating

Settling down to a meal with friends is one of life's great pleasures for the Portuguese, who take pride in simple but flavourful dishes. Seafood, roast meats, freshly baked bread and velvety wines are key staples in the everyday feast that is eating in Portugal. Every region has its own distinct specialities and themes – the Algarve is known for its seafood and *cataplana* (seafood stew), the north for its pork dishes, the Estremadura for its fish stews and Lisbon for its variety. One aspect of Portuguese cuisine visitors should not miss is its coffee and cake culture.

Drinking & Nightlife

Lisbon and Porto both have vibrant bars, lounges and dance clubs – Lisbon's scene is now a major European stop for all top

★ **Best Lisbon Fado Houses**

A Tasco do Chico (p84)

Senhor Fado (p84)

Parreirinha de Alfama (p84)

Mesa de Frades (p84)

A Baîuca (p85)

international DJs. In the Algarve, there's abundant nightlife all along the coast (Lagos is the epicentre for the party crowd) – drawing mostly a foreign clientele. Smaller cities such as Coimbra, Évora and Braga have smaller scenes, with a fairly laid-back vibe during the week, and livelier celebrations on weekends. In the small towns, things are generally pretty sedate.

From left: Praia de Dona Ana (p129), the Algarve; Pastries for sale at Feira de Barcelos (p188)

Plan Your Trip
Month by Month

February

Winter sees fewer crowds and lower prices along with abundant rainfall, particularly in the north. Coastal temperatures are cool but mild, while inland there are frigid days. Many resorts remain shuttered until spring.

♣ Carnaval

Portugal's Carnaval features much merry-making in the pre-Lenten celebrations. Loulé boasts the best parades, but Lisbon, Nazaré and Viana do Castelo all throw a respectable bash.

♣ Fantasporto

Porto's world-renowned two-week international festival (www.fantasporto.com) celebrates fantasy, horror and just plain weird films.

♣ Essência do Vinho

Oenophiles are in their element at this wine gathering (www.essenciadovinhoporto.com), held in late February in the sublime setting of Palácio da Bolsa. Some 3000 wines from 350 producers are available for tasting.

March

March days are rainy and chilly in much of Portugal, though the south sees more sunshine. Prices remain low, and travellers are few and far between.

♣ Festival Internacional do Chocolate

For several days early in the month Óbidos celebrates the sweet temptation of the cacao bean (www.festivalchocolate.cm-obidos.pt).

April

Spring arrives, bringing warmer temperatures and abundant sunshine in both the north and the south. Late April sees a profusion of wildflowers in the south.

♣ Semana Santa

The build-up to Easter is magnificent in the Minho's saintly Braga. During Holy Week, barefoot penitents process through the

★ **Best Festivals**

Carnaval, February

Queima das Fitas, May

Serralves em Festa, May

Festa de São João, June

Fado no Castelo, June

streets, past rows of makeshift altars, with an explosion of jubilation at the cathedral on the eve of Easter.

May

Lovely sunny weather and the lack of peak-season crowds make May an ideal time to visit. The beaches of the Algarve awake from their slumber and see a smattering of travellers passing through.

🎊 Queima das Fitas

Join the mayhem of the Burning of the Ribbons at the University of Coimbra (Portugal's Oxford), as students celebrate the end of the academic year with concerts, a parade and copious amounts of drinking (www.queimadasfitas.org).

🎊 Festa das Cruzes

Barcelos turns into a fairground of flags, flowers, coloured lights and open-air concerts at the Festival of the Crosses. The biggest days are 1 to 3 May. Monsanto, in

the Beiras, also celebrates, with singing and dancing beside a medieval castle.

🎊 Festa do Mar

Celebrating the age-old love of the sea (and the patron saints of fishers), this lively festival brings a flotilla of fishing boats to Nazaré's harbour, as well as a colourful parade of elaborately decorated floats. There's plenty of eating and drinking.

🎊 Fátima Romaris

Hundreds of thousands make the pilgrimage to Fátima each year to commemorate the apparitions of the Virgin (p287) that occurred on 13 May 1917. The pilgrimage also happens in October (12 and 13).

☆ Serralves em Festa

This huge cultural event (www.serralvesem festa.com) runs for 40 hours non-stop over one weekend in late May. Parque de Serralves hosts the main events, with concerts,

From left: Carnaval parade, Lisbon; Illuminated church facade during Festa das Cruzes, Barcelos avant-garde theatre and kids' activities. Other open-air events happen all over town.

June

Early summer is one of the liveliest times to visit, as the festival calendar is packed. Warm, sunny days are the norm, and while tourism picks up, the hordes have yet to arrive.

☆ Fado no Castelo

Lisbon's love affair with fado reaches a high point at this annual songfest held at the cinematic Castelo de São Jorge over three evenings in June.

⚒ Festa do Corpo de Deus

This religious fest happens all across northern Portugal on Corpus Christi but is liveliest in Monção, with an old-fashioned medieval fair, theatrical shows and over-the-top processions.

☆ Festival Med

Loulé's world-music festival (www.festival med.pt), held over three days, brings more than 50 bands playing an incredible variety of music. World cuisine accompanies the global beats.

⚒ Festa de São João

St John is the favourite up north, where Porto, Braga and Vila do Conde celebrate with elaborate processions, music and feasting, while folks go around whacking each other with plastic hammers.

⚒ Festas Populares

Celebrating the feast days of São João and São Pedro, Évora hosts a lively 12-day event that kicks off in late June. There's a traditional fairground, art exhibitions, gourmet food and drink, cultural events and sporting competitions.

July

The summer heat arrives, bringing sunseekers who pack the resorts of the Algarve. Lisbon and Porto also swell with crowds and prices peak in July and August.

☆ Festival Internacional de Folclore

The week-long International Folk Festival in late July brings costumed dancers and traditional groups to Porto.

⚔ Mercado Medieval

Don your armour and head to the castle grounds for this lively two-week medieval fair (www.mercadomedievalobidos.pt) in Óbidos. Attractions include wandering minstrels, jousting matches and plenty of grog. Other medieval fairs are held in Silves and other castle towns.

August

The mercury shoots up in August, with sweltering days best spent at the beach. This is Portugal's busiest tourist month, and reserving ahead is essential.

⚒ Festival do Marisco

Seafood lovers should not miss this grand culinary fest (www.festivaldomarisco.com) in Olhão. Highlights include regional specialities such as chargrilled fish, *caldeirada* (fish stew) and *cataplana* (a kind of Portuguese paella); there's also live music.

☆ Folkfaro

A musician's treat, Folkfaro (www.folkfaro. com) brings local and international folk performers to the city of Faro for staged and impromptu performances across town. Street fairs accompany the event.

☆ Noites Ritual Rock

Towards the end of summer, Porto hosts a free weekend-long rock bash that sees up-and-coming bands from around Portugal work big crowds at the Jardins do Palácio de Cristal.

⚒ Festa da Ria

Aveiro celebrates its canals and *moliceiros* (boats) in late August. Highlights include folk dancing and a *moliceiro* race, plus competitions for the best *moliceiro* murals.

Plan Your Trip
Get Inspired

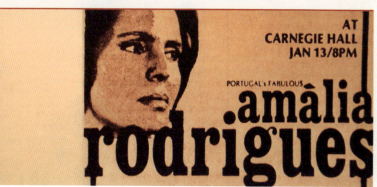

Read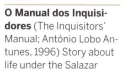

O Manual dos Inquisidores (The Inquisitors' Manual; António Lobo Antunes, 1996) Story about life under the Salazar dictatorship.

Memorial do Convento (Baltasar and Blimunda; José Saramago, 1982) Darkly comic 18th-century love story.

Livro do Desassossego (The Book of Disquiet; Fernando Pessoa, 1982) Literary masterpiece by Portugal's greatest poet.

Portugal: A Companion History (José Hermano Saraiva, 1997) An easily digestible history of the country written for the non-expert.

Food of Portugal (Jean Anderson, 1986) One of the best English-language Portuguese cookbooks.

Watch

A Lisbon Story (1994) Wim Wenders' love letter to Lisbon.

Letters from Fontainhas (1997–2006) Pedro Costa's art-house trilogy set in Lisbon.

Capitães de Abril (Captains of April; 2000) Overview of the 1974 Revolution of the Carnations.

Sangre de mi Sangre (Blood of My Blood; 2011) Oscar-nominated drama about the intricacies of life in poor suburban Lisbon.

Listen

Moura (2015) Latest album by fado (traditional song) superstar Ana Moura.

Art of Amália (1998) Compilation by one of fado's greats, Amália Rodrigues.

Best of Rui Veloso (2000) Portugal's legendary rock-balladeer.

10.000 Anos Depois Entre Vénus e Marte (10,000 Years Later Between Venus and Mars; 1978) José Cid's famous and oh-so-'70s progressive rock album.

Above: Poster for Amália Rodrigues exhibition, Centro Cultural de Belém, Lisbon

Plan Your Trip
Five-Day Itineraries

Lisbon & Around

Base yourself in Portugal's capital and explore its Manueline architecture, fado houses and museums before heading out to the chocolate-box vistas of Sintra, the walled town of Óbidos and the monastery at Batalha. This itinerary is possible by public transport.

4 Batalha (p251) A major monastery dating from the 15th century, but with many later Manueline additions making it one of the country's top architectural marvels.

3 Óbidos (p229) A quaintly beautiful walled town with heaps of architecture, interesting boutiques and a laid-back vibe.
🚌 50 mins to Batalha

2 Sintra (p217) A dramatic area of wooded hills, palaces and castles within easy reach of Lisbon. 🚌 40 mins to Lisbon then 🚌 1 hr to Óbidos

1 Lisbon (p37) Two days of vintage trams, fado, thumping nightlife, monasteries and museums.
🚌 40 mins to Sintra

South Coast

Sand, seafood and surfing are the three S's that define Portugal's holiday coast. The Algarve is an incredibly popular destination among British travellers, but it's not all about Irish pubs and fish 'n' chips – there's plenty of beauty and culture to discover, too.

3 Lagos (p140) This busy resort city has a superb beach, great nightlife and a tightly packed historical centre. 🚌 1 hr to Sagres

4 Sagres & Cabo de São Vicente (p239) Portugal's southwesternmost tip is a surfing centre as well as being steeped in history relating to the Age of Discoveries.

2 Faro (p136) Historical Faro is the buzzing gateway to the Algarve as well as the amazing Parque Natural da Ria Formosa. 🚌 2 hrs to Lagos

1 Tavira (p134) This eastern Algarve town is one of the coast's most charming. Take a day trip to the Ilha de Tavira. 🚌 1 hr to Faro

FROM LEFT: IRINASEN / GETTY IMAGES ©; HLPHOTO / SHUTTERSTOCK ©

Plan Your Trip
10-Day Itinerary

Porto & Around

Wine is the theme of this tipsy itinerary, from the wine bars of Porto to the ancient lodges of Vila Nova de Gaia to the vineyards of the Unesco-listed Douro Valley. Three or four days in Porto can be followed by a week exploring the Douro.

1 Porto (p89) Immerse yourself in historical Ribeira, do a spot of *azulejo*-spotting and visit the Museu da Misericórdia do Porto. 10 mins walk to Vila Nova de Gaia

2 Vila Nova de Gaia (p96) This hillside across the river from the city centre is where you'll find Porto's oldest wine lodges.
🚌 2 hrs to Douro Valley

3 Douro Valley (p165)
Spend a week sampling Portugal's best wines in its oldest wine-producing region, drinking in the dramatic views of the Douro Valley as you go. **3**

Plan Your Trip
Two-Week Itinerary

North to South

This odyssey from north to south takes in the vast majority of Portugal's major sights, including Lisbon, Porto and the Algarve. This journey is perfectly feasible by bus and train, but a hire car will, of course, speed things up considerably.

1 Braga (p179) Portugal's third-largest city is a place of narrow lanes, baroque churches, religious festivals and one remarkable cathedral. 🚌 1 hr to Porto

2 Porto (p89) Spend at least two days sampling Porto's heady mix of port wine, *azulejos* and impressive riverside location. 🚌 1¼ hrs to Coimbra

3 Coimbra (p191) Call in at the hilltop Velha Universidade (Old University) before enjoying some student nightlife and Coimbra's own take on fado. 🚌 2 hrs to Lisbon

5 Évora (p151) Few Portuguese cities boast the diversity of architecture that Évora does. A ring of defensive town walls contains Roman and medieval sites. 🚌 4 hrs to Faro

4 Lisbon (p37) You'll need at least three days to cover the basics in Lisbon, with regular breaks for the city's signature egg custard tarts. 🚌 2 hrs to Évora

6 Faro (p136) The de facto capital of the Algarve has history, food, architecture and an easy-going vibe. 🚌 to Lagos then 🚌 to Sagres 5 hrs

7 Sagres & Cabo de São Vicente (p239) The dramatic cliffs at Cabo de São Vicente mark Europe's most southwesterly point. It's also a big surfing location.

Plan Your Trip
Family Travel

Portugal for Kids

The great thing about Portugal for children is its manageable size and the range of sights and activities on offer. There's so much to explore and that can catch the imagination, even for those with very short attention spans.

The Algarve has to be the best kid-pleasing destination in Portugal, with endless beaches, zoos, water parks, horse-riding outfitters and boat trips on offer. Kids will also be happy in Lisbon and its outlying provinces. There are trams, puppet shows, a huge aquarium, a toy museum, horse-drawn carriages, castles, parks and playgrounds.

As for fairy-tale places, Portugal has these in spades. Some children enjoy visiting churches if it means they can light a candle, and they'll enjoy the make-believe of the castles and palaces sprinkled about the country. In towns, hop-on, hop-off tours can be good for saving small legs, and miniature resort trains often cause more excitement than you would have thought possible.

Kids are welcome just about everywhere and the Portuguese are generally very kind towards them. They even get literary: the late Nobel Prize–winning author José Saramago wrote a charming children's fable, *The Tale of the Unknown Island*, available in English.

Portugal for Babies

○ The Portuguese are generally quite laid-back about breastfeeding in public as long as some attempt at discretion is made.

○ Formula (including organic brands) and disposable nappies (diapers) are widely available at most pharmacies and grocery stores.

○ *Turismos* (tourist offices), as well as most hotels and guest houses, can recommend babysitters.

○ Keep your baby hydrated in the summer months, especially on the beaches of the Algarve and in big cities such as Lisbon and Porto.

MIKADUN / SHUTTERSTOCK ©

★ Best for Kids

Museu de Arte, Arquitetura e Tecnologia (p62)

Oceanário (p65)

Museu da Marioneta (p66)

Skygarden (p199)

Algarve beaches (p128)

Aveiro boat trips (p208)

Eating with Kids

Portuguese restaurateurs are consistently glad to see junior diners. Kids' portions are almost always available, high chairs can always be found and staff are very friendly and forgiving towards children. Less formal cafes and bakeries are superb places to feed tots – we've yet to encounter a child in Portugal who hadn't discovered the joys of a *pastel de nata* (custard tart)! A glass of warm milk can cost as little as €0.50 and kids love freshly squeezed juices.

Getting Around

Children aged under five travel for free; those aged from five to 12 go for half price. This is true on the trains and you'll find bus drivers on local services will often just wave you to a seat when they see a child getting on. Journeys are rarely long enough for niggliness to set in. Long-distance coaches always have a toilet on board.

Annoyances

Nothing is ever perfect and there are aspects of family travel in Portugal that can be irksome.

❍ The message about kids and sugar hasn't quite reached Portugal. Often children's drinks come with extra sachets of sugar.

❍ Some Portuguese have the habit of ruffling the hair of blond children they see in the street – some parents may not be comfortable with this.

❍ Health and safety is not a priority at most castles in Portugal – missing railings, exposed walkways etc abound. Keep hold of those tiny hands if you see a dangerous section coming up.

From left: Museu de Arte, Arquitetura e Tecnologia (p62); Oceanário (p65)

Castelo de
São Jorge

Padrão dos Descobrimentos, Belém

Arriving in Lisbon

Aeroporto de Lisboa Direct flights to major international hubs including London, New York, Paris and Frankfurt.

Sete Rios bus station The main long-distance bus terminal.

Gare do Oriente bus station Bus services to the north and to Spain.

Gare do Oriente train station Lisbon's largest train station.

Sleeping

Lisbon has an array of boutique hotels, upmarket hostels and both modern and old-fashioned guest houses. Be sure to book ahead for high season (July to September). A word to those with weak knees and/or heavy bags: many guest houses lack lifts, meaning you'll have to haul your luggage up three flights or more. If this disconcerts, be sure to book a place with a lift.

Miradouro (lookout) and rooftop bar

Lisbon's Nightlife

Late-night street parties in Cais do Sodré and Bairro Alto, sunset ginjinhas on Rossio's sticky cobbles, drinks with indie kids in Santa Catarina – Lisbon has one of Europe's most eclectic nightlife scenes.

Great For...

☑ Don't Miss

Savour a craft cocktail at Cinco Lounge (p82) courtesy of an award-winning, London-born mixologist.

Cais do Sodré

For years Cais do Sodré was the haunt of whisky-slugging sailors craving after-dark sleaze. In late 2011, the district went from seedy to stylish. Rua Nova do Carvalho was painted pink and the call girls were sent packing, but the edginess and decadence on which Lisbon thrives remains. Now party central, its boho bars, live-music venues and burlesque clubs are perfect for a late-night bar crawl. When someone refers to Pink Street, they mean here.

Bairro Alto & Harbour Area

Bairro Alto is like a student at a house party: wasted on cheap booze, flirty and everybody's friend. At dusk, the nocturnal hedonist rears its head with bars trying to out-decibel each other, hash peddlers

Rua Nova do Carvalho

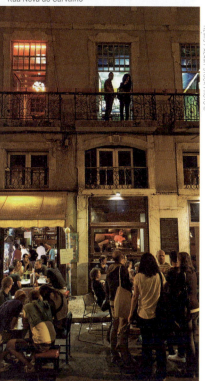

HEMIS / ALAMY STOCK PHOTO ©

❶ Need to Know

Top nightlife neighbourhoods are Cais do Sodré, Bairro Alto, Alfama and the harbour area.

✗ Take a Break

There are countless places to eat amid the revelry. **Cafe Tati** (☎213 461 279; www.cafetati.blogspot.com; Rua da Ribeira Nova 36; mains €7-8; ⊙11am-1am Tue-Sun; 🛜) has a hip retro feel and is a great place to grab a coffee.

★ Top Tip

Locals don't even think about showing up at a club before 2am.

lurking in the shadows and kamikaze taxi drivers forcing kerbside sippers to leap aside. For a more sophisticated and more artistically minded crowd, head a few blocks south to Bica.

The dockside duo of Doca de Alcântara and Doca de Santo Amaro harbour wall-to-wall bars with a preclubbing vibe. Many occupy revamped warehouses, with terraces facing the river and the lit-up Ponte 25 de Abril. Most people taxi here, but you can take the train from Cais do Sodré to Alcântara Mar or catch tram 15 from Praça da Figueira.

Clubbing Tips

Though getting in is not as much of a beauty contest as in other capitals, you'll stand a better chance of slipping past the

fashion police if you dress smartish and don't rock up on your lonesome. Most clubs charge entry (around €5 to €20, which usually includes a drink or two) and some operate a card-stamping system to ensure you spend a minimum amount. Many close Sunday and Monday.

Keep in mind club security has the right to dramatically inflate cover charges (€250 in some cases!) in order to discourage entry for those they deem to be potential trouble, whether due to level of intoxication or any other reason. Yes, it's discriminatory, but unfortunately it's perfectly legal.

Something different

Nightlife in Alfama revolves mostly around fado – the neighbourhood packs in a wide variety of atmospheric live-music venues. Just north of Bairro Alto, Príncipe Real is the epicentre of Lisbon's gay scene and home to some quirky drinking dens.

Ginjinha

Ginjinha is a sweet cherry liqueur served in tiny bars around the Largo de São Domingos and the adjacent Rua das Portas de Santo Antão.

The Alfama

This scenic route starts on tram 28 from Largo Martim Moniz or the Baixa, taking in the city's best tram route and avoiding uphill slogs. Take the tram up to Largo da Graça. From here, stroll north and turn left behind the barracks to Miradouro da Senhora do Monte.

Start Miradouro da Senhora do Monte
Distance 3km
Duration Two to three hours

1 The views of the city's red roofs from Lisbon's highest lookout point, **Miradouro da Senhora do Monte**, are simply breathtaking.

4 Towering dramatically above Lisbon, the mid-11th-century hilltop fortifications of **Castelo de São Jorge** sneak into almost every snapshot. One of the city's top attractions.

Take a Break
Cruzes Credo Café (Rua Cruzes da Sé 29; ⏰10am-2am) **is a handy stop for a drink.**

6 The 12th-century, fortress-like **Sé de Lisboa** was built on the site of a mosque soon after Christians recaptured the city from the Moors.

7 The urban space, **Praça do Comércio**, claims to be Europe's largest square, though it has many rivals.

Tram 28/Largo
Martim Moniz

Costa do
Castelo

Rossio Ⓜ

BAIXA

Costa do Castelo

Ⓜ Baixa-
Chiado

Tram 28/
Baixa

R Áurea

R Augusta

R da Alfândega

FINISH
7

R do Arsenal

Pç do
Comércio

Av Infante Dom Henrique

Classic Photo of the old yellow tram 28 hauling itself up to Largo da Graça.

2 From the Miradouro da Senhora do Monte walk south and right to pine-shaded **Miradouro da Graça**, where central Lisbon spreads out before you.

3 The exquisitely tiled interiors of **Mosteiro de São Vicente de Fora** house an eerie mausoleum holding the tombs of Portugal's last kings.

5 There are more fine vistas from bougainvillea-clad lookout point **Miradouro de Santa Luzia**.

START

Cç do Monte

R Damasceno Monteiro

Jardim da Cerca da Graça

R da Graça

Tram 28/Largo da Graça

GRAÇA

Cç de Sto André

Tv das Mónicas

R de São Vicente

CASTELO

Santa Apolónia

ALFAMA

R Terreiro do Trigo

R Augusto Rosa

Doca do Jardim do Tabaco

R de São João da Praça

Doca da Marinha

Rio Tejo

N 0 400 m
0 0.2 miles

© SAMUEL BORGES PHOTOGRAPHY / SHUTTERSTOCK ©, 2 MATT MUNRO / LONELY PLANET ©, 5 ALLIX / SHUTTERSTOCK ©, 6 PHOTOCONIX / SHUTTERSTOCK ©

Fado Vadio mural, curated by M.A.S.C. – Movimento os Amigos de São Cristóvão

NICK F / 500PX ©

Fado

Portugal's most famous style of music is fado (Portuguese for 'fate'), a simple, wistful genre that emerged in the 19th century working-class neighbourhoods of Lisbon.

No visit to the Portuguese world is complete without an evening of fado music, the traditional music of Lisbon. A performance in a typical fado house provides an insight into the Portuguese soul, the lilting guitar and vocals evoking a melancholic yearning for the past.

What is Fado?

Although fado is something of a national treasure – in 2011 it was added to Unesco's list of the World's Intangible Cultural Heritage – it's really the music of Lisbon (Coimbra has its own, slightly different version). Fados are traditionally sung by one performer accompanied by a 12-string Portuguese *guitarra* (pear-shaped guitar). When two *fadistas* (singers of traditional Portuguese song) perform, they

Great For...

☑ Don't Miss

The greatest *fadista*, Amália Rodrigues, was given a place in the Panteão Nacional.

Fado performers

MARTIN THOMAS PHOTOGRAPHY / ALAMY STOCK PHOTO ©

the mainstream. Fado's popularity slipped in the post-revolution days, when the Portuguese were eager to make a clean break with the past. (Salazar spoke of throwing the masses the three F's – fado, football and Fátima – to keep them happily occupied.) The 1990s, however, saw a resurgence of fado's popularity, with the opening of new fado houses and the emergence of new performers.

sometimes engage in *desgarrada*, a bit of improvisational one-upmanship where the singers challenge and play off one another. At fado houses there are usually a number of singers, each one traditionally singing three songs.

History of Fado

No one quite knows fado's origins, though African and Brazilian rhythms, Moorish chants and the songs of Provençal troubadours may have influenced the sound. What is clear is that by the 19th century fado could be heard all over the working-class neighbourhoods of Mouraria and Alfama. It was the anthem of the poor and it maintained an unsavoury reputation until the late 19th century, when the upper classes took an interest and brought it into

Amália Rodrigues

One singer who played a major role in its popularisation was Amália Rodrigues, the 'queen of fado', who became a household name in the 1940s. Born to a poor family in 1920, Amália took the music from the tavern to the concert hall, and then into households via radio and onto film screens, starring in the 1947 film *Capas Negras* (Black Capes).

Cover Charges and Menus

Most fado places have a minimum cover charge of €15 to €25, though a fixed menu can cost anything up to €50. The quality of food can be hit and miss; if in doubt, it might be worth asking if you can just order a bottle of wine.

View across to Mosteiro dos Jerónimos

CHIARA SALVADORI / GETTY IMAGES ©

Mosteiro dos Jerónimos

One of Lisbon's top attractions is this Unesco-listed monastery, one of the finest examples of the elaborate Manueline style.

Great For...

☑ Don't Miss

The monastery is one of the finest examples of the short Manueline period in Portuguese architecture.

The Monastery's Story

Belém's undisputed heart-stealer is the stuff of pure fantasy; a fusion of Diogo de Boitaca's creative vision and the spice and pepper dosh of Manuel I, who commissioned it to trumpet Vasco da Gama's discovery of a sea route to India in 1498. The building embodies the golden age of Portuguese discoveries and was funded using the profits from the spices Vasco da Gama brought back from the subcontinent. It was begun in 1502 but not completed for almost a century. Wrought for the glory of God, Jerónimos was once populated by monks of the Order of St Jerome, whose spiritual job for four centuries was to comfort sailors and pray for the king's soul. The monastery withstood the 1755 earthquake but fell into disrepair when the order was dissolved in 1833. It was later used as a

Sculptural detail, Mosteiro dos Jerónimos

ℹ️ **Need to Know**

Map p63; www.mosteirojeronimos.pt; Praça do Império; adult/child €10/5, 1st Sun of month free; ⊙10am-6.30pm Tue-Sun, to 5.30pm Oct-May

✕ **Take a Break**

Pão Pão Queijo Queijo (Map p63; 📞213 626 369; Rua de Belém 124; mains €4-8; ⊙10am-midnight Mon-Sat, to 8pm Sun; 🛜📶) is a popular fast-food stop selling traditional sandwiches and other snacks.

★ **Top Tip**

A €12 admission pass is valid for both the monastery and the nearby Torre de Belém.

school and orphanage until about 1940. In 2007 the now much-discussed Treaty of Lisbon was signed here.

The Church

Entering the church through the western portal, you'll notice tree-trunk-like columns that seem to grow into the ceiling, which is itself a spiderweb of stone. Windows cast a soft golden light over the church. Superstar Vasco da Gama is interred in the lower chancel, just left of the entrance, opposite venerated 16th-century poet Luís Vaz de Camões. From the upper choir, there's a superb view of the church; the rows of seats are Portugal's first Renaissance woodcarvings.

Vasco Da Gama

Born in Alentejo in the 1460s, Vasco da Gama was the first European explorer to reach India by ship. This was a key moment in Portuguese history as it opened up trading links to Asia and established Portugal's maritime empire, the wealth from which made the country into a world superpower. Da Gama died from malaria on his third voyage to India in 1524.

The Cloisters

There's nothing like the moment you walk into the honey-stone Manueline cloisters, dripping with organic detail in their delicately scalloped arches, twisting auger-shell turrets and columns intertwined with leaves, vines and knots. It will simply wow. Keep an eye out for symbols of the age such as the armillary sphere and the cross of the Military Order, plus gargoyles and fantastical beasties on the upper balustrade.

Azulejo-decorated wall, Museu Nacional do Azulejo

ALEX TREADWAY / GETTY IMAGES ©

Azulejos & Museu Nacional do Azulejo

Few visitors fail to be impressed by the exquisite tiles the Portuguese have traditionally used to decorate their buildings. There's even a museum that tells the story of these azulejos.

Great For

☑ Don't Miss

The museum shop has a superb range of ceramic souvenirs and beautiful coffee-table books.

Azulejos

Portugal's favourite decorative art is easy to spot. Polished painted tiles called *azulejos* (after the Arabic *al zulaycha*, meaning polished stone) cover everything from churches to train stations. The Moors introduced the art, having picked it up from the Persians, but the Portuguese wholeheartedly adopted it.

Portugal's earliest tiles are Moorish, from Seville. These were decorated with interlocking geometric or floral patterns. After the Portuguese captured Ceuta in Morocco in 1415, they began exploring the art themselves. The 16th-century Italian invention of maiolica, in which colours are painted directly onto wet clay over a layer of white enamel, gave works a fresco-like brightness.

The earliest home-grown examples date from the 1580s, and may be seen in churches

Wall decorated with *azulejos*, Lisbon

RUSINKA / GETTY IMAGES ©

ℹ Need to Know

www.museudoazulejo.pt; Rua Madre de Deus 4; adult/child €5/2.50, free 1st Sun of the month; ⊘10am-6pm Tue-Sun)

✕ Take a Break

The museum has its own restaurant.

★ Top Tip

Admission to the museum is free on the first Sunday of the month.

and interiors for shops, restaurants and residential buildings. Today, *azulejos* still coat contemporary life.

The Museum

Housed in a sublime 16th-century convent, Lisbon's **Museu Nacional do Azulejo** covers the entire *azulejo* spectrum. Star exhibits feature a 36m-long panel depicting pre-earthquake Lisbon, a Manueline cloister with web-like vaulting and exquisite blue-and-white *azulejos* and a gold-smothered baroque chapel. Here you'll find every kind of *azulejo* imaginable, from early Ottoman geometry to zinging altars, scenes of lords a-hunting to Goan intricacies. Bedecked with food-inspired *azulejos* – ducks, pigs and the like – the restaurant opens onto a vine-clad courtyard.

such as Lisbon's Igreja de São Roque, providing an ideal counterbalance to fussy baroque.

The late 17th century saw a fashion for huge panels depicting everything from saints to seascapes. As demand grew, mass production became necessary and the Netherlands' blue-and-white Delft tiles started appearing.

Portuguese tile makers rose to the challenge of this influx, and the splendid work of virtuosos António de Oliveira Bernardes and his son Policarpo in the 18th century springs from this competitive creativity. You can see their work in Évora, in the Igreja de São João.

By the end of the 18th century, industrial-scale manufacture began to affect quality. There was also massive demand for tiles after the 1755 Lisbon earthquake.

From the late 19th century, the art-nouveau and art-deco movements took *azulejos* by storm, providing fantastic facades

Tile Spotting in the Metro

Maria Keil (1914–2012) designed 19 of Lisbon's stations, from the 1950s onwards – look out for her wild modernist designs at the stations of Rossio, Restauradores, Intendente, Marquês de Pombal, Anjos and Martim Moniz.

Historic tram 28 passes Sé de Lisboa (p57)

CARLOS SANCHEZ PEREYRA / DESIGN PICS / GETTY IMAGES ©

Lisbon's Trams

For a quintessentially Lisbon experience, don't leave the city without riding one of the city's typical yellow trams. Tram 28 that climbs through the Alfama is a must for every visitor.

Great For

☑ Don't Miss

In addition to tram 28, other city-centre tram routes include numbers 12, 15, 18 and 25.

Lisbon's Old Trams

Lisbon's old yellow streetcars are a nostalgic throwback to the early days of urban public transport and would have long since been pensioned off to a transport museum in most other European countries. They have survived largely as they were specially designed for a specific task – to trundle up and down central Lisbon's steep gradients (just like their San Francisco cousins) and would be much too expensive to replace. These roller-coaster vintage trams date from the 1930s and are called *Remodelados* (remodelled). The name comes from the fact the cars were slightly upgraded in the 1990s to include such luxuries as late 20th-century brakes. There were once 27 lines in the city, but the construction of the metro put the system into decline. Today there are only five lines left – *remodelados* run on all of them.

Tram in Lisbon's Cais do Sodré neighbourhood

CLAUDIA CASAL / GETTY IMAGES ©

ℹ️ Need to Know

Companhia Carris de Ferro de Lisboa
(Carris; ☎213 500 115; www.carris.trans-
porteslisboa.pt) operates all transport in
Lisbon proper except the metro.

✖ Take a Break

Many cafes and restaurants line the
route of the No 28 tram – take
your pick.

★ Top Tip

Ride tram 28 early in the morning or
at night to avoid the tourist mobs.

Tram 28

The famous tram 28, Lisbon's longest tram
route, is extremely popular with tourists as
it heads through Baixa, Graça, Alfama and
Estrela, climbing the steep hill from Baixa
to the castle and Alfama as well as three of
the city's seven other hills en route. There
are 34 stops between Campo Ourique
in the west of the city centre to Martim
Monique, though the most interesting
section is between Estrela and Graça.
Trams depart every 11 minutes, though the
last leaves fairly early, around 9pm. The
experience on the museum-piece tram
can be an uncomfortable one for some,
with varnished wooden benches, steps and
crowds of tourists getting in each other's
way. But it's worth it for the ride, there's no
cheaper tour in town and it's a great option
to take when the weather is not playing ball.

Tram Stops and Fares

Lisbon's tram stops are marked by a small
yellow *paragem* (stop) sign hanging from a
lamp post or from the overhead wires. You'll
pay more for a tram ride if you buy your
ticket on board rather than purchasing a
prepaid card. On-board one-way prices are
€2.85, but a day pass costs just €6 and is
valid on all of the city's public transport for
24 hours.

Pickpockets

With groups of tourists crammed into a
small space, sadly tram 28 is a happy hunting ground for pickpockets. Take the usual
precautions to avoid being parted from
your possessions.

⊙ SIGHTS

At the riverfront is the grand Praça do Comércio. Behind it march the pedestrian-filled streets of Baixa (lower) district, up to Praça da Figueira and Praça Dom Pedro IV (aka Rossio). From Baixa it's a steep climb west, through swanky shopping district Chiado, into the narrow streets of night-life-haven Bairro Alto. Eastwards from the Baixa it's another climb to Castelo de São Jorge and the Moorish, labyrinthine Alfama district around it. The World Heritage Sites of Belém lie further west along the river – an easy tram ride from Praça do Comércio.

◎ Alfama, Castelo & Graça

Castelo de São Jorge   Castle
(Map p54; www.castelodesaojorge.pt; adult/student/child €8.50/5/free; ☉9am-9pm Mar-Oct, to 6pm Nov-Feb) Roam Castelo de São Jorge's snaking ramparts and pine-shaded courtyards for superlative views over the city's red rooftops to the river. Three guided tours daily (Portuguese, English and Span-

ish) at 1pm and 5pm are included in the admission price.

These smooth cobbles have seen it all – Visigoths in the 5th century, Moors in the 9th century, Christians in the 12th century, royals from the 14th to 16th centuries, and convicts in every century.

Inside the Ulysses Tower, a camera obscura offers a unique 360-degree angle on Lisbon, with demos every 20 minutes. There are also a few galleries displaying relics from past centuries, including traces of the Moorish neighbourhood dating from the 11th century at the Archaeological Site. But the standout attraction is the view – as well as the anachronous feeling of stepping back in time amid fortified courtyards and towering walls. There are a few cafes and restaurants to while away time in as well.

Bus 737 from Sé or Praça Figueira goes right to the gate. Tram 28 also passes nearby. An escalator traversing the hill from Praça Martim Moniz is planned to be in operation by 2017.

View of Castelo de São Jorge from Graça

Jardim da Cerca da Graça   Park

(Map p54; Calçada Do Monte 46; 📷) Closed
for centuries, this 1.7-hectare green space
debuted in 2015 and clocks in as Lisbon's
second-biggest park, offering a lush transition between the neighbourhoods of Graça
and Mouraria. There are superb city and
castle views from several points and a shady
picnic park along with a playground, an
orchard and a peaceful kiosk with a terrace.

Largo das Portas do Sol   Viewpoint

(Map p54; Largo das Portas do Sol) This
original Moorish gateway affords stunning
angles over Alfama's jumble of red rooftops
and pastel-coloured houses, underscored
by the true blue Tejo.

Miradouro da Graça   Viewpoint

(Map p54; Largo da Graça) A much-loved
summertime hangout of *lisboêtas* (people
who live in Lisbon), this *miradouro* (lookout) sidles up to the baroque Igreja da
Graça. It has an incredible view of the castle
sitting plump on the hillside, the river and
the Ponte 25 de Abril. Sunset is prime-time
viewing at the kiosk terrace.

Miradouro da Senhora do Monte   Viewpoint

(Map p54; Rua da Senhora do Monte) Lisbon
spreads out before you at Graça's highest of
the high, Miradouro da Senhora do Monte.
Come for the relaxed vibe and the best
views of the castle on the hill opposite. It's a
short walk west (along Rua da Senhora do
Monte) of the tram 28 stop on Rua da Graça.

Miradouro de Santa Luzia   Viewpoint

(Map p54; Largo Santa Luzia) Your gaze drifts
over a mosaic of rooftops and spires to the
river below from Miradouro de Santa Luzia.

Mosteiro de São Vicente de Fora   Church

(Map p54; Largo de São Vicente; adult/
child €5/free; ⏰10am-6pm Tue-Sun) Graça's
Mosteiro de São Vicente de Fora was
founded in 1147 and revamped by Italian architect Felipe Terzi in the late 16th century.
Since the adjacent church took the brunt
of the 1755 earthquake (the church's dome

 Neighbourhoods in a Nutshell

Baixa, near the riverfront, and Rossio,
just north of there, are the heart of old
Lisbon, with pedestrian streets and picturesque plazas. Follow the rattling trams
to the east and you'll reach Alfama, with
its medina-like lanes, and tiny, fado-filled
restaurants. Above the Alfama looms the
ramparts of an ancient castle, with great
viewpoints here and in other parts of the
aptly named Castelo neighbourhood.

A steep climb west of Baixa leads
into the swanky shopping and dining
district of Chiado; further uphill lie the
narrow streets of nightlife-haven Bairro
Alto. Nearby Santa Catarina with its tiny
bars and old-fashioned funicular has a
more laid-back vibe. Further downhill
towards the river is Cais do Sodré, a red-
light-district-turned hipster centre, with
late-night bars and eateries.

The World Heritage sites of Belém lie
further west along the river – an easy
tram ride from Baixa or Cais do Sodré.

Waterfront promenade Ribeira das Naus

crashed through the ceiling of the sacristy,
but emerged otherwise unscathed), elaborate blue-and-white *azulejos* dance across
almost every wall, echoing the building's
architectural curves.

On the 1st floor you'll find a one-off
collection of panels depicting La Fontaine's
moral tales of sly foxes and greedy wolves.
Under the marble sacristy lie graves of
Moorish-era *lisboêta* Christians. Seek out
the weeping, cloaked woman holding stony
vigil in the eerie mausoleum, which houses

Alfama, Castelo & Graça

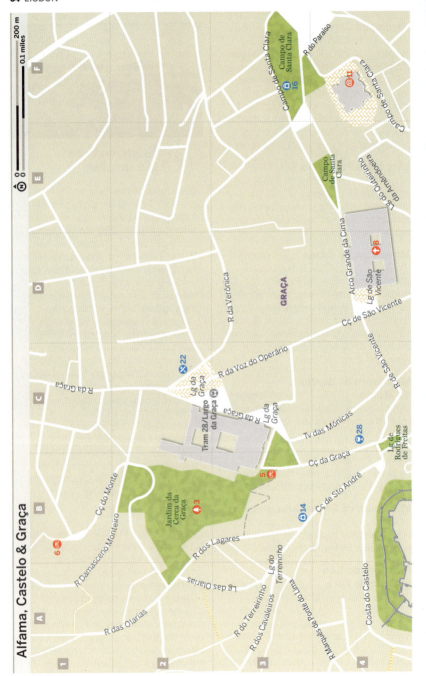

N

0   200 m
0   0.1 miles

F
Campo de Santa Clara

Campo de Santa Clara **16**

R do Paraíso

11 Campo de Santas Clara

E
Campo de Santa Clara

Lg do Outeirinho

Lg da Amendoeira

Arco Grande da Cima

8

Lg de São Vicente

D
R da Verónica

GRAÇA

Cç de São Vicente

R de São Vicente

C
R da Graça
R da Graça

22

Lg da Graça

R da Voz do Operário

R da Graça

Lg da Graça

Tv das Mónicas

Lg de Rodrigues de Freitas

Tram 28/Largo da Graça

Cç da Graça

28

B
Cç do Monte

Jardim da Cerca da Graça

3

5

14

Cç de Sto André

6

R Damasceno Monteiro

R dos Lagares

A
R das Olarias

Lg das Olarias

R do Terreirinho

Lg do Terreirinho

R dos Cavaleiros

R Marquês de Ponte do Lima

Costa do Castelo

1

2

3

4

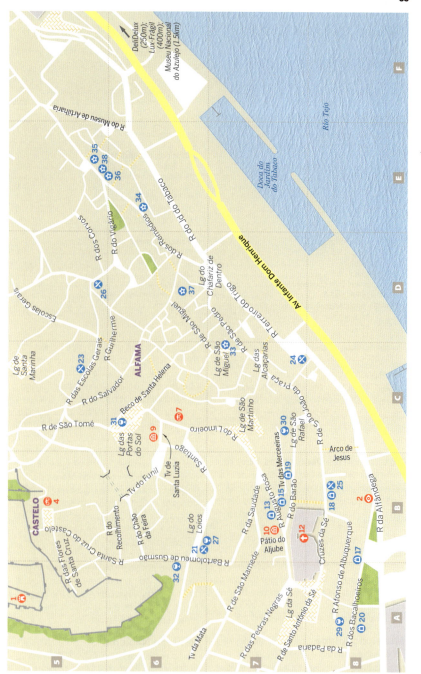

Alfama, Castelo & Graça

the lion's share of the tombs of Portugal's last kings. Enjoy the serene and gorgeous atmosphere throughout – there are more *azulejos* here than the Museu Nacional do Azulejo – and have your camera handy for the superb views from the tower. Multilingual guided tours run at 11am and 3pm every day except Sunday.

Museu de Artes Decorativas   Museum

(Museum of Decorative Arts; Map p54; www. fress.pt; Largo das Portas do Sol 2; adult/child €4/free; ⊙10am-5pm Wed-Mon) Set in a petite 17th-century palace, the Museu de Artes Decorativas creaks under the weight of treasures including blingy French silverware, priceless Qing vases and Indo-Chinese furniture, a collection amassed by a wealthy Portuguese banker from the age of 16. It's worth a visit alone to admire the lavish apartments, embellished with baroque *azulejos*, frescoes and chandeliers.

Museu do Aljube   Museum

(Map p54; www.museudoaljube.pt; Rua do Augusto Rosa 42; ⊙10am-6pm Tue-Sun) **FREE** Both poignant and haunting, this new and

highly important museum has turned the former Portuguese dictatorship's political prison of choice into a museum of truth and consequence, memorial and remembrance – it's a must-see.

Disturbing tales of authoritarian dictatorship (beginning with the *Ditadura Militar* in 1926; and evolving into the *Estado Novo*, or New State, from 1933 to 1974), including those of government torture, eavesdropping, oppression, coercion, informants and censorship, are found among three floors of exhibitions divided among topics such as Political Courts, Prison Circuit and Resistance, finally leading to the Carnation Revolution that eventually released the country into the arms of democracy after 41 downright scary years. By the time you reach that point, you're nearly as relieved as the Portuguese. Don't miss the panoramic views from the 4th-floor cafe – you'll need a breath of fresh air.

Panteão Nacional   Museum

(Map p54; www.patrimoniocultural.pt; Campo de Santa Clara; adult/child €4/free, free 1st Sun of the month; ⊙10am-6pm Tue-Sun, to 5pm Oct-

Mar) Perched high and mighty above Graça's Campo de Santa Clara, the porcelain-white Panteão Nacional is a baroque beauty. Originally intended as a church, it now pays homage to Portugal's heroes and heroines, including 15th-century explorer Vasco da Gama and *fadista* Amália Rodrigues.

Lavishly adorned with pink marble and gold swirls, its echoing dome resembles an enormous Fabergé egg. Trudge up to the 4th-floor viewpoint for vertigo-inducing views over Alfama and the river.

Sé de Lisboa   Cathedral

(Map p54; Largo de Sé; ☉9am-7pm Tue-Sat, to 5pm Mon & Sun) **FREE** One of Lisbon's icons is the fortress-like Sé de Lisboa, built in 1150 on the site of a mosque soon after Christians recaptured the city from the Moors.

It was sensitively restored in the 1930s. Despite the masses outside, the rib-vaulted interior, lit by a rose window, is calm. Stroll around the cathedral to spy leering gargoyles peeking above the orange trees.

History buffs shouldn't miss the less-visited **Gothic cloister** (Map p54; admission €2.50; ☉10am-5pm Mon, to 6.30pm Tue-Sat Apr-Sep, 10am-5pm Mon-Sat Oct-Mar), which opens onto a deep pit full of archaeological excavations going back more than 2000 years. You have to squint hard to imagine it, but you'll see remnants of a Roman street and shopfronts, an Islamic-era house and dump, as well as a medieval cistern. The **Treasury** (Map p54; admission €2.50; ☉10am-5pm Mon-Sat) showcases religious artwork.

The plaza in front of the church is home to one of Lisbon's most adorable kiosks, Quiosque de Refresco.

◉ Bairro Alto & Chiado

Convento do Carmo & Museu Arqueológico   Ruins, Museum

(Map p58; Largo do Carmo; adult/child €3.50/ free; ☉10am-7pm Mon-Sat, to 6pm Oct-May) Soaring above Lisbon, the skeletal Convento do Carmo was all but devoured by the 1755 earthquake and that's precisely what makes it so captivating. Its shattered pillars and wishbone-like arches are completely exposed to the elements. The Museu

Arqueológico shelters archaeological treasures, such as 4th-century sarcophagi, griffin-covered column fragments, 16th-century *azulejo* panels and two gruesome 16th-century Peruvian mummies.

Igreja & Museu São Roque   Church, Museum

(Map p58; www.museu-saoroque.com; Largo Trindade Coelho; church free, museum adult/ child €2.50/free, free 10am-2pm Sun; ☉2-7pm Mon, 10am-7pm Tue-Wed & Fri-Sun, 10am-8pm Thu) The plain facade of 16th-century Jesuit Igreja de São Roque belies its dazzling interior of gold, marble and Florentine *azulejos* – bankrolled by Brazilian riches. Its star attraction is Capela de São João Baptista, a lavish confection of amethyst, alabaster, lapis lazuli and Carrara marble. The museum adjoining the church is packed with elaborate sacred art and holy relics.

Free guided tours are offered in four languages. For English, arrive on Thursdays (3pm), Fridays (11.30am and 4.30pm), Saturdays (10am) and Sundays (3pm).

Miradouro de São Pedro de Alcântara   Viewpoint

(Map p58; Rua São Pedro de Alcântara; ☉viewpoint 24hr, kiosk 10am-midnight Mon-Wed, to 2am Thu-Sun) Hitch a ride on vintage **Ascensor da Glória** (Map p58; www. transporteslisboa.pt; Praça dos Restauradores; return €3.60; ☉7am-midnight Mon-Thu, 7am-12.30pm Fri, 8.30am-12.30am Sat, 9am-midnight Sun) from Praça dos Restauradores, or huff your way up steep Calçada da Glória to this terrific hilltop viewpoint. Fountains and Greek busts add a regal air to the surroundings, and the open-air kiosk doles out wine, beer and snacks, which you can enjoy while taking in the castle views and live music.

◉ Baixa & Rossio

Arco da Rua Augusta   Landmark

(Map p58; Rua Augusta 2-10; admission €2.50; ☉9am-7pm) This triumphal arch was built in the wake of the 1755 earthquake. A lift whisks you to the top, where fine views of Praça do Comércio, the river and the castle await. Admission for kids under five is free.

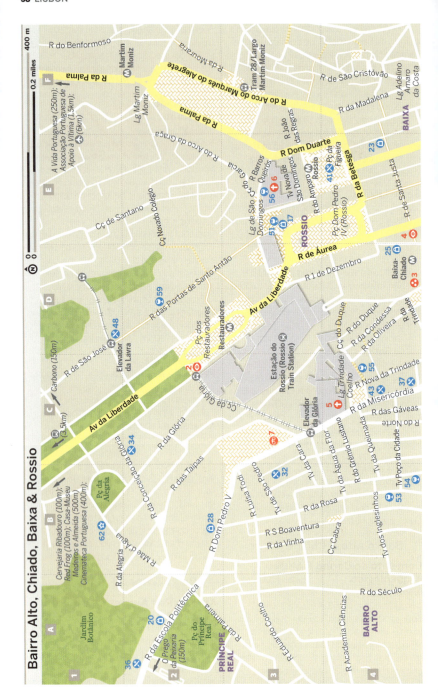

Bairro Alto, Chiado, Baixa & Rossio

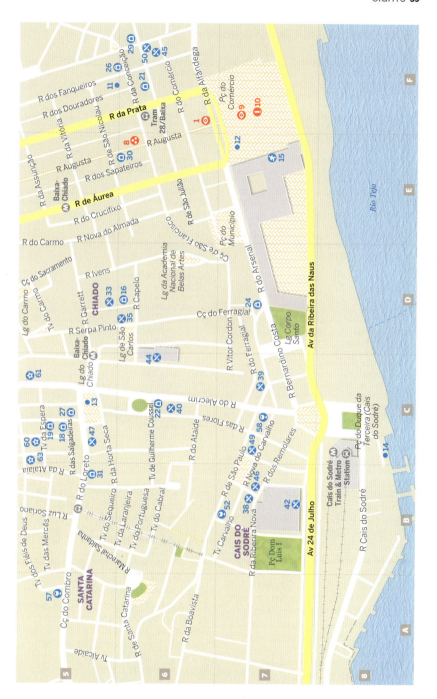

Bairro Alto, Chiado, Baixa & Rossio

Elevador de Santa Justa   Elevator

(Map p58; www.transporteslisboa.pt; cnr Rua de Santa Justa & Largo do Carmo; return trip €5; ⊙7am-11pm, to 10pm Oct-May) If the lanky, wrought-iron Elevador de Santa Justa seems uncannily familiar, it's probably because the neo-Gothic marvel is the handiwork of Raul Mésnier, Gustave Eiffel's apprentice. It's Lisbon's only vertical street lift, built in 1902 and steam-powered until 1907. Get there early to beat the crowds and zoom to the top for sweeping views over the city's skyline.

Bear in mind, however, some call the €5 fee Santa Injusta! You can save €3.50 by entering the platform from the top (behind Convento do Carmo) and paying just €1.50 to access the viewing platform.

Igreja de São Domingos   Church

(Map p58; Largo de São Domingos; ⊙1-5pm) **FREE** It's a miracle that this baroque church still stands, having barely survived the 1755 earthquake, then fire in 1959. Dating to 1241, its sea of tea lights illuminates gashed pillars, battered walls and ethereal sculptures in its musty, yet enchanting, interior. Note the Star of David memorial outside marking the spot of a bloody anti-Semitic massacre in 1506.

The square is a popular hang-out for Lisbon's African community.

Núcleo Arqueológico da Rua dos Correeiros · Ruins

(Map p58; ☎211 131 004; http://ind.millennium bcp.pt; Rua Augusta 96; ⏱10am-noon & 2-5pm Mon-Sat) FREE Hidden under the Millennium BCP bank building are layers of ruins dating from the Iron Age, discovered on a 1991 parking-lot dig. Fascinating archaeologist-led tours, run by Fundacão Millennium, descend into the depths (departing on the hour; booking ahead year-round is highly advisable). The extremely well-done site is now rightfully a National Monument.

You'll visit a small museum of artefacts found on premises before heading down into the web of tunnels, the majority of which are believed to be the remnants of a Roman sardine factory (and its owner's home) dating from the 1st century AD. It's worth noting that archaeologists had to remove Medieval and Islamic ruins (among others) to reach these startling structures. Highlights include Lisbon's only visible Roman mosaic, dating to the 3rd century; numerous baths and fish-preservation tanks and a Visigoth burial site with a remarkably preserved 30-year-old male skeleton. The entire 850-sq-metre site is notably well-maintained and is easily one of the city's most fascinating (and free) attractions.

Praça do Comércio · Plaza

(Map p58; Terreiro do Paço) With its grand 18th-century arcades, lemon-meringue facades and mosaic cobbles, the riverfront Praça do Comércio is a square to out-pomp them all. Everyone arriving by boat used to disembark here and it still feels like the gateway to Lisbon, thronging with activity and rattling trams.

At its centre rises the dashing equestrian **statue of Dom José I**, (Map p58) hinting at the square's royal roots on the pre-earthquake site of Palácio da Ribeira. In 1908, the square witnessed the fall of the monarchy, when anarchists assassinated Dom Carlos I and his son. The biggest crowd-puller is Verissimo da Costa's triumphal Arco da Rua Augusta (p57),

crowned with bigwigs such as 15th-century explorer Vasco da Gama; come at dusk to see the arch glow gold.

◉ Belém

Torre de Belém · Tower

(Map p63; www.torrebelem.pt; adult/child €6/3, 1st Sun of month free; ⏱10am-6.30pm Tue-Sun, to 5.30pm Oct-Apr) Jutting out onto the Rio Tejo, this Unesco World Heritage–listed fortress epitomises the Age of Discoveries. You'll need to breathe in to climb the narrow spiral staircase to the tower, which affords sublime views over Belém and the river.

Francisco de Arruda designed the pearlygrey chess piece in 1515 to defend Lisbon's harbour and nowhere else is the lure of the Atlantic more powerful. The Manueline show-off flaunts filigree stonework, meringue-like cupolas and – just below the western tower – a stone rhinoceros.

The ungulate depicts the one Manuel I sent Pope Leo X in 1515, which inspired Dürer's famous woodcut. Crowds can be intense on weekends (especially Sunday) – a warning to claustrophobes.

Palácio Nacional da Ajuda · Palace

(Map p63; ☎213 637 095; www.palacioajuda. pt; Largo da Ajuda; adult/child €5/free, free 1st Sun of month; ⏱10am-6pm Thu-Tue) Built in the early 19th century, this staggering neoclassical palace served as the royal residence from the 1860s until the end of the monarchy (1910). You can tour private apartments and state rooms and get an eyeful of gilded furnishings and exquisite artworks dating back five centuries; and, since 2014, the queen's chapel, home to Portugal's only El Greco painting.

It's a long uphill walk from Belém, or you can take tram 18 or several buses from downtown, including 760 from Praça do Comércio.

Museu Nacional dos Coches · Museum

(Map p63; www.museudoscoches.pt; Av da Índia 136; adult/child €6/3, free 1st Sun of month; ⏱10am-6pm Tue-Sun) Cinderella wannabes delight in Portugal's most-visited museum, which dazzles with its world-class collection of 70 17th- to 19th-century coaches in a new ultramodern (and some might say inappropriately contrasting) space that debuted in 2015. Don't miss Pope Clement XI's stunning ride, the scarlet-and-gold *Coach of the Oceans,* or the old royal riding school, Antigo Picadeiro Real (p62), across the street.

The easily missable upper level hosts temporary contemporary-art exhibitions.

Museu de Arte, Arquitetura e Tecnologia   Museum

(Art, Architecture & Technology Museum; MAAT; Map p63; www.maat.pt; Av Brasília, Central Tejo; from €5; ☺noon-8pm, closed Tue) Lisbon's latest riverfront star is this low-rise, glazed-tiled structure that intriguingly hips and sways into ground-level exhibition halls. Visitors can walk over and under its reflective surfaces, which play with water, light and shadow and pay homage to the city's intimate relationship with the sea.

The striking building was designed by UK-based Amanda Levete (famed for winning the rights to design London's Victoria & Albert Museum expansion on Exhibition Rd). The museum, which has absorbed former Museu da Electricidade (and some of its massive coal-burning generators) in the red-brick building and former 1900 power station next door, hosts a permanent science and electricity exhibit as well as temporary exhibitions on visual arts, media, architecture, technology and science. By March 2017, extensive gardens will connect the old and new buildings, and a footbridge will cross Av Brasília, allowing for direct access from Belém proper.

Museu da Presidência da República   Museum

(Museum of the Presidency of the Republic; Map p63; www.museu.presidencia.pt; Praça Afonso de Albuquerque, Palácio de Belém; adult/child €2.50/free; ☺10am-6pm Tue-Sun) Portugal's small presidential museum is worth a look for its fascinating state gifts exhibit – note the outrageous 1957 offering from Brazil's Juscelino Kubitschek, a massive tortoise-shell depicting handpainted Brazilian

scenes; Saudi swords and a gorgeous traditional Japanese dance depiction scene. Don't miss the official presidential portrait of Mário Soares, either – that guy looks like fun!

The museum is located in the official residence and office of the President, **Palácio de Belém** (Map p63; Belém Palace; ☎213 614 660; www.presidencia.pt; Praça Afonso de Albuquerque; €5/free; ☺10am-6pm Sat), and was inaugurated in 2004, the brainchild of then President Jorge Sampaio.

Museu Colecção Berardo   Museum

(Map p63; www.museuberardo.pt; Praça do Império; ☺10am-7pm Tue-Sun) **FREE** Culture fiends get their contemporary-art fix for free at Museu Colecção Berardo, the star of the Centro Cultural de Belém. The ultrawhite, minimalist gallery displays millionaire José Berardo's eye-popping collection of abstract, surrealist and pop art, including Hockney, Lichtenstein, Warhol and Pollack originals.

Temporary exhibitions are among the best in Portugal. Also in the complex is a cafe-restaurant that faces a grassy lawn, a bookshop and a crafty museum store.

Antigo Picadeiro Real   Museum

(Old Royal Riding School; www.museudoscoches.pt; Praça Afonso de Albuquerque; adult/child €4/free, free 1st Sun of month; ☺10am-6pm Tue-Sun) Lisbon's original coach museum is now home to just seven of these majestic 18th-century four-wheeled works of art, but it's worth also visiting the stuccoed, frescoed halls of the former royal riding stables built by Italian architect Giacomo Azzolini in 1726 – a far more fitting and palatial rest home than the modern monolith, Museu Nacional dos Coches (p61), across the street.

You can save €2 by purchasing a combination ticket with the Museu Nacional dos Coches.

 **Lapa & Alcântra**

Museu Nacional de Arte Antiga   Museum

(Ancient Art Museum; Map p64; www.museude arteantiga.pt; Rua das Janelas Verdes; adult/ child €6/3, 1st Sun of month free; ☺10am-6pm

Belém

Tue-Sun) Set in a lemon-fronted, 17th-century palace, the Museu Nacional de Arte Antiga is Lapa's biggest draw. It presents a star-studded collection of European and Asian paintings and decorative arts.

Keep an eye out for highlights such as Nuno Gonçalves' naturalistic *Panels of São Vicente*, Dürer's *St Jerome* and Lucas Cranach's haunting *Salomé* as well as period furniture pieces like King Afonso V's ceremonial 1470s armchair and the elaborate lacquered wood, silver-gilt and bronze late-16th-century casket.

Other gems include golden wonder the *Monstrance of Belém*, a souvenir from Vasco da Gama's second voyage, and 16th-century Japanese screens depicting the arrival of the Namban (southern barbarians), namely big-nosed Portuguese explorers.

Biannual temporary themed exhibitions (priced separately at around €7) are reached via a **second entrance** (Map p64) on Rua das Janelas Verdes, as is the stone-arched cafe and wonderfully peaceful gardens with river views.

Lapa, Alcântra, Príncipe Real, Santos & Estrela

LX Factory   Arts Centre

(Map p64; www.lxfactory.com; Rua Rodrigues de Faria 103) Lisbon's hub of cutting-edge creativity hosts a dynamic menu of events from live concerts and film screenings to fashion shows and art exhibitions. There's a rustically cool cafe as well as a restaurant, bookshop and design-minded shops. Weekend nights see parties with a dance- and art-loving crowd.

Ponte 25 de Abril   Bridge

(Map p64; Doca de Santo Amaro) Most
people experience déjà vu the first time
they clap eyes on the bombastic suspen-
sion bridge Ponte 25 de Abril. It's hardly
surprising given that it's the spitting image
of San Francisco's Golden Gate Bridge, was
constructed by the same company in 1966
and, at 2.27km, is almost as long.

The thundering bridge dwarfs Lisbon's
docks and is dazzling when illuminated by
night. It was called Ponte Salazar until the
1974 Revolution of the Carnations, when a
demonstrator removed the 'Salazar' and
daubed '25 de Abril' in its place; the name
stuck, the dictatorship crumbled.

Marquês de Pombal & Around

Museu Calouste
Gulbenkian   Museum

(www.museu.gulbenkian.pt; Av de Berna 45;
adult/child €5/free, Sun free; ☉10am-6pm Wed-
Mon) Famous for its outstanding quality and
breadth, the world-class Museu Calouste
Gulbenkian showcases an epic collection
of Western and Eastern art – from Egyptian
treasures to old master and impressionist
paintings.

The chronological romp kicks off with
highlights such as gilded Egyptian mummy
masks, Mesopotamian urns, elaborate
Persian carpets, Qing porcelain (note the
grinning *Dogs of Fo*) and a fascinating
Roman gold-medallion collection. Going
west, art buffs admire masterpieces by
Rembrandt (*Portrait of an Old Man*), Van
Dyck and Rubens (including the frantic
Loves of the Centaurs). Be sure to glimpse
Rodin's passionate *Eternal Springtime*. The
grand finale is the collection of exquisite
René Lalique jewellery, including the other-
worldly *Dragonfly*.

Casa-Museu Medeiros
e Almeida   Museum

(www.casa-museumedeirosealmeida.pt; Rua Rosa
Araújo 41; adult/child €5/free, free 10am-1pm Sat;
☉1-5.30pm Mon-Fri, 10am-5.30pm Sat) Housed
in a stunning early-19th-century mansion,
this little-known museum presents António

Medeiros e Almeida's exquisite fine- and
decorative-arts collection. Highlights
include Han ceramics and Ming- and
Qing-dynasty porcelain, Thomas Gainsbor-
ough paintings, a 300-strong stockpile of
watches and clocks (one of the best private
collections in Europe), and a dinner service
that once belonged to Napoleon Bonaparte.

◉ Parque das Nações

Ponte Vasco da Gama   Bridge

(Vasco da Gama Bridge; www.lusoponte.pt)
Vanishing into a watery distance, Ponte
Vasco da Gama is Europe's longest bridge,
stretching 17.2km across the Rio Tejo.

Gare do Oriente   Notable Building

(Oriente Station; Av Dom João II) Designed
by acclaimed Spanish architect Santiago
Calatrava, the space-age Gare do Oriente
is an extraordinary vaulted structure, with
slender columns fanning out into a con-
certina roof to create a kind of geometric,
crystalline forest.

Oceanário   Aquarium

(www.oceanario.pt; Doca dos Olivais; adult/child
€14/9, incl temporary exhibition €17/11; ☉10am-
8pm, to 7pm winter) The closest you'll get to
scuba diving without a wetsuit, Lisbon's
Oceanário is mind-blowing. No amount of
hyperbole can do justice to the 8000 marine creatures splashing in 7 million litres of
seawater. Huge wrap-around tanks make
you feel as if you are underwater, as you
eyeball zebra sharks, honeycombed rays,
gliding mantas and schools of neon fish.

Keep an eye out for oddities such as
filigree sea dragons, big ocean sunfish,
otherworldly jellyfish, frolicsome sea otters
and squiggly garden eels. You'll also want to
see the re-created rainforest, Indo-Pacific
coral reef and Magellan penguins on ice.
In light of the 2013 documentary *Black-
fish*, entertainment aquariums have fallen
out of favour, but for what it's worth, this
conservation-oriented oceanarium offers
no entertainment shows; it reproduces, as
opposed to capturing, in the wild wherever
possible and runs the largest environmental education program in Portugal.

Príncipe Real, Santos & Estrela

Basílica da Estrela   Church

(Map p64; Praça da Estrela; basilica free, nativity scene €1.50, roof €4; ⊘basilica 7.30am-7.45pm, terrace 10am-6.40pm, presépio 10-11.30am & 3-5pm, closed Mon afternoon & Sun morning) The curvaceous, sugar-white dome and twin belfries of Basílica da Estrela are visible from afar. The echoing interior is awash with pink-and-black marble, which creates a kaleidoscopic effect when you gaze up into the cupola. The neoclassical beauty was completed in 1790 by order of Dona Maria I (whose tomb is here) in gratitude for a male heir.

Don't miss the *presépio*, home to the incredibly elaborate 500-piece Nativity Scene made of cork and terracotta by celebrated 18th-century sculptor Joaquim Machado de Castro; it's in a room just beyond the tomb. Climb the 112 steps of the dome for far-reaching views over Lisbon.

Casa Museu de Amália Rodrigues   Museum

(Map p64; www.amaliarodrigues.pt; Rua de São Bento 193; adult/child €5/3.50; ⊘10am-1pm & 2-6pm Tue-Sun) A pilgrimage site for fado fans, Casa Museu de Amália Rodrigues is where the Rainha do Fado (Queen of Fado) Amália Rodrigues lived; note graffiti along the street announcing it as Rua Amália. Short tours take in portraits, glittering costumes and crackly recordings of her performances.

Born in Lisbon in 1920, the diva popularised the genre with her heartbreaking trills and poetic soul.

Museu da Marioneta   Museum

(Puppet Museum; Map p64; www.museuda marioneta.pt; Rua da Esperança 146; adult/child €5/3, free 10am-1pm Sun; ⊘10am-1pm & 2-6pm Tue-Sun) Discover your inner child at the surprisingly enchanting Museu da Marioneta, a veritable Geppetto's workshop housed in the 17th-century Convento das Bernardas. Alongside superstars such as impish Punch and his Portuguese equiva-

lent Dom Roberto, you will also find some rarities: Vietnamese water puppets, Sicilian opera marionettes and intricate Burmese shadow puppets. Check out the fascinating exhibit of the making of animation film, *A Suspeita*.

Tots can try their hand at puppetry. The museum also hosts puppet-making workshops, free weekend puppet shows from October to December and charged shows in the open-air cloister in summer. Check the website for details.

🏃 ACTIVITIES

Sipping away summer on numerous hilltop and waterfront terraces *(esplanadas)* and plaza kiosks is a quintessential Lisbon experience. Fancy some football? Two of Portugal's big three clubs, Benfica and Sporting, call Lisbon home. Guided tours are extremely popular and, for certified beach bums, idyllic sands at Carcavelos, Parede, Estoril and Cascais are easy train rides away.

ViniPortugal   Wine

(Map p58; www.winesofportugal.info; Praça do Comércio; ⊘11am-7pm Tue-Sat) Under the arcades on Praça do Comércio, this viticultural organisation offers €6 themed wine tastings, if booked in advance. Otherwise, pop in and grab a €3 enocard, which allows you to taste between two and four Portuguese wines, from Alentejo whites to full-bodied Douro reds.

Kiss the Cook   Cooking

(Map p64; ☎968 119 652; www.kissthecook. pt; Rua Rodrigues Faria 103, LX Factory; class €65; ⊘noon-3pm) If you're into Portuguese food in a big way and fancy picking up a few tips and tricks from the experts, why not pass by Kiss the Cook? Here you can prepare (and devour) traditional dishes. The cookery classes are totally hands-on and the price includes lunch and wine.

Jardins d'Água   Water Park

(Water Gardens; Passeio de Neptuno; ⊘24hr) FREE These themed water gardens are a great spot to cool off in summer. When the sun shines, parents and their overexcited kids get soaked ducking behind the raging waterfalls and misty geysers, and testing out the hands-on water activities.

Teleférico   Cable Car

(Telecabine Lisboa; www.telecabinelisboa. pt; Passeio do Tejo; 1-way adult/child €3.95/2; ⏱10.30am-8pm, 11am-7pm off season) Hitch a ride on this 20m-high cable car, linking Torre Vasco da Gama to the Oceanário. The ride affords bird's-eye views across Parque das Nações' skyline and the glittering Tejo that will have you burning up the pixels on your camera.

Zeev   Cycling

(Map p64; 📱915 100 242; www.rent.zeev. pt; Rua da Boavista 166; bike hire per 3/8/24hr €16/22/30; ⏱9am-7pm Mon-Sat) 🏴 Rents electric bikes (you'll appreciate the pedal-assist on Lisbon's hills), Renault Twizy electric two-person buggies, as well as full-size electric cars. Charging is free as is parking for electric vehicles within Lisbon city limits.

TOURS

Lisbon is all about getting out and about, so you're never far from an inventive way to peel back thousands of years of history. There are walking, cycling and boat tours, which provide the ideal welcome mat to the city; or you can lose time on less-academic endeavours such as wine-fuelled food tours (or food-fuelled wine tours!), pub crawls and fado tours. The artistically inclined shouldn't skip Lisbon's street-art tours, either, which offer fascinating insight into the city's indelible public-art scene, one of Europe's most dynamic.

HIPPOtrip   Adventure

(Map p64; 📱211 922 030; www.hippotrip. com; Doca de Santo Amaro; adult/child €25/15; ⏱9am-6pm) This fun 90-minute tour takes visitors on a land and river tour in an amphibious vehicle that drives straight into the Tejo! It begins and ends at Docas de Santo Amaro. From April to September, tours depart at 10am, noon, 2pm, 4pm and 6pm (the last departure falls off the schedule from October to March).

Torre de Belém (p61)

GoCar minicars

We Hate Tourism Tours   Tours

(Map p64; ☏ 913 776 598; www.wehatetourism
tours.com; Rua da Silva 27; per person from
€30; ⏱ 11am-7pm Mon & Thu) One memorable way to explore the city is aboard an
open-topped UMM (a Portuguese 4WD
once made for the army). In addition to the
weekend King of the Hills tour, this alternative outfit organises dinners followed by a
night tour around Lisbon, plus responsible
walks, longer city tours and excursions to
Sintra. Most trips depart from Praça Luís
de Camões.

You can always find these folks hanging
out and drinking wine at their quirky HQ,
dubbed the Armazém Geral, on Mondays
and Thursdays.

GoCar Touring   Driving

(Map p58; ☏ 210 965 030; www.gocartours.
pt; Rua dos Douradores 16; per hr/day €29/89;
⏱ 9.30am-6.30pm) These self-guided
tours put you behind the wheel of an
open-topped, two-seater minicar with a
talking GPS that guides you along one of
several predetermined routes. Helmets
included.

The same company runs Segway and
convertible-classic VW Beetle tours out of
the same address.

Lisbon Walker   Walking

(Map p58; ☏ 218 861 840; www.lisbonwalker.
com; Rua dos Remédios 84; 3hr walk adult/child
€15/free; ⏱ 10am & 2.30pm) This excellent
company, with well-informed, English-
speaking guides, offers themed walking
tours through Lisbon, which depart from
the northwest corner of Praça do Comércio.

Themed tours include 'Old Town' (the
history and lore of the Alfama) and 'Legends and Mysteries'. Check the website for
scheduling.

Sandemans
New Lisbon   Walking

(Map p58; www.newlisbontours.com; ⏱ 10am,
11am & 2pm) **FREE** For the inside scoop on
the city, Sandemans' fun, informative and
free 2½-hour walking tours of downtown
Lisbon are hard to beat. You'll do the
rounds of all the major landmarks and get
versed in history and city tips as you stroll.
The tours begin at the scheduled time

(book online) at the monument on Praça Luís de Camões.

Guides appreciate the odd tip, naturally, and are decidedly deserving.

Eco Tuk Tours   Tours
(☎914 925 450; www.ecotuktours.com; 60/90/120min tour for 6 people €50/70/90) 🏍 Lisboêtas love them or hate them, but tourists do enjoy travelling around Lisbon in a small, open-topped tuk tuk – those quaint, three-wheel vehicles popular in India and southeast Asia. If this is your thing, the least you can do is go for the quieter, eco-friendly electric version.

You can select from a range of circuits, the best of which head up to various lookouts, giving you dazzling views over the city without the serious legwork. Reserve ahead.

Lisbon Bike Tour   Cycling
(☎912 272 300; www.lisbonbiketour.com; adult/child €32.50/15; �﹖9.30am-1pm) It's all downhill on this 3½-hour guided bike ride from Marquês de Pombal to Belém.

Underdogs Public Art Store Tours
(Map p58; www.under-dogs.net; Rua da Cintura do Porto de Lisboa, Armazém A; tours from €35; �﹖11am-8pm Mon-Sat) Witness the strength of street knowledge at this part gallery, part Montana-street-art paint store and cafe behind Cais do Sodre. Underdogs specialises in high-profile public art and are the go-to guys for Lisbon's street-art tours, the best of which hit the road via e-bike. Themes include central Lisbon, greater Lisbon and Vhils, the artist behind the underdogs.

All tours must be prebooked in person or by email.

🔒 SHOPPING

Le freak, c'est retro *chic* in grid-like Bairro Alto, attracting vinyl lovers and vintage devotees to its cluster of late-opening boutiques. Alfama, Baixa and Rossio have frozen-in-time stores dealing exclusively in buttons and kid gloves, tawny port and tinned fish. Elegant Chiado is the go-to

place for high-street and couture shopping to the backbeat of buskers.

Loja das Conservas   Food
(Map p58; www.facebook.com/lojadas conservas; Rua do Arsenal 130; �﹖10am-9pm Mon-Sat, noon-8pm Sun) What appears to be a gallery is on closer inspection a fascinating temple to tinned fish (or *conservas* as the Portuguese say), the result of an industry on its deathbed revived by a savvy marketing about-face and new generations of hipsters. The retro-wrapped tins, displayed along with the history of each canning factory, are the artworks.

They make terrific gifts and you can try them at the tastings from 4pm to 8pm every Tuesday and Wednesday. The most popular? Brisa's boneless/skinless sardines in olive oil, lime and basil.

A Vida Portuguesa Gifts & Souvenirs
(Map p58; www.avidaportuguesa.com; Rua Anchieta 11; �﹖10am-8pm Mon-Sat, from 11am Sun) A flashback to the late 19th century with its high ceilings and polished cabinets, this former warehouse and perfume factory lures nostalgics with all-Portuguese products from retro-wrapped Tricona sardines to Claus Porto soaps, and heart-embellished Viana do Castelo embroideries to Bordallo Pinheiro porcelain swallows. Also in **Intendente** (Largo do Intendente 23; �﹖10.30am-7.30pm).

Sky Walker   Clothing
(Map p58; www.facebook.com/skywalkerlx; Rua do Norte 12; �﹖10am-9pm Mon-Thu, to 10pm Fri-Sat, 3-8pm Sun) This small hipster men's boutique is a well-curated hotspot for picking up slimming Bellroy wallets from Australia, adult backpacks from Herschel Supply Co and Fjällräven, cool hats from Penfield and Komono sunglasses, as well as a stylish selection of sneakers, jackets, tees and other accessories.

Azevedo Rua   Hats
(Map p58; ☎213 470 817; www.azevedorua. com; Praça Dom Pedro IV 73; �﹖9.30am-7.30pm Mon-Fri, 10am-2.30pm Sat) Lisbon's maddest hatters have been covering bald spots

More Info, Please!

Lonely Planet (www.lonelyplanet.com/lisbon) Destination information, hotel bookings, traveller forum and more.

Visit Lisboa (www.visitlisboa.com) Comprehensive tourist office website.

Lisbon Lux (www.lisbonlux.com) Trendy city guide.

Spotted by Locals (www.spottedbylocals.com/lisbon) Insider tips.

Go Lisbon (www.golisbon.com) Dining, drinking and nightlife insight.

Aerial view of Rua Augusta
SAM74100 / GETTY IMAGES ©

since 1886. Expect old-school service and wood-panelled cabinets full of flat caps and Ascot-worthy headwear.

Luvaria Ulisses — Clothing

(Map p58; www.luvariaulisses.com; Rua do Carmo 87A; gloves €49-170; ☺10am-7pm Mon-Sat) So tiny it's almost an optical illusion, this magical art-deco store is chock-full of soft handmade leather gloves for men and women in kaleidoscope shades. A Lisbon legend since 1925.

Vellas Loreto — Candles

(Map p58; www.cazavellasloreto.com.pt; Rua do Loreto 53; ☺9am-7pm Mon-Fri, to 1pm Sat) *Lisboêtas* have been waxing lyrical about this specialist candle-maker since 1789. The wood-panelled, talc-scented store sells myriad candles, from cherubs and peppers to Christmas trees and water lilies.

Fábrica Sant'Ana — Arts & Crafts

(Map p58; www.santanna.com.pt; Rua do Alecrim 95; azulejos from €5; ☺9.30am-7pm Mon-Fri, 10am-7pm Sat) Handmaking and painting *azulejos* since 1741, this is the place to get some eye-catching porcelain tiles for your home.

The Lisbon Walker — Shoes

(Map p58; www.thelisbonwalker.com; Rua da Madalena 68; shoes from €95; ☺10am-1pm & 2-8pm Mon-Sat, 2-8pm Sun) This cool new concept shop hawks handcrafted Portuguese men's shoes in unique styles that everyone else at home won't also be wearing. Pick more formal wing-tips, casual boots and sneakers. They throw in a bottle of wine with every pair, which is sort of gimmicky, but the shoes are pretty jazzy.

If they don't have your size, they'll have it custom made and shipped to your home at no extra charge.

Typographia — Clothing

(Map p58; www.typographia.com; Rua Augusta 93; T-shirts €16-24; ☺10am-9pm) With shops in Porto and Madrid as well, this high-design T-shirt shop is one of Europe's best. It features a select, monthly-changing array of clever and artsy, locally designed T-shirts.

LX Market — Market

(Map p64; http://lxmarket.com.pt; Rua Rodrigues de Faria 103, LX Factory; ☺11am-6pm Sun) Vintage clothing, antiques, crafts, food and weird and wonderful plants – the LX Factory market is the place to find them. Live music keeps the Sunday shoppers entertained.

Napoleão — Wine

(Map p58; www.napoleao.co.pt; Rua dos Fanqueiros 70; ☺9am-8pm Mon-Sat, 1-8pm Sun) Of the two Napoleão shops on this corner, this friendly, English-speaking cellar specialises in Portuguese-only wines, ports and spirits with hundreds of bottles to choose from (and other homegrown gourmet products). Ships worldwide.

Ler Devagar   Books

(Map p64; ☎213 259 992; www.lerdevagar.com; Rua Rodrigues de Faria 103, LX Factory; ⊙noon-9pm Mon, noon-midnight Tue-Thu, noon-2am Fri-Sat, 11am-9pm Sun) Late-night bookworms and anyone who likes a good read will love this floor-to-ceiling temple of books at the LX Factory (p64). Art, culture and foreign-language titles are well represented.

Garrafeira Nacional   Wine

(Map p58; www.garrafeiranacional.com; Rua de Santa Justa 18; ⊙9.30am-7.30pm Mon-Fri, to 7.30pm Sat) This Lisbon landmark has been slinging Portuguese juice since 1927 and is easily the best spot to pick up a bevy of local wines and spirits. It is especially helpful and will steer you towards lesser-known boutique wines and vintage ports in addition to the usual suspects. The small museum features vintages dating to the 18th century.

They have a second, smaller outlet in the Mercado da Ribeira.

Espaço Açores   Food

(Map p58; www.espacoacores.pt; Rua de São Julião 58; ⊙10am-2pm & 3-7pm Mon-Sat) The closest you can get to actually visiting the Azores is this attractive shop, where a taste of the islands comes in the form of cheeses, honeys, preserves, passion-fruit liqueurs and, apparently, the oldest tea produced in Europe.

Embaixada   Shopping Centre

(Map p58; www.embaixadalx.pt; Praça do Príncipe Real 26; ⊙noon-8pm, restaurants to 2am) Take an exquisite 19th-century neo-Moorish palace, fill it with fashion, design and concept stores on the cutting edge of cool and you have one of Lisbon's most exciting new shopping experiences: Embaixada. Centred on a grand sweeping staircase and courtyard are boutiques selling everything from vintage records to organic cosmetics, eco-homewares, contemporary Portuguese ceramics and catwalk styles.

There is a wonderful gin-centric bar-cafe in the atrium (Gin Lovers) and a good steakhouse hidden below, to the back (O Talho).

Solar   Antiques

(Map p58; www.solar.com.pt; Rua Dom Pedro V 70; azulejos €15-200; ⊙10am-7pm, closed Sat & Sun Jul-Aug) Hawking antique *azulejos* for seven decades, Solar offers row after row and pile after pile of precious Portuguese tiles dating from the 1500s to 1900s, many of which were salvaged from old churches and palaces.

Carbono   Music

(www.carbono.com.pt; Rua do Telhal 6B; ⊙11am-7pm Mon-Sat) The staff may be grumpy, but it's hard not to like Carbono, with its impressive selection of new and second-hand vinyl and CDs. World music – West African boogaloo, Brazilian tropicalia – is especially well represented.

Cork & Company   Gifts & Souvenirs

(Map p58; www.corkandcompany.pt; Rua das Salgadeiras 10; ⊙11am-7pm Mon-Thu, to 9pm Fri-Sat) ⚑ At this elegantly designed shop, you'll find cork put to surprisingly imaginative uses, with well-made and sustainable cork handbags, pens, wallets, journals, candleholders, hats, scarves, place mats, umbrellas, iPhone covers and even chaise longues!

Verso Branco   Design

(Map p64; www.versobranco.pt; Rua da Boavista 132-134; ⊙11.30am-8pm Tue-Sat) 'Free verse' is the name of this split-level design store, where Fernando has a story for every object. The high-ceilinged space showcases Portuguese contemporary arts, crafts and furnishings, from Burel's quality wool creations to limited edition La.Ga bags by designer Jorge Moita – the beautifully crafted bags made from Tyvek weigh just 40 grams and can hold 55 kilos.

Arte da Terra   Gifts & Souvenirs

(Map p54; www.aartedaterra.pt; Rua Augusto Rosa 40; ⊙11am-8pm) In the stables of a centuries-old bishop's palace, Arte da Terra brims with authentic Portuguese crafts including Castello Branco embroideries, nativity figurines, hand-painted *azulejos*, fado CDs and quality goods (umbrellas, aprons, writing journals) made from cork. Some goods are beautifully lit in former troughs.

Cortiço & Netos   Homewares

(Map p54; www.corticoenetos.com; Calçada de Santo André 66; ☺10am-1pm & 2-7pm Mon-Sat) A wonder wall of fabulous *azulejos* greets you as you enter this very special space. It's the vision of brothers Pedro, João, Ricardo and Tiago Cortiço, whose grandfather dedicated more than 30 years to gathering, storing and selling discontinued Portuguese industrial tiles. Reviving the family trade, they are experts on the *azulejo* and how it can be interpreted today.

El Dorado   Vintage Cothing

(Map p58; ☎213 423 935; Rua do Norte 23; ☺noon-9pm Mon-Sat, 5-9pm Sun) A gramophone plays vinyl classics as divas bag vintage styles from psychedelic prints to 6-inch platforms and pencil skirts at this Bairro Alto hipster shop. There's also a great range of club wear.

Fabula Urbis   Books

(Map p54; www.fabula-urbis.pt; Rua Augusto Rosa 27; ☺10am-1pm & 3-8pm) A great little bookshop that celebrates works about Portugal, both by home-grown and expat authors. All the best works by Lobo Antunes, Saramago, Pessoa, Richard Zimler and Robert C Wilson are here and available in English, French, Spanish, Italian, German and, of course, Portuguese.

Feira da Ladra   Market

(Map p54; Campo de Santa Clara; ☺6am-5pm Tue & Sat) Browse for back-of-the-lorry treasures at this massive flea market. You'll find old records, coins, baggy pants, dog-eared poetry books and other attic junk. Haggle hard and watch your wallet – it isn't called 'thief's market' for nothing.

Silva & Feijóo   Food

(Map p54; www.facebook.com/silvaefeijoo; Rua dos Bacalhoeiros 117; ☺10am-7pm Mon-Sat) Planning a picnic? Stop by this nearly 100-year-old brand's shop, one of several in the area, for sheep's cheese from the Seia mountains, sardine pâté, rye bread,

salsichas (sausages) and other Portuguese goodies.

Loja dos Descobrimentos   Arts & Crafts

(Map p54; www.loja-descobrimentos.com; Rua dos Bacalhoeiros 14A; ☺9am-7pm Mon-Sat) Watch artisans carefully painting hand-made *azulejos* at this workshop and store near the **Casa dos Bicos** (Map p54; www.josesaramago.org; Rua dos Bacalhoeiros 10; adult/child €3/free; ☺10am-6pm Mon-Sat). Fruits and flowers, boats, culinary motifs or geometric – tiles are available in myriad colours and designs.

O Voo da Andorinha/ Era Uma Vez Um Sonho   Gifts & Souvenirs

(Map p54; Rua do Barão 22; ☺10am-8pm Mon-Sat) Candy-bright beads, hand-stitched swallows, embroidered accessories and quirky furnishings made with recycled junk – you'll find all of this and more at this adorable boutique near the cathedral. It shares space with the unique handcrafted puppets, stuffed animals, puzzles and illustrated books of Era Uma Vez Um Sonho. It's great for kids.

MO&TA CA.SA   Fashion & Accessories

(Map p54; ☎937 133 093; Rua São João da Praça 97, 1st fl; ☺9am-10pm) To meet Portuguese designer Jorge Moita and see the full array of his La.Ga bags – which he affectionately calls his UFOs – visit his new design workshop in Alfama. The striking tear-shaped handbags made of super-lightweight, incredibly resistant Tyvek, bear the creatively unique hallmarks of female prisoners, designers and artists.

✪ EATING

Ti-Natércia   Portuguese €

(Map p54; ☎218 862 133; Rua Escola Gerais 54; mains €5-12; ☺7pm-midnight Mon-Fri, noon-3pm & 7pm-midnight Sat) A decade in and a legend in the making, 'Aunt' Natércia and her downright delicious Portuguese home cooking is a tough ticket: there are

Bookshop, LX Market (p70)

but a mere six tables and they fill up fast. She'll talk your ear off (and doesn't mince words!) while you devour her excellent take on the classics. Reservations essential (and cash only).

If you do manage to get a seat, you're in for a treat, especially with the *bacalhau com natas* (shredded codfish with bechamel, served au gratin) or *à Brás* (shredded codfish with eggs and potatoes) or, well, anything else you might order. President Marcelo Rebelo de Sousa approved – his photo is on the wall.

Alma   Contemporary, Portuguese €€€

(Map p58; 213 470 650; www.almalisboa. pt; Rua Anchieta 15; mains €25-29, tasting menus €60-80; noon-3pm & 7-11pm Tue-Sun;) Henrique Sá Pessoa, one of Portugal's most talented chefs, moved his flagship Alma from Santos to more fitting digs in Chiado in 2015. The casual space exudes understated style amid its original stone flooring and gorgeous hardwood tables, but it's Pessoa's outrageously good nouveau Portuguese cuisine that draws the foodie flock from far and wide.

Seasonal menus focus on the freshest Iberian flavours possible. Standout dishes include charred red peppers in an exquisite red-pepper coulis and suckling-pig confit that will bring you to your knees in unadulterated culinary joy. Portions are bigger than average at this level and the sommelier isn't afraid to pick bold, unorthodox wines to round out your evening.

100 Maneiras   Fusion €€€

(Map p58; 910 307 575; www.restaurante 100maneiras.com; Rua do Teixeira 35; tasting menu €58, with classic/premium wine pairing €93/118; 7.30pm-2am;) How do we love 100 Maneiras? Let us count the 100 ways... The nine-course tasting menu changes twice yearly and features imaginative, delicately prepared dishes. The courses are all a surprise – part of the charm – though somewhat disappointingly, the chef will only budge so far to accommodate special diets and food allergies. Reservations are essential for the elegant and small space.

Sea Me   Seafood €€€

(Map p58; ☑213 500 115; www.peixaria
moderna.com; Rua do Loreto 21; mains €17-28;
⊙12.30-3.30pm & 7.30pm-midnight Mon-Fri,
12.30pm-1am Sat, 12.30pm-midnight Sun; 🛜)
This urban-cool space serves grilled fish
by the kilo (market price; check out the
tempting fresh selection in the back),
Portuguese-leaning sushi (fresh *bacalhau*
with olive oil, cilantro and almonds; seared
sardines with sea salt) and dishes with
occasional Asian accents, among other
standouts.

An easy-listening soundtrack is delivered
from a DJ console.

Belcanto   Portuguese €€€

(Map p58; ☑213 420 607; www.belcanto.pt;
Largo de São Carlos 10; mains €45, tasting menu
€125-145, with 5/7 wines €50/60; ⊙12.30-3pm
& 7.30-11pm Tue-Sat; 🛜) Fresh off a 2016 inti-
macy upgrade, José Avillez' two-Michelin-
starred cathedral of cookery wows diners
with painstaking creativity, polished service
and first-rate sommelier. Standouts among
Lisbon's culinary adventure of a lifetime
include suckling pig with orange puree,

sea bass with seaweed and bivalves and
a stunning roasted butternut squash with
miso; paired wines sometimes date to the
'70s! Reservations essential.

There's palatable casualness to your
dining experience here, but thankfully it
does not come at the sacrifice of service or
execution – a refreshing detour at this level.

Bistro 100 Maneiras   Fusion €€€

(Map p58; ☑910 307 575; www.restaurante
100maneiras.com; Largo da Trindade 9; mains
€17-33; ⊙7.30pm-2am Mon-Sat; 🛜) The Bos-
nian mastermind behind Bairro Alto's 100
Maneiras (p73) also oversees this creatively charged Chiado bistro. Start with the
namesake 100 Maneiras Strong cocktail in
the beautiful downstairs bar, then head upstairs for beautifully prepared dishes showcasing high-end Portuguese ingredients.
Classics such as truffled mushroom risotto
with wild shrimp are astounding; options
for braver souls include lamb brains.

It stays open late (though the kitchen
closes around 12.30am), making it a good
option for late-night dining. Reserve ahead.

Outdoor dining, Bairro Alto

Gelataria Nannarella   Ice Cream €

(Map p64; www.facebook.com/gelateria
nannarella; Rua Nova da Piedade 68; small/
medium/large €2/2.50/3; ⊘noon-10pm) This
is where you'll get Lisbon's best gelato.
Seatless Nannarella is squeezed into
little more than a doorway, where Roman
transplant Constanza Ventura churns out
some 25 perfect, spatula-slabbed flavours
of traditional gelato/sorbet daily to anxious
lines of *lisboêtas*. Nailing both consistency
and flavour, this sweet, sweet stuff from
which heaven is made seemingly emerges
straight from Ventura's kitchen.

Its name is the nickname of famous
Academy Award–winning Roman actress,
Anna Magnani.

Landeau   Sweets €

(Map p58; www.landeau.pt; Rua das Flores 70;
cake €3.50; ⊘noon-7pm; 🛜) The Portuguese
love to self-proclaim (by name, no less!)
their product to be the Best This or the
Best That in the World, but this don't-miss
cafe puts its chocolate where its mouth is,
serving up as flawless a piece of chocolate
cake as you'll ever encounter.

Sofia Landeau's version was so popular
at her previous restaurant of employ,
she had to go and open her own place
dedicated solely to this wondrously gooey,
perfectly moist, just-sweet-enough piece of
chocolate perfection.

Bota Feijão   Portuguese €

(✆218 532 489; Rua Conselheiro Lopo Vaz
5; half/whole portion €8.50/12; ⊘noon-3pm
Mon-Fri) Don't be fooled by the nondescript
decor and railroad-track views – when a
tucked-away place is this crowded with
locals at lunchtime midweek, they must
be doing something right. They're all here
for one thing and one thing only: *leitão*,
suckling pig spit-roasted on an open fire
until juicy and meltingly tender, doused in a
beautiful peppery garlic sauce. You can take
home the whole hog for €125!

Landeau   Desserts €

(Map p64; www.landeau.pt; Rua Rodrigues de
Faria 103, LX Factory; cake €3.50; ⊘11am-7pm;
🛜) Landeau is quite simply about having

Great Escapes

Some of Lisbon's greenest and most
peaceful *praças* (town squares) are
perfect for a crowd-free stroll or picnic.
A few of our favourites:

Praça da Alegria Swooping palms and
banyan trees shade tranquil Praça da
Alegria, which is actually more round
than square. Look out for the bronze
bust of 19th-century Portuguese painter
and composer Alfredo Keil.

Praça do Príncipe Real A century-old
cedar tree forms a giant natural parasol
at the centre of this palm-dotted square,
popular among grizzled card players by
day and gay cruisers by night. There's a
kids' playground and a relaxed cafe with
al fresco seating.

Praça das Flores Centred on a fountain,
this romantic, leafy square has cobbles,
pastel-washed houses and enough
doggie-do to make a Parisian proud.

Campo dos Mártires da Pátria Framed
by elegant buildings, this grassy square
is dotted with pine, weeping willow and
jacaranda trees, with a pond for ducks
and a pleasant indoor-outdoor cafe. *Lisboêtas* in search of cures light candles
before the statue of Dr Sousa Martins,
who was renowned for his healing work
among the poor.

Park, Príncipe Real

your cake and eating it. The industro-cool
cafe at the LX Factory (p64) is famous
for its dark, dense, deliciously moist chocolate cake, which is also now available in
their Chiado outlet as well.

Craft Beer

Lisboêtas have finally been released from the decades-long suds purgatory imposed on them by commoner lagers Super Bock and Sagres. IPAs, stouts, porters, *saisons* and sours are booming – keep an eye out for an ever-expanding list of local standouts that includes Dois Corvos, Oitava Colina, Passarola, Mean Sardine, Amnesia and Musa. Drink in the local scene at several new craft-beer bars and brewpubs. The hops revolution has begun!

Feitoria   Modern Portuguese €€€

(Map p63; ☏210 400 208; www.restaurante feitoria.com; Altis Belém Hotel, Doca do Bom Sucesso; mains €33-38, tasting menus €75-120, with wine €110-175; ☺7.30-11pm Mon-Sat; ☏) A defining dining experience awaits at chef João Rodrigues' slick, contemporary Michelin-starred restaurant overlooking the riverfront. Rich textures and clean, bright flavours dominate throughout three tasting menus (Land, Tradition and Travel) showcasing Portugal's rich and vibrant bounty. Egg-yolk, cheese and spinach ravioli with mushrooms and truffles, and Iberian pork neck with smoked eel, progressively exhilarate on every bite.

From the onset (excellent bread with Joaquim Arnaud olive oil poured over lacquered seashells) and through to engaging wine choices and a few surprises along the way (roasted lettuce hearts over smoking Northern Portugal river stones, a cruelty-free nod to Peru's *anticuchos*, a

skewered-meat street snack), this is where your palette meets paradise. Those springing for tasting menus receive a wax-sealed menu of their evening signed by the chef.

Solar dos Presuntos   Portuguese €€€

(Map p58; ☏213 424 253; www.solardos presuntos.com; Rua das Portas de Santo Antão 150; mains €16-27.50, seafood per kg €29-70; ☺12.30-3.30pm & 7-11pm Mon-Sat; ☏) Don't be fooled by the smoked *presunto* (ham) hanging in the window, this iconic restaurant is renowned for its excellent seafood too. Start with the excellent *pata negra* (cured ham), *paio* smoked sausage and cheese *couvert*, then dig into a fantastic lobster *açorda* (bread and shellfish stew), delectable seafood paella or crustacean curry. Go easy on their homespun piri-piri (hot sauce) – it bites back!

There's a pleasant buzz to the folksy and welcoming space, with photos and caricatures of celebrity admirers lining the walls.

Mercado da Baixa   Market €

(Map p58; www.adbaixapombalina.pt; Praça da Figueira; ☺10am-10pm Fri-Sun) This tented market/glorious food court on Praça da Figueira has been slinging cheese, wine, smoked sausages and other gourmet goodies since 1855. It takes place on the last weekend of each month and it is fantastic fun to stroll the stalls eating and drinking yourself into a gluttonous mess.

Mercado da Ribeira   Market €

(Map p58; www.timeoutmarket.com; Av 24 de Julho; ☺10am-midnight Sun-Wed, to 2am Thu-Sat; ☏) Doing trade in fresh fruit and veg, fish and flowers since 1892, this oriental-dome-topped market hall is the word on everyone's lips since Time Out transformed half of it into a gourmet food court in 2014. Now it's like Lisbon in microcosm, with everything from Garrafeira Nacional wines to Conserveira de Lisboa fish, Arcádia chocolate and Santini gelato.

Follow the lead of locals and come for a browse in the morning followed by lunch at one of 35 kiosks – there's everything from Café de São Bento's famous steak and fries to a stand by top-chef Henrique Sá Pessoa. Do not miss it.

Bettina & Niccolò Corallo Sweets €

(Map p58; www.claudiocorallo.com; Rua da Escola Politécnica 4; chocolate per kg from €90; ⊙10am-7pm Mon-Sat) Few chocolates command such undying devotion, but this family-run transplant from São Tomé and Príncipe elicits freakish enthusiasm for their thin artisan chocolate bars. Indeed, in ginger, orange, sea salt and pepper, sesame, and toffee and sea salt varieties, this is heart-stoppingly good stuff. Try a free sample with the excellent espresso before committing.

Both the *cacau* (from Venezuela, Bolivia and Dominicana) and coffee (from São Tomé) are roasted in-house. Family members run the show and are always willing to give you the lowdown on their sweet homespun journey.

O Prego da Peixaria Portuguese €

(www.opregodapeixaria.com; Rua da Escola Politécnica 40; sandwiches €8.50-13; ⊙12.30pm-midnight, to 1am Fri-Sat; 🛜) Grab a seat on rustic, reclaimed-hardwood cinema seats at this hotspot specialising in gourmet *pregos* (steak sandwiches). A perfect lunch here starts with the best *pica-pau* we've found in Lisbon (bite-size pieces of steak swimming in garlic-white-wine sauce and then sopped up with garlic-butter-slathered *bolo de caco* bread), followed by the excellent Azores tuna sandwich with sweet-potato fries.

You'll find additional outlets at Mercado da Ribeira and Saldanha.

Chapitô à Mesa Portuguese €€

(Map p54; ☏218 875 077; www.facebook.com/chapitoamesa; Rua Costa do Castelo 7; mains €18-21; ⊙noon-11pm Mon-Fri, 7.30-11pm Sat-Sun; 🛜) Up a spiral iron staircase from this circus school's casual cafe, the decidedly creative menu of Chef Bertílio Gomes is served alongside views worth writing home about. His modern takes include classic dishes (*bacalhau à Brás*, stewed veal cheeks, suckling pig), plus daring ones (rooster testicles – goes swimmingly with a drop of Quinta da Sllveira Reserva).

DeliDelux Cafe €

(www.delidelux.pt; Av Infante Dom Henrique, Armazém B, Loja 8; mains €6.90-10.40; ⊙10am-10pm Sun-Thu, to midnight Fri-Sat; 🛜) Despite a bounty of wine, cheeses, olive oils and other gourmet goodies, this deli's wonderful waterfront patio has yet to be discovered by tourists (even though this string of converted warehouses is attached to – though not accessible from – the cruise-ship terminal). The charcuterie plates, salads, sandwiches and other light bites are all of exceptional quality.

Os Gazeteiros Modern European €€

(Map p54; ☏939 501 211; www.osgazeteiros.pt; Rua das Escolas Gerais 114-116; prix-fixe lunch/dinner €14/20; ⊙noon-3pm Tue-Wed, noon-3pm & 6pm-2am Thu-Fri, 11am-3pm & 6pm-2am Sat-Sun; 🛜) 🍃 French chef David Eyguesier honed his skills at Pois Café, then his own underground restaurant at home before opening this sorely needed Alfama gem whose name loosely translates as 'The Truants' (he 'skipped' culinary school!). His daily changing, market-fresh set menus delight under a spiderweb of modern lighting, beautiful geometric cabinetry and an open kitchen. No microwave. No freezer!

Pois Café Cafe €

(Map p54; www.poiscafe.com; Rua de São João da Praça 93; mains €7-10; ⊙noon-11pm Mon, 10am-11pm Tue-Sun; 🛜) Boasting a laid-back vibe under dominant stone arches, atmospheric Pois Café has creative salads, sandwiches and fresh juices, plus a handful of heartier daily specials (salmon quiche, sirloin steak). Its sofas invite lazy afternoons spent reading novels and sipping coffee, but you'll fight for space with the laptop brigade.

Placete Chafariz d'el Rei Breakfast €€

(Map p54; ☏218 886 150; www.chafarizdelrei.com; Tv do Chafariz de El-Rei 6; brunch €19; ⊙noon-6pm Wed-Fri, 11am-6pm Sat-Sun; 🛜) Entering the stained-glass-draped and palm-covered entrance hall of this hidden 20th-century mansion feels like a discovery, though the secret that this is one of Lisbon's top brunches is certainly out.

Mercado da Ribeira (p76)

The exquisite tea room books up fast with socialites and foodies gnawing on towers of creamy cheeses and house-baked breads, savoury cold cuts, warm croissants and freshly squeezed juices.

Mercantina   Pizza €€

(Map p58; ☎231 070 013; www.mercantina. pt; Rua da Misericórdia 114; pizza €8.70-14, pasta €10.80-13.40; ⊗noon-3.30pm & 7.30-11.30pm Mon-Thu, noon-3.30pm & 7pm-midnight Fri, 12.30-3.30pm & 7pm-midnight Sat, 12.30-3.30pm & 7-11.30pm Sun; ⭤) You'll find Lisbon's best pizza – uncut, certified by Napoli's strict *Associazione Verace Pizza Napoletana* – at this cosy Chiado hotspot whose hardwood-heavy decor vaguely approaches skilodge territory. The spicy *diavola* (tomato, mozzarella, ventricina, Parmesan and basil) and *mercantina* (tomato, mozzarella, ham, salami, mushrooms and Parmesan) are both showstoppers, but don't discount the phenomenal lasagna. Reserve ahead online.

Sala de Corte   Steak €€

(Map p58; ☎213 460 030; www.saladecorte. pt; Rua da Ribeira Nova 28; steaks €11.50-29; ⊗noon-3pm & 7pm-midnight Mon-Fri, noon-

midnight Sat-Sun; ⭤) The not-to-be-missed 'cut room' in Cais do Sodré dishes out succulent, perfectly seasoned imported beef in six cuts (entrecôte, *picanha*, sirloin, chateaubriand etc), which are chargrilled in a small, world-class Josper grill/oven hybrid, then prepped and beautifully presented on wooden planks in an intimate open kitchen. When you're sick of seafood, run here – but not without a reservation!

Pssst...the bathrooms are behind that walk-in freezer door.

Mini Bar   Fusion €€

(Map p58; ☎211 305 393; www.minibar.pt; Rua António Maria Cardoso 58; small plates €2.40-12.50, tasting menus €39-48.50; ⊗7pm-2am; ⭤) Trendy and fun, Mini Bar is the most approachable and hippest entry point into the innovative cuisine of Michelin-starred chef José Avillez, who has several restaurants in the vicinity. Billed as a gourmet bar amid theatre-inspired decor, it's a trendy mashup of nightlife and fine dining, where you'll enjoy exceptional craft drinking alongside small, chef-driven *petiscos* (small plates).

The two tasting menus are the way to go. Standout dishes? Exploding El Bulli olives, oxtail with maize porridge, beef tartar with mustard emulsion and the lemon-lime globe for dessert. There's great wine and exceptional service as well.

Cervejaria Ribadouro   Seafood €€

(☏213 549 411; www.cervejariaribadouro.pt; Rua do Salitre 2; mains €10-28, seafood per kg €41-180; ⏰noon-12.30am; 🛜) Bright, noisy and full to the gills, this bustling beer hall is popular with local seafood fans, some of whom just belly up to the bar, chase their fresh shrimp and *tremoços* (Lupin beans) with an ice-cold *imperial* (draft beer) and call it a night. The shellfish are plucked fresh from the tank, weighed and cooked to lip-smacking perfection.

The highlights are long: anything *à Brás* (mixed with eggs and potatoes), Bulhão Pato–style clams (with olive oil, coriander and garlic) and done-with-love versions of cheaper staples such as *bitoque* (steak and eggs).

As Velhas   Portuguese €€

(Map p58; ☏213 422 490; www.facebook. com/restaurante.as.velhas; Rua da Conceição da Glória 21; mains €17-23; ⏰noon-3pm & 7-10pm) No airs, no graces, just hearty helpings of Portuguese soul food served by delightfully old-school servers are what you can expect at this beamed restaurant. The monkfish and clams in garlic and coriander sauce is superb, as is the duck rice. Don't skip that dessert cart!

Antiga Confeitaria de Belém   Patisserie €

(Map p63; ☏213 637 423; www.pasteisde belem.pt; Rua de Belém 84-92; pastries from €1.05; ⏰8am-11pm Oct-Jun, to midnight Jul-Sep) Since 1837, this patisserie has been transporting locals to sugar-coated nirvana with heavenly *pastéis de belém*. The crisp pastry nests are filled with custard cream, baked at 200°C for that perfect golden crust, then lightly dusted with cinnamon. Admire *azulejos* in the vaulted rooms or devour a still-warm tart at the counter and try to guess the secret ingredient.

Go early midweek to avoid nasty lines.

Top Tips for Lisbon

○ Visit museums on the first Sunday of the month – many are free! Avoid Monday, when many are closed.

○ Reserve ahead at popular restaurants. Without reservations, you'll often be turned away at hotspots, even in low season or midweek.

○ Keep cash on hand. Some small shops, restaurants and guesthouses will only accept Portuguese-issued plastic (Multibanco).

○ Those tempting olives, cheeses and bread baskets your server slaps down at your table unsolicited? Those are *not* free! Send them back if you do not want them.

○ Save €3.50 by entering the Elevador de Santa Justa from the top side behind Convento do Carmo and paying just €1.50 to access the platform.

Casa de Pasto   Portuguese €€

(Map p58; ☏963 739 979; www.casade pasto.com; Rua do São Paulo 20, 1st fl; mains €10-22; ⏰12.30-3pm & 6-11pm Mon-Wed, to midnight Thu-Sat; 🛜) Up the stairs behind a not-very-triumphant facade lays this surprising treasure trove of 19th-century Portuguese bric-a-brac – seashell nightlights, ceramic taxidermy, gaudy mirrors – which fascinate while Diogo Noronha, a former Per Se intern and one of Lisbon's top upstart chefs, does decidedly delightful things with his charcoal oven. The tuna? The pork cheeks? The grilled veggies? Perfect.

Tasca Kome   Japanese €€

(Map p58; ☏211 340 117; www.kome-lisboa. com; Rua da Madalena 57; mains €7-15, sushi plates from €15; ⏰noon-2.30pm & 7-10pm Mon-Thu, noon-3pm & 7-10pm Fri, 12.30-3pm & 7-10pm Sat; 🛜) This blink-and-you'll-miss-it Japanese *tasca* is one of Lisbon's few turning out authentic cuisine from the

When to go to Lisbon

The peak summer season (June to August) serves up hot weather and is the best time for open-air festivals, beach days and al fresco dining. However, the perfect season for exploring may be spring (March to May) – it has milder but often sunny days, and accommodation is still reasonably priced.

Patterned cobblestones, Belém

Land of the Rising Sun. The menu doesn't overwhelm with options; instead, there's exquisite sushi, *tonkatsu* (breaded pork cutlets), *shime saba* (mackerel ceviche), slow-cooked pork belly and the like (eggplant bolognese for vegetarians), all nicely washed down with sake or *mugi-cha* (roasted barley tea).

The €9.50 lunch specials are perfect little deals.

Nova Pombalina   Portuguese €

(Map p58; www.facebook.com/anovapomba lina; Rua do Comércio 2; sandwiches €2.20-4; ⊙7am-7.30pm, closed Sun) The reason this bustling traditional restaurant is always packed around midday is its delicious *leitão* (suckling pig) sandwich, served on freshly baked bread in 60 seconds or less by the lightning-fast crew behind the counter.

A fresh juice and a light and delicious cheese tart made with artisanal sheep cheese from Seia round out this classic cheapie quite nicely.

Taberna Tosca   Tapas €€

(Map p58; ☑218 034 563; www.taberna tosca.com; Praça São Paulo 21; tapas €7-15.50; ⊙noon-midnight) A peaceful retreat from nearby Rua Nova do Carvalho mayhem, Tosca is an enticing spot for Portuguese tapas and bold Douro reds (but don't be afraid to spring for a pitcher of fabulous port sangria). Open-air seating is on leafy Praça São Paulo in front, opposite an 18th-century church, making it feel like a hidden Lisbon highlight.

The owners have opened the more bar-oriented Mercearia Tosca next door. If you aren't planning to eat, head there as we received some food-order pressure on our visit.

Rio Maravila   Fusion €€

(Map p64; ☑966 028 229; www.riomaravilha. pt; Rua Rodrigues de Faria 103, LX Factory; small plates €5-20; ⊙6pm-2am Tue, 12.30pm-2am Wed-Sat, 12.30pm-6pm Sun) In the former break room on the top floor of LX Factory (p64), Diogo Noronha's Portuguese-Brazilian small-plate party frames outstanding views of Cristo Rei, Ponte 25 de Abril and the Rio Tejo.

Kitschy hi-tech elements such as interactive bathtubs aside, dishes here are prepared by one of Lisbon's top young chefs. Go-to shared plates include the rich egg BT (with pancetta, Parmesan and cheese), a creamy duck rice and a decadent 70% chocolate dessert. Creative cocktails and fun young servers egg on the festivities, along with live *forró* (accordion-driven Northeastern Brazilian music) and reggae on Saturday nights.

Enoteca de Belém   Portuguese, Wine Bar €€

(Map p63; ☑213 631 511; www.travessada ermida.com; Travessa do Marta Pinto 10; mains €16.50-18; ⊙1-11pm Tue-Sun; 🛜) Tucked down a quiet lane just off Belém's main thoroughfare, this casual wine bar serves modernised Portuguese classics (fantastic octopus, Iberian pork), matched by an excellent selection of full-bodied Douro reds and refreshing Alentejan whites. The experience – led by well-trained servers particularly adept at gravitating you towards a juice that marries with your tastes – is distinctively memorable.

Churrasco da Graça Portuguese €€

(Map p54; Largo da Graça 43; mains €8.50-13.50; ⊙11am-midnight Mon-Sat) This cheerful, no-nonsense grill sits bang in the heart of Graça. At lunchtime the place bustles with hungry locals, who come for grilled seafood and steaks cooked to a T and served with a mound of fries and savoury rice.

 DRINKING & NIGHTLIFE

Portas do Sol Bar

(Map p54; www.portasdosol.pt; Largo das Portas do Sol; cocktails €6; ⊙10am-1am, to 2am Fri-Sat; 🛜) Near one of Lisbon's iconic viewpoints, this spacious sun-drenched terrace has a mix of sofas and white patio furniture, where you can sip cocktails while taking in magnificent river views. DJs bring animation to the darkly lit industrial interior on weekends.

Red Frog Cocktail Bar

(www.facebook.com/redfrogspeakeasy; Rua do Salitre 5A; cocktails €8-12.50; ⊙6pm-2am Sun-Thu, to 4am Fri-Sat) In true speakeasy fashion, sign-less Red Frog is accessed via a 'Press Here for Cocktails' doorbell. Enter a sophisticated world of mixology, where craft cocktails are king and appropriate behaviour, dress and glassware are tenants. The exquisite seasonal cocktail menu is perfectly balanced and the dark and classy room (including the intriguing secret one) is a perfect accompaniment.

Park Bar

(Map p58; www.facebook.com/OOpark; Calçada do Combro 58; cocktails €6.50-8; ⊙1pm-2am Tue-Sat, 1-8pm Sun; 🛜) If only all multistorey car parks were like this... Take the elevator to the 5th floor, and head up and around to the top, which has been transformed into one of Lisbon's hippest rooftop bars, with sweeping views reaching right down to the Tejo and over the bell towers of Santa Catarina Church.

The vibe is cool and creative and DJs spin hip hop, jazz and house at all hours. Plopping yourself down on the sunset-facing wooden chairs in the late afternoon is a Lisbon must.

Pensão Amor Bar

(Map p58; www.pensaoamor.pt; Rua do Alecrim 19; cocktails €5.50-13; ⊙noon-3am Mon-Wed, to 4am Thu-Sat, to 3am Sun) Set inside a former brothel, this cheeky bar pays homage to its passion-filled past with colourful wall murals, a library of erotic-tinged works and a small stage where you can sometimes catch burlesque shows. The Museu Erótico de Lisboa (MEL) was on the way at time of research.

Memmo Alfama Bar

(Map p54; www.memmoalfama.com; Travessa das Merceeiras 27; cocktails €8-9.50; ⊙noon-11pm; 🛜) Wow what a view! Alfama unfolds like origami from the stylishly decked roof terrace of the Memmo Alfama hotel. It's perfect sundowner material, with dreamy views over the rooftops, spires and down to the Rio Tejo.

Lux-Frágil Club

(www.luxfragil.com; Av Infante Dom Henrique, Armazém A - Cais de Pedra, Santo Apolónia; ⊙11pm-6am Thu-Sat) Lisbon's ice-cool, must-see club, Lux hosts big-name DJs spinning electro and house. It's run by ex-Frágil maestro Marcel Reis and part-owned by John Malkovich. Grab a spot on the terrace to see the sun rise over the Tejo; or chill like a king on the throne-like giant interior chairs.

Style policing is heartwarmingly lax but arrive after 4am at weekends and you might have trouble getting in because of the crowds.

A Tabacaria Bar

(Map p58; Rua de São Paulo 75; cocktails €7.50-16; ⊙4pm-2am) Small and intimate (and simultaneously sleek and grungy), this Cais do Sodré newcomer boasts a beautiful hardwood back bar and stained glass originally from this space when it opened as an exchange bureau in 1885. No tourists are here (well, until now, anyway...) and it serves mostly beer and gin and tonics

The Great Lisbon Earthquake

At 9.40am on All Saints' Day, 1 November 1755, Lisbon was forever changed. Three major earthquakes hit, as residents celebrated Mass, in what is considered one of the most powerful earthquake sequences in recorded human history, measuring between an estimated 8.5 and 9.1 on the moment magnitude scale. The tremors brought an even more devastating fire and tsunami. Some estimate that as many as 90,000 of Lisbon's 270,000 inhabitants died. Much of the city was ruined, never to regain its former status. Dom João I's chief minister, the formidable Marquês de Pombal, immediately began rebuilding in a simple, cheap, earthquake-proof style that created today's formal grid around the Pombaline downtown area known as Baixa.

Arco da Rua Augusta (p57)
JOSÉ LUIS VEGA / 500PX ©

(made with unique house-macerated tinctures).

BA Wine Bar do Bairro Alto   Wine Bar

(Map p58; ☎213 461 182; bawinebar@gmail.com; Rua da Rosa 107; wines from €3, tapas from €12; ☻6-11pm Tue-Sun; ☞) Reserve ahead unless you want to get shut out of Bairro Alto's best wine bar, where the genuinely welcoming staff will offer you three fantastic choices to taste based on your wine proclivities. The cheeses (from small artisanal producers) and charcuterie (melt-in-your-mouth black-pork *presuntos*) are not to be missed, either. You could spend the night here.

Ginjinha Rubi   Ginjinha Bar

(Map p58; Rua Barros Queirós 27; ☻7am-10.30pm Mon-Sat) Squeeze into this hole-in-the-wall bar to natter with locals over a *ginjinha* (cherry liqueur; €1.40) or three and admire the *azulejos*.

A Ginjinha   Ginjinha Bar

(Map p58; Largo de Saõ Domingos 8; ☻9am-10pm) Hipsters, old men in flat caps, office workers and tourists all meet at this microscopic *ginjinha* bar for that moment of cherry-licking, pip-spitting pleasure (€1.40 a shot).

Watch the owner line 'em up at the bar under the beady watch of the drink's 19th-century inventor, Espinheira. It's less about the grog, more about the event.

Foxtrot   Bar

(Map p64; www.barfoxtrot.com; Travessa Santa Teresa 28; cocktails €7-15; ☻6pm-3am Mon-Sat, 8pm-2am Sun; ☞) A cuckoo-clock doorbell announces new arrivals to this dark, decadent slither of art-nouveau glamour, in the bar business since 1978. Foxtrot keeps the mood mellow with jazzy beats, excruciatingly attentive mixology detailed on a tracing-paper menu and a chilled feline that isn't afraid to belly up to the bar. It's a wonderfully moody spot for a chat.

Cinco Lounge   Lounge

(Map p64; www.cincolounge.com; Rua Ruben António Leitão 17; cocktails from €7.50; ☻9pm-2am) Take an award-winning London-born mixologist, Dave Palethorpe, add a candlelit, turquoise-kissed setting and give it a funky twist – *et voilà* – you have Cinco Lounge. Come here to converse, sip legendary cocktails or join a cocktail-mixing workshop. Cash only.

Chapitô   Bar

(Map p54; ☎218 875 077; www.chapito.org; Costa do Castelo 7; mains €18-24; ☻terrace noon-2am, restaurant 7pm-2am; ☞) This alternative theatre/circus school occupies a former female prison and offers fantastic views from its bar. It's a top choice for a sundowner or a late-night drink overlooking the city. More serious foodies will want to

book a table at the restaurant, Chapitô
à Mesa (p77), in the hands of Bertílio
Gomes, one of the city's top chefs.

When school is in session, the terrace is
reserved for students during school hours.

Wine Bar do Castelo   Wine Bar
(Map p54; ☎218 879 093; www.winebardo
castelo.blogspot.pt; Rua Bartolomeu de Gusmão
13; wines by the glass €4-30; ☺1-10pm) Located
near the entrance to the Castelo de São
Jorge (p52), this laid-back wine bar
serves more than 150 Portuguese wines
by the glass, along with gourmet smoked
meats, cheeses, olives and other tasty
accompaniments. Nuno, the multilingual
owner, is a welcoming host and a fount of
knowledge about all things wine-related.

Graça do Vinho   Wine Bar
(Map p54; www.facebook.com/gracadovinholx;
Calçada da Graça 10; ☺noon-11pm Mon-Fri,
12.30pm-12.30am Sat) This former pharmacy
serves a refreshing variety of wines (at
least 50 by the glass), which go nicely with
cheeses, sardines, smoked meats and
other appetisers.

LisBeer   Beer Hall
(Map p54; www.facebook.com/lisbeerbar;
Beco do Arco Escuro 1; pints €4-7; ☺4am-1am
Thu-Thu, to 3am Fri-Sat; 🛜) The loungiest
and least beer-geeky of Lisbon's craft beer
bars, Sé's LisBeer offers six artisanal brews
on tap and another 250 or so in the bottle,
divided by style and country with an obvious emphasis on Portugal's rising scene.
It's a good spot to get hopped up among
various rooms of tattered leather sofas and
mismatched tables.

Capela   Bar
(Map p58; www.facebook.com/acapelabar;
Rua da Atalaia 45; ☺8pm-2am Sun-Thu, to 3am
Fri-Sat) According to (questionable) legend
this was once a Gothic chapel, but today
Capela's gospel is an experimental line-up
of electronica and funky house. Get there
early (before midnight) to appreciate the
DJs before the crowds descend. Frescoes,
Renaissance-style nude murals and dusty
chandeliers add a boho-chic touch.

Duque Brewpub   Brewery
(Map p58; www.duquebrewpub.com; Duques
da Calçada 49; pints €5.50-8.90; ☺noon-1am;
🛜) Lisbon's first brewpub debuted in 2016
with 10 taps, five of which will be eventually
dedicated to on-site suds (under the ban-
ner of Cerveja Aroeira) brewed in true craft-
beer style: no two batches are the same.
Additional taps feature invited Portuguese
craft beers such as Passarola, Dois Corvos
and Letra.

Take a load off with a hoppy IPA on the
pleasant sidewalk seating or hang out in
the cosy indoor space, where the tunes pop
seamlessly between early '80s Depeche
Mode to solo Morrissey to sexy modern
fado from Gisela João.

Primeiro Andar   Bar
(Map p58; Rua das Portas de Santo Antão
110, Ateneu Comercial de Lisboa; ☺7pm-2am;
🛜) Although it's right above a touristy
pedestrian street, this delightful cafe-bar
remains well-concealed from the masses.
Despite initial appearances, it's a welcoming, laid-back place. To get here, follow the
small alley about 30m south of the Ateneu
Comercial de Lisboa building, go to the
end and head inside the dark entrance
and cross a basketball court: *voila!* Local's
secret jackpot!

Bosq   Club
(Map p64; ☎210 938 029; www.facebook.
com/bosqlx; Rua Rodrigues Faria 103, LX Factory;
☺11pm-5am Fri-Sat) The newest tenant for
LX Factory (p64) is this hyper-cool
two-storey nightclub, which features a
120-sq-metre vertical garden above the
upstairs bar and duelling environments
that bounce between dance, R&B and hip
hop. Lisbon's bold and beautiful flock here
to dance under the guise of nightlife-ready
animal portraits and 3D wallpaper.

⭐ ENTERTAINMENT

Hot Clube de Portugal   Jazz
(Map p58; ☎213 460 305; www.hcp.pt; Praça
da Alegria 48; ☺10pm-2am Tue-Sat) As hot
as its name suggests, this small, poster-

plastered cellar (and newly added garden) has staged top-drawer jazz acts since the 1940s. It's considered one of Europe's best.

A Tasco do Chico   Fado
(Map p58; ☏961 339 696; www.facebook.com/atasca.dochico; Rua Diário de Notícias 39; ☺noon-2am, to 3am Fri-Sat) This crowded dive (reserve ahead), full of soccer banners and spilling over with people of all ilk, is a fado free-for-all. It's not uncommon for taxi drivers to roll up, hum a few bars, and hop right back into their cabs, speeding off into the night. Portugal's most famous fado singer, Mariza, brought us here in 2005. It's legit.

Bar da Velha Senhora   Live Music
(Map p58; www.facebook.com/bardavelha senhora; Rua Nova do Carvalho 40; ☺6pm-2am Tue-Thu, to 3am Fri-Sat) The fabulously burlesque Bar da Velha Senhora whisks you back to those crazy days of the 1920s, with its low-lit interior and glittering revue shows. Tapas and cocktails with risqué names get the crowd in the mood for fado, cabaret, Latin jazz, flamenco, erotic poetry recitals and more.

Senhor Fado   Fado
(Map p54; ☏218 874 298; www.sr-fado.com; Rua dos Remédios 176; ☺8pm-2am Wed-Sat) Small and lantern-lit, this is a cosy spot for *fado vadio* (street fado). *Fadista* Ana Marina and guitarist Duarte Santos make a great double act.

Parreirinha de Alfama   Fado
(Map p54; ☏218 868 209; www.parreirinhade alfama.com; Beco do Espírito Santo 1; minimum €30; ☺8pm-2am) Owned by fado legend Argentina Santos, this place offers good food amid candlelit ambience; it attracts an audience that often falls hard for the top-quality *fadistas* (three singers and two guitarists per night, sometimes appearing straight from the crowd). Book by 4pm.

Mesa de Frades   Fado
(Map p54; ☏917 029 436; www.facebook.com/mesadefradeslisboa; Rua dos Remédios 139A; ☺8pm-2.30am Mon-Sat) A magical place to hear fado, tiny Mesa de Frades used to be a chapel. It's tiled with exquisite *azulejos* and has just a handful of tables. The show

Fado performance at A Baîuca

begins around 11pm. Skip the food (which is hit-or-miss) and stick to drinks.

A Baîuca
Fado

(Map p54; ☎218 867 284; Rua de São Miguel 20; ⊗8pm-midnight Thu-Mon) On a good night, walking into A Baîuca is like gate-crashing a family party. It's a special place with *fado vadio*, where locals take a turn and spectators hiss if anyone dares to chat during the singing. There's a €25 minimum spend, which is as tough to swallow as the food, though the fado is spectacular. Reserve ahead.

Cinemateca Portuguesa
Cinema

(www.cinemateca.pt; Rua Barata Salgueiro 39; films €3.20) Screens offbeat, art-house, world and old films.

Fundação Calouste Gulbenkian
Live Music

(☎217 823 000; https://gulbenkian.pt; Av de Berna 45A) Home to the Gulbenkian Orchestra, this classical-music heavyweight stages first-rate concerts and ballets.

Bela
Fado

(Map p54; ☎926 077 511; Rua dos Remédios 190; ⊗8pm-3am Tue-Sun) This intimate spot features live fado on Wednesday, Friday, Saturday and Sunday, and eclectic cultural fare (poetry readings, jazz nights) on other nights. Although there is a €15-minimum consumption, unlike most fado houses, you won't have to buy a pricey meal as it's an appetisers-and-drinks kind of place. Fado begins at 9.15pm.

Senhor Vinho
Fado

(Map p64; ☎213 972 681; www.srvinho.com; Rua do Meio á Lapa 18; minimum €15; ⊗7.30pm-2am) Fado star Maria da Fé owns this small place, welcoming first-rate *fadistas*. Go for the fado (from 7pm), not the food, and feel free to refuse menu extras.

Adega dos Fadistas
Fado

(Map p54; ☎211 510 368; Rua dos Remédios 102; ⊗noon-2am Tue-Sun) One of the top newer fado houses in the Alfama, the Adega dos Fadistas serves up first-rate fado in a medieval-like stone-walled dining room.

⇱ Off the Beaten Track

The neighbourhood of Madragoa, west of Baixa, with its narrow lanes and charming restaurants, is reminiscent of the Alfama, but with a fraction of the tourists. Take tram 25 from Praça do Comércio to get there.

Colourful houses in Madragoa
MAURICIO ABREU / GETTY IMAGES ©

Mains cost around €17 and the added music charge is €10. Shows start at 9pm most nights.

Fado in Chiado
Fado

(Map p58; ☎961 717 778; www.fadoinchiado.com; Espaço Chiado, Rua da Miséricordia 14; admission €17; ⊗7pm Mon-Sat) Inside a small theatre, the 50-minute nightly shows feature high-quality fado – a male and a female singer and two guitarists – and it is held early so you can grab dinner afterwards.

Zé dos Bois
Live Music

(ZDB; Map p58; www.zedosbois.org; Rua da Barroca 59; cover €6-10; ⊗expositions 6-11pm Wed-Sat, concerts from 10pm) Focusing on tomorrow's performing-arts and music trends, Zé dos Bois is an experimental venue with a graffitied courtyard and an eclectic line-up of theatre, film, visual arts and live music.

Meo Arena
Concert Venue

(☎218 918 471; www.arena.meo.pt; Rossio dos Olivais, Parque das Nações) Sporting an energy-efficient zinc roof, this UFO-shaped arena is Portugal's largest, hosting big international acts Dave Matthews Band, Lady Gaga, Beyoncé and beyond.

ℹ️ INFORMATION

Mind your wallet on tram 28 – a major hotspot for pickpockets – and at other tourist hubs such as Rua Augusta.

In an emergency, dial:

Police 📞112
Fire 📞112
Ambulance 📞112
Lisbon Tourist Police 📞213 421 623

ℹ️ GETTING THERE & AWAY

AIR

Situated around 6km north of the centre, the ultramodern **Aeroporto de Lisboa** (p301) operates direct flights to major international hubs including London, New York, Paris and Frankfurt. Several low-cost carriers (Easyjet, Ryanair, Transavia, Norwegian etc) leave from the less-efficient terminal 2 – you'll need to factor in extra time for the shuttle ride if arriving at the airport on the metro.

BUS

Lisbon's main long-distance bus terminal is **Rodoviário de Sete Rios** (Praça General Humberto Delgado, Rua das Laranjeiras), adjacent to both Jardim Zoológico metro station and Sete Rios train station. The big carriers, **Rede Expressos** (📞707 223 344; www.rede-expressos.pt) and **Eva** (📞707 223 344; www.eva-bus.com), run frequent services to almost every major town. You can buy your ticket up to seven days in advance.

Domestic services:

Coimbra €14.50, 2½ hours, 15 to 25 daily.
Évora €12.50, 1½ hours, 10 to 20 daily.
Faro €20, 3½ hours, four to eight daily.
Porto €20, 3½ hours, 10 to 20 daily.

Intercentro (📞707 200 512; www.intercentro.pt; Gare do Oriente) runs coaches to destinations all over Europe, beginning at Sete Rios and stopping at Gare do Oriente 15 minutes later. In addition to Madrid, there are direct connections to Paris (€91, 28 hours, 9.15am) and Amsterdam (€147, 35 hours, 7am).

TRAIN

Lisbon is linked by train to other major cities. Check the **Comboios de Portugal** website (www.cp.pt) for schedules. Express services:

Coimbra €20, two hours, 10 to 20 daily.
Évora €12, 1½ hours, three to four daily.
Faro €21, three hours, three to six daily.
Porto €24, three hours, seven to 18 daily.

Lisbon has several major train stations.

ℹ️ GETTING AROUND

BUS, TRAM & FUNICULAR

Companhia Carris de Ferro de Lisboa (p51) operates all transport in Lisbon proper except the metro. Its buses and trams run from about 5am or 6am to about 10pm or 11pm; there are some night bus and tram services.

Pick up a transport map, *Rede de Transportes de Lisboa*, from tourist offices. The Carris website has timetables and route details.

Board tram 28 at Praça Martim Moniz. You'll increase your chances of a seat and avoid waiting at heavier trafficked tourist areas where packed trams skip stops.

METRO

The **metro** (www.metro.transporteslisboa.pt; single/day ticket €1.40/6; ⏱6.30am-1am) is useful for short hops and to reach the stations.

Buy tickets from metro ticket machines, which have English-language menus. The Lisboa Card is also valid.

Entrances are marked by a big red 'M'. Useful signs include *correspondência* (transfer between lines) and *saída* (exit to the street).

TICKETS & PASSES

On-board one-way prices are €1.80 for buses, €2.85 for trams and €3.60 (return) for funicular rides (one-way tickets not available). A day pass for all public transport is €6.

Where to Stay

You're spoilt for choice in the Portuguese capital when it comes to places to unpack your duffle bag. Each neighbourhood has its own noise level so choose carefully. Room rates tend to be lower than in most of Western Europe.

Neighbourhood	Atmosphere
Alfama, Castelo & Graça	The Alfama's cobbled streets and lanes generally offer fairly peaceful slumber, though choose wisely or else you might find yourself being serenaded to sleep by a warbling *fadista*. On its hilltop perch above Lisbon, leafy Graça has wonderfully dramatic views.
Bairro Alto, Chiado & Around	Well-heeled Chiado has high-quality top-end and budget options, but little in between. Bairro Alto is nightlife central, meaning you won't get much rest amid the late-night (early-morning) revelry. The hip Santa Catarina district has a few sound options.
Baixo & Rossio	Sandwiched between the Alfama and Bairro Alto, this central area is packed with options, including high-end hotels, modest and upper-end guesthouses and first-rate backpacker and party hostels. You can walk everywhere and the area is served well by Lisbon's public transport system.
Príncipe Real, Santos & Estrela	Leafy neighbourhoods and plenty of style set the scene for an overnight stay in the top-notch boutique hotels here. It's ideal for escapists who prefer pin-drop peace to central bustle.

PORTO

Porto at a Glance...

Opening up like a pop-up book from the Rio Douro at sunset, humble-yet-opulent Porto entices with its higgledy-piggledy medieval centre, divine food and wine, and charismatic locals. Porto's charms are as subtle as the nuances of an aged tawny port, best savoured slowly on a romp through the hilly backstreets of Miragaia, Ribeira and Massarelos. It's the quiet moments of reflection and the snapshots of daily life that you'll remember most: the slosh of the Douro against the docks; the sound of wine glasses clinking. The city also has some of Portugal's top festivals and restaurants.

Porto in Two Days

Spend day one exploring the **Ribeira**'s knot of alleyways, churches and palaces, including the Romanesque **Sé** (p100), the **Palácio da Bolsa** (p100)and the **Igreja de São Francisco** (p101). On day two take a culinary tour of the city and take in more of its architecture, *azulejos* spotting as you go. End the day at a pavement cafe on the **Cais da Ribeira**, (p95) followed by dinner.

Porto in Four Days

Take your taste buds on day three across the Rio Douro to the **Vila Nova de Gaia** (p96) where you'll discover many old port-wine cellars, some still belonging to the original British merchant families who established them. Spend day four exploring some of Porto's other superb attractions such as the exquisitely tiled **São Bento Train Station** (p105) and the waterfront.

Central Porto Map (p102)

Arriving in Porto

Francisco de Sá Carneiro Airport
Linked to many European hubs.

Bus station There is no central bus station – bus companies arrive and depart from a variety of places throughout the city.

Campanhã train station 3km east of the city centre – handles long-distance trains.

São Bento train station Local train services.

Sleeping

Porto's sleeping scene has experienced an incredible renaissance in the last couple of years, due to the influx of weekend visitors arriving on low-cost flights. Time-worn *residenciales* (guest houses) are slowly being replaced, and hipsterish hostels, retro-cool guest houses and slickly modern apartments (look for the 'AL' sign) are now plentiful.

Wine, Tiles & Custard Tarts

The cultural trinity that intrigues every visitor to Portugal's second city is its unique wines, eye-catching tiles and addictive custard tarts.

Great For...

☑ Don't Miss

The exquisite *azulejos* at the city's São Bento train station.

Wine

You can't say you've been to Porto until you've tasted the Douro's oak-barrel-aged nectar. Ever since the 17th century, lodges in Vila Nova de Gaia have been the nerve centre of port production. It was probably Roman soldiers who first planted grapes in the Douro Valley. According to legend, British merchants invented port when they added brandy to the wine to preserve it for shipment back to England. Something about the fortification of the wine and the time it spent in hot barrels at sea turned the wine into the wonderful beverage we know today. Madeira's famous desert wine was 'accidentally' produced in the same way.

Igreja do Carmo

MATT MUNRO / LONELY PLANET ©

Train Station (p105), a veritable ode to tile art with over 20,000 azulejos adorning the station's vestibule. Dating from 1905 to 1916, they are the romantic work of tile painter Jorge Colaço and depict scenes from Portugal's history. Another of Colaço's *azulejos* masterpieces in Porto is the façade of the **Church of Saint Ildefonso** (Praça da Batalha; 🕑9am-noon & 3-6.30pm Mon-Sat, 9am-1pm Sun).

Wine Tasting

For an insightful primer on port, hook onto a tasting at Touriga (p113) or Vinologia (p119), where the learned owners give an enlightening lesson with each glass they pour, or sample fine ports by the glass at Prova (p119). From here, head across the Douro to Vila Nova de Gaia, the steep banks of which are speckled with grand port-wine lodges.

Azulejos

Azulejos greet you on almost every corner in Porto. One of the delights of taking a stroll through the centre is the tiles you will encounter. Old and new, utilitarian and decorative, plain and geometrically patterned. Some of the finest grace Porto's churches, but Porto's crowning *azulejos* glory is undoubtedly the resplendent São Bento

Pastel de Nata

Though native to Lisbon, Porto is as good a place as any to try the ubiquitous *pastel de nata*, often rather drearily translated into English as 'custard tart', which barely does this irresistible treat justice. Made with egg custard and cinnamon, baked in a cup of flaky pastry, once you've tried one you'll be hooked – many develop a 'one-a-day' habit throughout their time in Portugal. It doesn't help that they are so cheap as well – you'll have overpaid if you part with €1 for this most typical of Portuguese tooth-rotters. Porto's cafes are, of course, brimming with other traditional cakes and pastries, ideal for a cheap and filling breakfast accompanied by a cup of smooth and frothy Portuguese coffee.

Igreja de São Francisco (p101)

Ribeira

Ribeira is Porto's biggest heart stealer, with its Unesco World Heritage maze of medieval alleys that zigzag down to the Douro River. Exploring this postcard-perfect neighbourhood is a must for every visitor.

Great For...

☑ Don't Miss

Ponte de Dom Luís I – admire, photograph and walk across Porto's main bridge.

Churches & Palaces

Sitting on Praça Infante Dom Henrique, Igreja de São Francisco (p101) looks from the outside to be an austerely Gothic church, but inside it hides one of Portugal's most dazzling displays of baroque finery. Hardly an inch escapes unsmothered, as otherworldly cherubs and sober monks are drowned by nearly 100kg of gold leaf. If you see only one church in Porto, make it this one.

Porto's Sé (p100) is a hulking, hilltop fortress of the cathedral, founded in the 12th century though largely rebuilt a century later and extensively altered during the 18th century. You can still make out the church's Romanesque origins in the barrel-vaulted nave. Inside, a rose window and a 14th-century Gothic cloister also remain from its early days.

Ponte de Dom Luís I

ℹ Need to Know

The local metro stop is São Bento (yellow metro line D).

✕ Take a Break

Centrally located Mercearia das Flores (p115) is a delicatessen/food store serving Azores tea and light lunches.

★ Top Tip

Take a *barcos rabelos* tour to see the sights of Ribeira and Vila Nova de Gaia from the water.

The splendid neoclassical Palácio da Bolsa (p100) honours Porto's past and present money merchants. Just past the entrance is the glass-domed Pátio das Nações (Hall of Nations), where the exchange once operated. But this pales in comparison with rooms deeper inside; to visit these, join one of the half-hour guided tours (every 30 minutes).

Ponte de Dom Luís I

Completed in 1886 by a student of Gustave Eiffel, this **bridge's** (Map p102) top deck is now reserved for pedestrians, as well as one of the city's metro lines; the lower deck bears regular traffic, as well as narrow walkways for those on foot. The views of the river and Old Town are simply stunning, as are the daredevils who leap from the lower level. The bridge's construction was

significant, as the area's foot traffic once navigated a bridge made from old port boats lashed together. To make matters worse, the river was wild back then, with no upstream dams.

Cais da Ribeira

This riverfront **promenade** (Map p102) is postcard Porto, taking in the whole spectacular sweep of the city, from Ribeira's pastel houses stacked like Lego bricks to the *barcos rabelos* (flat-bottomed boats) once used to transport port from the Douro. Early evening buskers serenade crowds and chefs fire up grills in the hole-in-the-wall fish restaurants and *tascas* (taverns) in the old arcades.

Waterfront of Vila Nova de Gaia

Vila Nova de Gaia

Vila Nova de Gaia (simply 'Gaia' to locals) takes you back to the 17th-century beginnings of port-wine production, when British merchants transformed wine into the post-dinner tipple of choice.

Great For...

☑ Don't Miss

A tasting session at Graham's, Porto's finest port-wine lodge.

Wine Lodges

One of the main reasons to head to Porto is to sample port-wine, and the place to do this is Gaia. A good place to start is the **Espaço Porto Cruz** (Map p102; www.myportocruz. com; Largo Miguel Bombarda 23; ⊙11am-7pm Tue-Sun), a swanky emporium inside a restored 18th-century riverside building which celebrates all things port. In addition to a shop where tastings are held (€7.50 for three ports), there are exhibition halls, a rooftop terrace with panoramic views and a restaurant. **Graham's** (Map p102; ☑223 776 484; www.grahams-port.com; Rua do Agro 141; tours incl tasting €10-100; ⊙9.30am-6pm) is one of the original British-founded Gaia wine cellars, established way back in 1820. The complex has been totally revamped and now features a small museum. It's a big

Wine barrels at Croft

RICHARD SEMIK / GETTY IMAGES ©

❶ Need to Know

Metro line D runs through the Jardim do Morro stop.

✕ Take a Break

Dovrvm (☏ 220 917 910; Avenida Diogo Leite 454; mains €8-12; ⊗ noon-11pm) is a cosy bistro literally a stone's throw from the Ponte Dom Luís I.

★ Top Tip

For a less touristy feel, head higher up the hill to Graham's, Taylor's and Croft.

---

name and a popular choice for tours (30 minutes) where you can dip into atmospheric barrel-lined cellars and conclude with a tasting of three to eight port wines. British-run **Taylor's** (☏ 223 742 800, 223 772 956; www.taylor.pt; Rua do Choupelo 250; tours incl tasting €12; ⊗ 10am-6pm) boasts lovely, oh-so-English grounds with tremendous views of Porto. Its one-hour tours include a tasting of three top-of-the-range port wines. Its cellars are simply staggering, piled to the rafters with huge barrels, including the big one containing 100,000L of late bottled vintage. **Croft** (www.croftport.com; Rua Barão de Forrester 412; tours incl tasting €7; ⊗ 10am-6pm) and **Cálem** (Map p102; ☏ 223 746 660; www.calem.pt; Avenida Diogo Leite 344; tours incl tasting €6; ⊗ 10am-7pm May-Oct, to 6pm Nov-Apr) are other recommended places.

Teleférico de Gaia

Don't miss a ride on the **Teleférico de Gaia** (Map p102; www.gaiacablecar.com; one-way/ return €5/8; ⊗ 10am-8pm May-Sep, to 6pm Oct-Mar), an aerial gondola that provides fine views over the Douro and Porto on its short, five-minute jaunt between the southern end of the Ponte de Dom Luís I and the riverside. At the bridge end of the teleférico is a hilltop park called the **Jardim do Morro** (p105), which can also be reached by crossing the upper level of Ponte de Dom Luís I.

Mosteiro da Serra de Pilar

Watching over Gaia is this 17th-century hilltop **monastery** (Map p102; Rampa do Infante Santo; adult/child €3/1; ⊗ 10am-6.30pm Tue-Sun Apr-Oct, to 5.30pm Nov-Mar), with its striking circular cloister, church with gilded altar and stellar river views. Requisitioned by the future Duke of Wellington during the Peninsular War (1807–14), it still belongs to the Portuguese military and can only be visited on the 40-minute guided tours leaving hourly between 10.30am and 12.30pm and 2.30pm and 5.30pm.

Porto City Centre

This walking tour winds its way through the city centre, skirting the edge of the Ribeira before running along the river to Porto's main river bridge. The route takes in some of the city's architectural highlights and two of the best waterfront dining areas.

Start Torre dos Clérigos
Distance 2km
Duration Two to three hours

1 Begin at the baroque **Torre dos Clérigos** (p105), which offers unrivalled views over Porto from its 76m-high tower.

4 Near the end of Rua das Flores stands Nicolau Nasoni's baroque masterpiece, the **Igreja da Misericórdia**, part of the new Museu da Misericórdia do Porto (p101).

5 At the neoclassical **Palácio da Bolsa** (p100) check out the main courtyard (once Porto's stock exchange) for free, or stay on for a tour.

6 Just next door to the Palácio da Bolsa is the **Igreja de São Francisco** (p101), a severe Gothic facade hiding a jaw-dropping golden interior.

7 In Rua da Alfândega you'll find the medieval **Casa do Infante** (p105), the birthplace of Henry the Navigator and the site of some remarkable Roman ruins.

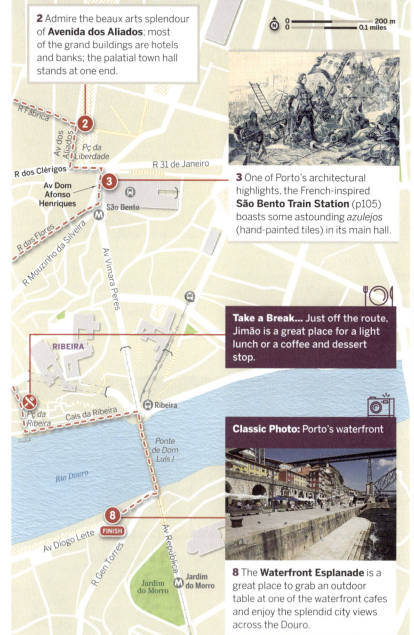

2 Admire the beaux arts splendour of **Avenida dos Aliados**; most of the grand buildings are hotels and banks; the palatial town hall stands at one end.

3 One of Porto's architectural highlights, the French-inspired **São Bento Train Station** (p105) boasts some astounding *azulejos* (hand-painted tiles) in its main hall.

Take a Break... Just off the route, Jimão is a great place for a light lunch or a coffee and dessert stop.

Classic Photo: Porto's waterfront

8 The **Waterfront Esplanade** is a great place to grab an outdoor table at one of the waterfront cafes and enjoy the splendid city views across the Douro.

⊙ SIGHTS

With the exception of the blockbuster Museu de Arte Contemporânea, Porto's must-sees cluster in the compact centre and are easily walkable. Many of the big hitters huddle in the Unesco-listed Ribeira district and Aliados, while hilltop Miragaia has some peaceful pockets of greenery and knockout views. For port-wine lodges aplenty, cross the river to Gaia.

◉ Ribeira

Sé   Cathedral

(Map p102; Terreiro da Sé; cloisters adult/ student €3/2; ⊘9am-12.30pm & 2.30-7pm Apr-Oct, to 6pm Nov-Mar) From Praça da Ribeira rises a tangle of medieval alleys and stairways that eventually reach the hulking, hilltop fortress of the cathedral. Founded in the 12th century, it was largely rebuilt a century later and then extensively altered during the 18th century. However, you can still make out the church's Romanesque origins in the barrel-vaulted nave. Inside, a rose window and a 14th-century Gothic cloister also remain from its early days.

History lends the cathedral gravitas – this is where King John I married his beloved Philippa of Lancaster in 1387, and where Prince Henry the Navigator was baptised in 1394, the fortune of far-flung lands but a distant dream.

Palácio da Bolsa   Historic Building

(Stock Exchange; Map p102; www.palacioda bolsa.com; Rua Ferreira Borges; tours adult/ child €8/4.50; ⊘9am-6.30pm Apr-Oct, 9am-12.30pm & 2-5.30pm Nov-Mar) This splendid neoclassical monument (built from 1842 to 1910) honours Porto's past and present money merchants. Just past the entrance is the glass-domed **Pátio das Nações** (Hall of Nations), where the exchange once operated. But this pales in comparison with rooms deeper inside; to visit these, join one of the half-hour guided tours, which set off every 30 minutes.

The highlight is a stupendous ballroom known as the **Salão Árabe** (Arabian Hall), with stucco walls that have been teased into complex Moorish designs, then gilded with some 18kg of gold.

Palácio da Bolsa

SAIKO3P / SHUTTERSTOCK ©

Igreja de São Francisco   Church

(Map p102; Praça Infante Dom Henrique; adult/child €4/2; ⊙9am-8pm Jul-Sep, to 7pm Mar-Jun & Oct, to 6pm Nov-Feb) Sitting on Praça Infante Dom Henrique, Igreja de São Francisco looks from the outside to be an austerely Gothic church, but inside it hides one of Portugal's most dazzling displays of baroque finery. Hardly a centimetre escapes unsmothered, as otherworldly cherubs and sober monks are drowned by nearly 100kg of gold leaf. If you see only one church in Porto, make it this one.

High on your list should be the nave, interwoven with vines and curlicues, dripping with cherubs and shot through with gold leaf. Peel back the layers to find standouts such as the Manueline-style Chapel of St John the Baptist, the 13th-century statue of St Francis of Assisi and the 18th-century Tree of Jesse, a polychrome marvel of an altarpiece. The church museum harbours a fine, well-edited collection of sacred art.

In the atmospheric catacombs, the great and the good of Porto were once buried. Look out for sculptural works by Italian master Nicolau Nasoni and prolific Portuguese sculptor António Teixeira Lopes.

Museu da Misericórdia do Porto   Church, Museum

(MMIPO; Map p102; www.mmipo.pt; Rua das Flores 5; adult/child €5/2.50; ⊙10am-6.30pm Apr-Sep, to 5.30pm Oct-Mar) All hail Porto's newly reopened Museu da Misericórdia do Porto, which harmoniously unites cutting-edge architecture, a prized collection of 15th- to 17th-century sacred art and portraiture, and one of Ribeira's finest churches, Igreja da Misericórdia. Bearing the hallmark of Italian baroque architect Nicolau Nasoni, the church's interior is adorned with blue-and-white *azulejos*. The museum's biggest stunner is the large-scale Flemish Renaissance painting, *Fons Vitae* (Fountain of Life), depicting Dom Manuel I and family around a fountain of blood from the crucified Christ.

The museum centres on a sky-lit atrium, and a visit begins on the 3rd floor, gradually working down to the church (be sure to get a photogenic glimpse of it from the gallery).

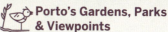

Porto's Gardens, Parks & Viewpoints

Whether it's the sparkle of the Rio Douro glimpsed from a perkily perched *miradouro* or a reviving stroll in a botanical garden, Porto effortlessly combines the urban and the outdoors.

Miradouro da Vitória (p108) See Porto spread scenically before you from this Jewish-quarter *miradouro*.

Jardim do Morro (p105) Slung high above the city in Gaia, these pretty gardens command stellar views of the historic centre.

Parque da Cidade (p106) Porto's urban escape is this mammoth lake-dotted park, complete with cycling and walking trails.

Jardim do Passeio Alegre (p106) Breathe in the pure Atlantic air as you saunter through these graceful 19th-century gardens.

Jardim Botânico do Porto (www.jardimbotanico.up.pt; Rua do Campo Alegre 1191; ⊙9am-5pm Mon-Fri, 10am-6pm Sat & Sun) **FREE** Green-fingered students tend these romantic and secluded botanical gardens.

Jardim das Virtudes (Map p102; Passeio das Virtudes; ⊙9am-7pm) Sloping lawns ideal for picnicking and river gazing.

Jardim da Cordoaria (Map p102; Rua Campo dos Mártires da Pátria) Find leafy respite in this sculpture-strewn park.

Jardim do Palácio de Cristal (p107) Secret gardens, flowery parterres, pockets of woodland and drop-dead gorgeous city views await.

Jardim do Palácio de Cristal (p107)
SAIKO3P / SHUTTERSTOCK ©

Central Porto

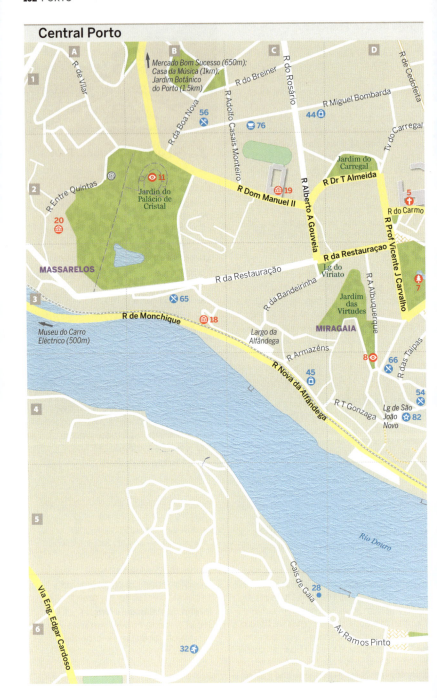

Mercado Bom Sucesso (650m);
Casa da Música (1km);
Jardim Botânico
do Porto (1.5km)

R de Vilar

R da Boa Nova

R Adolfo Casais Monteiro

R do Breiner

R do Rosário

R Miguel Bombarda

Tv do Carregal

R de Cedofeita

56

76

44

R Entre Quintas

11

Jardim do
Palácio de
Cristal

R Dom Manuel II

R Alberto A Gouveia

19

Jardim do
Carregal

R Dr T Almeida

5

R do Carmo

R Prof Vicente J Carvalho

20

R da Restauração

Lg do
Viriato

7

MASSARELOS

R da Restauração

R da Bandeirinha

Jardim
das
Virtudes

R A Albuquerque

65

R de Monchique

18

Largo da
Alfândega

MIRAGAIA

Museu do Carro
Eléctrico (500m)

R Armazéns

R Nova da Alfândega

45

8

66

R das Taipas

54

R T Gonzaga

Lg de São
João
Novo

82

Rio Douro

Via Eng. Edgar Cardoso

Cais de Gaia

28

Av Ramos Pinto

32

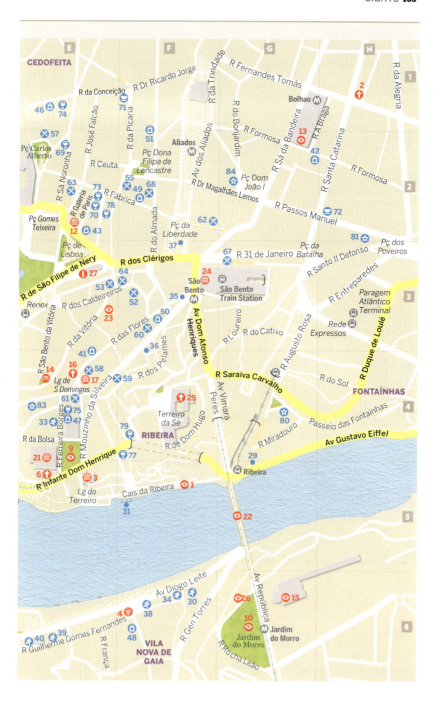

Central Porto

Sights

1	Cais da Ribeira	F5
2	Capela das Almas	H1
3	Casa do Infante	E5
4	Espaço Porto Cruz	F6
5	Igreja das Carmelitas	D2
6	Igreja de São Francisco	E5
7	Jardim da Cordoaria	D3
8	Jardim das Virtudes	D4
9	Jardim do Infante Dom Henrique	E4
10	Jardim do Morro	G6
11	Jardim do Palácio de Cristal	B2
12	Livraria Lello	E2
13	Mercado do Bolhão	G2
14	Miradouro da Vitória	E4
15	Mosteiro da Serra de Pilar	G6
16	Museu da Misericórdia do Porto	E4
17	Museu das Marionetas	E4
18	Museu do Vinho do Porto	B3
19	Museu Nacional Soares dos Reis	C2
20	Museu Romântico	A2
21	Palácio da Bolsa	E4
22	Ponte de Dom Luís I	G5
23	Rua de São Bento da Vitória	E3
24	São Bento Train Station	F3
25	Sé	F4
26	Teleférico de Gaia	G6
27	Torre dos Clérigos	E3

Activities, Courses & Tours

28	Barcadouro	C6
29	Blue Dragon Tours	G5
30	Cálem	F6
31	Douro Azul	F5
	eFun GPS Tours	(see 4)
32	Graham's	B6
33	Instituto dos Vinhos do Douro e do Porto	E4
34	Kopke	F6
35	Living Tours	F3
36	Other Side	F4
37	Porto Walkers	F3
38	Quinta do Noval	F6
39	Ramos Pinto	E6
40	Sogevinus	E6
	ViniPortugal	(see 21)

Shopping

41	43 Branco	E4
42	A Pérola Do Bolhão	G2

43	A Vida Portuguesa	E2
44	águas furtadas	C1
45	Armazém	C4
46	Coração Alecrim	E1
47	Oliva & Co	E4
48	Porto Wine House	F6
49	Touriga	F2
50	Tradições	F3
51	Workshops Pop Up	F1

Eating

52	A Sandeira	F3
53	All In Porto	E3
54	Belos Aires	D4
55	Book	F2
56	BUGO Art Burgers	B1
57	Camafeu	E2
58	Cantina 32	E4
59	Cantinho do Avillez	E4
60	Da Terra	F3
61	DOP	E4
62	Flor dos Congregados	F2
63	Leitaria da Quinta do Paço	E2
64	Miss'Opo	F3
65	Sardinha Alfândega	B3
66	Taberna de Santo António	D4
67	Tapabento	G3
68	Tascö	F2

Drinking & Nightlife

69	Aduela	E2
70	Café Au Lait	E2
71	Café Candelabro	F1
72	Café Majestic	H2
73	Era Uma Vez No Paris	E2
74	Museu d'Avó	E1
	Pinguim Café	(see 54)
75	Prova	E4
76	Rota do Chá	C1
77	Vinologia	F4
78	Wall	E2
79	Wine Box	F4

Entertainment

	Fado in Porto	(see 30)
80	Hot Five Jazz & Blues Club	G4
81	Maus Hábitos	H2
82	Restaurante O Fado	D4
83	Teatro Marionetas do Porto	E4
84	Teatro Municipal Rivoli	G2

It showcases an impressive stash of religious art, most of which has ties to the Santa Casa da Misericórdia (Holy House of Our Lady of Mercy), founded in 1499 by order of King Manuel I. This charitable organisation cared for the infirm, sick and poor for 500 years. On display are portraits of its benefactors, lab equipment (including electroshock apparatus to treat psychiatric disorders), and the treasures it amassed over centuries – sculpture, glass- and silverware, liturgical vestments etc.

The ultimate tribute to this old-meets-new medley is Portuguese artist Rui Chafes' eye-catching, curvaceous iron sculpture *My Blood is Your Blood* (2015), which hooks through the building to the facade.

Casa do Infante   Historic Building

(Map p102; Rua Alfândega 10; adult/child €2.20/free; ⏰9.30am-1pm & 2-5.30pm Tue-Sun) Just back from the river is this handsomely renovated medieval townhouse where, according to legend, Henry the Navigator was born in 1394. The building later served as Porto's first customs house. Today it boasts three floors of exhibits. In 2002 the complex was excavated, revealing Roman foundations and some remarkable mosaics – all of which are now on display.

Jardim do Infante Dom Henrique   Gardens

(Map p102; Rua Ferreira Borges) Presided over by the late 19th-century market hall **Mercado Ferreira Borges** and neoclassical Palácio da Bolsa (p100), these gardens are named after the centrepiece statue. Lifted high on a pedestal, the monument depicts Prince Henry the Navigator (1394–1460) – a catalyst in the Age of Discoveries and pioneer of the caravel, who braved the battering Atlantic in search of colonies for Portugal's collection.

Museu das Marionetas   Museum

(Map p102; www.marionetasdoporto.pt; Rua das Flores 22; €2; ⏰11am-1pm & 2-6pm; 👪) Porto's marionette museum turns the spotlight on the remarkable puppet creations that have taken to the stage at the **Teatro Marionetas do Porto** (Map p102; 📞222 089 175; www.marionetasdoporto.pt; Rua de Belmonte 57) over the past 25 years. Rotating exhibitions present marionettes from productions such as *Macbeth, Faust* and *Cinderella.*

◎ Vila Nova de Gaia

Jardim do Morro   Gardens

(Map p102; Avenida da República) The cable car swings up to this hilltop park, which can also be reached by crossing the upper level of Ponte Dom Luís I. Shaded by palms, these gardens are all about the view. From here, Porto is reduced to postcard format,

with the pastel-hued houses of Ribeira on the opposite side of the Douro and the snaking river below.

◎ Aliados & Bolhão

São Bento Train Station   Historic Building

(Map p102; Praça Almeida Garrett; ⏰5am-1am) One of the world's most beautiful train stations, beaux arts São Bento wings you back to a more graceful age of rail travel. Completed in 1903, it seems to have been imported from 19th-century Paris with its mansard roof. But the dramatic *azulejo* panels of historic scenes in the front hall are the real attraction. Designed by Jorge Colaço in 1930, some 20,000 tiles depict historic battles (including Henry the Navigator's conquest of Ceuta), as well as the history of transport.

Mercado do Bolhão   Market

(Map p102; Rua Formosa; ⏰7am-5pm Mon-Fri, to 1pm Sat) The 19th-century, wrought-iron Mercado do Bolhão does a brisk trade in fresh produce, including cheeses, olives, smoked meats, sausages, breads and more. At its lively best on Friday and Saturday mornings, the market is also sprinkled with inexpensive stalls where you can eat fish so fresh it was probably swimming in the Atlantic that morning, or taste or sample local wines and cheeses.

Torre dos Clérigos   Tower

(Map p102; www.torredosclerigos.pt; Rua de São Filipe de Nery; €3; ⏰9am-7pm) Sticking out on Porto's skyline like a sore thumb – albeit a beautiful baroque one – this 76m-high tower was designed by Italian-born baroque master Nicolau Nasoni in the mid-1700s. Climb its 225-step spiral staircase for phenomenal views over Porto's tiled rooftops, spires and the curve of the Douro to the port-wine lodges in Gaia. It also harbours an exhibition that chronicles the history of the tower's architects and residents.

Capela das Almas   Church

(Map p102; Rua Santa Catarina 428; ⏰7.30am-1pm & 3.30-7pm Mon, Tue & Sat, 7.30am-7pm Wed-Fri, 7.30am-1pm & 6-7pm Sun) On Rua

Santa Catarina stands the strikingly ornate, azulejo-clad Capela das Almas. Magnificent panels here depict scenes from the lives of various saints, including the death of St Francis and the martyrdom of St Catherine. Interestingly, Eduardo Leite painted the tiles in a classic 18th-century style, though they actually date back only to the early 20th century.

Livraria Lello — Historic Building
(Map p102; Rua das Carmelitas 144; €3; ⊙10am-7.30pm Mon-Sat, 11am-7pm Sun) Ostensibly a bookshop, but even if you're not after books, don't miss this exquisite 1906 neo-Gothic confection, with its lavishly carved plaster resembling wood and stained-glass skylight. Feels magical? Its intricately wrought, curiously twisting staircase was supposedly the inspiration for the one in the Harry Potter books, which JK Rowling partly wrote in Porto while working here as an English teacher from 1991 to 1993.

◎ Boavista

Mercado Bom Sucesso — Market
(www.mercadobomsucesso.com; Praça Bom Sucesso; ⊙10am-11pm Sun-Thu, to midnight Fri & Sat) For a snapshot of local life and a bite to eat, nip into Boavista's revamped Mercado Bom Sucesso. A complete architectural overhaul has brought this late 1940s market hall bang up to date. Now bright, modern and flooded with daylight, the striking curved edifice harbours a fresh produce market, a food court, cafes and the slick design hotel, Hotel da Música.

The fresh-produce market does a brisk trade in fish and shellfish, meat, fruit and vegetables and flowers from 10am to 8pm Monday to Saturday.

Gastronomes are in their element in the food court, which is perfect grazing territory, with stands selling everything from fresh sushi to piadine (Italian flat-bread sandwiches), tapas, ice cream and Portuguese sparkling wine. The **Traveller Café** is a good pit stop for freshly pressed juices and smoothies or coffee and pastries. If you're looking for edible gifts to take home, stop by **Sabores e Tradição**, which stocks gourmet products from the Trás-os-Montes, such as cheese, olive oil and honey.

The market also has a cultural slant, with events from live music to free monthly workshops (in Portuguese) ranging from cookery demos to gardening for kids.

◎ Foz do Douro & Serralves

Serralves — Museum
(www.serralves.pt; Rua Dom João de Castro 210; adult/child museums & park €10/free, park only €5/free, 10am-1pm 1st Sun of the month free; ⊙10am-7pm Tue-Fri, to 8pm Sat & Sun May-Sep, reduced hours Oct-Mar) This fabulous cultural institution combines a museum, a mansion and extensive gardens. Cutting-edge exhibitions, along with a fine permanent collection featuring works from the late 1960s to the present, are showcased in the **Museu de Arte Contemporânea**, an arrestingly minimalist, whitewashed space designed by the eminent Porto-based architect Álvaro Siza Vieira. The delightful, pink **Casa de Serralves** is a prime example of art deco, bearing the imprint of French architect Charles Siclis. One ticket gets you into both museums.

The museums sit within the marvellous 18-hectare **Parque de Serralves**. Lily ponds, rose gardens, formal fountains and whimsical touches – such as a bright-red sculpture of oversized pruning shears – make for a bucolic outing in the city. The estate is located 6km west of the city centre; take bus 201 from in front of Praça Dom João I, one block east of Av dos Aliados.

Jardim do Passeio Alegre — Gardens
(Rua Passeio Alegre) A joy for the aimless ambler, this 19th-century garden is flanked by graceful old buildings and dotted with palms, sculptures, fountains and a bandstand that occasionally stages concerts in summer. Listen to the crash of the ocean as you wander its tree-canopied avenues.

Parque da Cidade — Park
(Avenida da Boavista) The hum of traffic on the Avenida da Boavista soon fades as you enter the serene, green Parque da Cidade,

Portugal's largest urban park. Laced with 10km of walking and cycling trails, this is where locals come to unplug and recharge, picnic (especially at weekends), play ball, jog, cycle, lounge in the sun and feed the ducks on the lake.

Masserelos

Jardim do Palácio de Cristal   Gardens

(Map p102; Rua Dom Manuel II; ☉8am-9pm Apr-Sep, to 7pm Oct-Mar) Sitting atop a bluff, this gorgeous botanical garden is one of Porto's best-loved escapes, with lawns interwoven with sun-dappled paths and dotted with fountains, sculptures, giant magnolias, camellias, cypress and olive trees. It's actually a mosaic of small gardens that open up little by little as you wander – as do the stunning views of the city and Douro River.

The park is also home to a domed **sports pavilion**, the hi-tech **Biblioteca Municipal Almeida Garrett** (Map p102; Jardim do Palácio de Cristal; ☉2-6pm Mon, 10am-6pm Tue-Sat; 🛜) and the **Museu Romântico**

(Quinta da Macieirinha; Map p102; Rua Entre Quintas 220; adult/child €2.20/free, Sat & Sun free; ☉10am-5.30pm Mon-Sat, 10am-12.30pm & 2-5.30pm Sun).

Museu do Vinho do Porto   Museum

(Port Wine Museum; Map p102; Rua de Monchique 45; adult/child €2.20/free, Sat & Sun free; ☉10am-5.30pm Tue-Sat, 10am-12.30pm & 2-5.30pm Sun) Down by the river in a re-modelled warehouse, this modest museum traces the history of wine- and port-making with an informative short film, models and exhibits, though it doesn't offer much insight into the wine itself.

Museu do Carro Eléctrico   Museum

(Tram Museum; www.museudocarroelectrico.pt; Alameda Basílio Teles 51; adult/child €8/4; ☉2-6pm Mon, 10am-6pm Tue-Sun) Housed in an antiquated switching house, this museum is a tram-spotter's delight. It displays dozens of beautifully restored old trams – from early 1870s models once pulled by mules to streamlined, bee-yellow 1930s numbers.

Cityscape with Torre dos Clérigos (p105) in the background

SAIKO3P / SHUTTERSTOCK ©

Museu Nacional Soares dos Reis

⊚ Miragaia

Museu Nacional
Soares dos Reis   Museum

(Map p102; www.museusoaresdosreis.pt; Rua
Dom Manuel II 44; adult/child €5/free, 1st Sun of
the month free; ◷10am-6pm Tue-Sun) Porto's
best art museum presents a stellar collection ranging from Neolithic carvings to
Portugal's take on modernism, all housed in
the formidable Palácio das Carrancas.

Requisitioned by Napoleonic invaders,
the neoclassical palace was abandoned so
rapidly that the future Duke of Wellington
found an unfinished banquet in the dining
hall. Transformed into a museum of fine
and decorative arts in 1940, its best works
date from the 19th century, including
sculptures by António Teixeira Lopes and
António Soares dos Reis – seek out his
famous *O Desterrado* (The Exile), and the
naturalistic paintings of Henrique Pousão
and António Silva Porto.

Rua de São Bento da Vitória   Area

(Map p102) With its cobblestones polished
smooth by centuries of shoe leather and
pretty tiled houses with little wrought-iron
balconies and window boxes brimming
with pot plants, this narrow, gently curving
street was the beating heart of Jewish Porto in late medieval times. Keep your eyes
peeled for telltale sights of Jewish heritage,
such as bronze Hamsa (protective hand)
door knockers.

Igreja das Carmelitas   Church

(Map p102; Rua do Carmo; ◷7.30am-7pm
Mon-Fri, 9am-6.45pm Sat & Sun) Blink and you
might miss that this is a church in its own
right, snuggled as close as it is to the Igreja
do Carmo. The twin churches are separated
only by a 1m-wide house, once the dividing
line between the monks of Carmo and the
Carmelite nuns. Dating to the 17th century,
its modest classical facade belies its lavishly gilded nave.

Miradouro da Vitória   Viewpoint

(Map p102; Rua São Bento da Vitória) Porto is
reduced to postcard format at this *miradouro* (viewpoint), perched high and mighty
above a mosaic of terracotta rooftops that
tumble down to the Douro. It's a highly
atmospheric spot at dusk when landmarks

such as the Ponte Dom Luís I bridge are illuminated and the lights on Vila Nova de Gaia's wine lodges flick on one by one.

⚙ ACTIVITIES

Taste Porto Food Tours   Tours

(📞967 258 750; www.tasteportofoodtours.com; food tour adult/child €59/39; ⊙food tours 10am, 10.30am & 4pm Tue-Sat) Loosen a belt notch for these superb half-day food tours, where you'll sample everything from Porto's best slow-roast-pork sandwich to éclairs, fine wines, cheese and coffee. Friendly, knowledgeable André and his team lead these indulgent 3½-hour walking tours, which take in viewpoints, historic back lanes and the Mercado do Bolhão en route to restaurants, grocery stores and cafes.

Taste Porto have branched out recently to offer other experiences that immerse you fully in Porto's growing food scene. Among them are the fun, hands-on cookery classes (€79) at **Rosa Et Al Townhouse** (📞916 000 081; www.rosaetal.pt; Rua do Rosário 233; ste €118-228; 📶), where you'll whip up a three-course, all-Portuguese feast with Patricia before getting to sample what you've prepared along with some top wines (and of course taking home some recipes to perfect at your leisure); see the website for class details.

The 1½-hour olive-oil tastings (€29; 11.30am Monday to Saturday) at Oliva & Co (p112) will give you an entirely new appreciation of olive oil, and how it can be used to enhance food flavours. Gain great insight into the country's six DOP (PDO; Protected Designation of Origin) regions producing the finest extra-virgin varieties.

Barcadouro   Boating

(Map p102; 📞223 722 415; www.barcadouro. pt; Avenida Ramos Pinto 240, Cais de Gaia) Barcadouro runs cruises along the river to the Douro Valley (conditions permitting), including a round trip to Régua (€77.50), departing Porto at 8am and returning at 6.50pm. It's a wonderfully relaxed way to take in the steeply terraced vineyards from the water.

Festa de São João

In the sweet heat of midsummer, Porto pulls out all the stops, the bunting and the plastic hammers for one of Europe's wildest street parties – the Festa de São João, celebrated in riotous style on 23 and 24 June. If ever the full force of love is going to hit you when you least expect it, it's going to be here – one of the festival's unique traditions is to thwack whomever you fancy over the head with a squeaky plastic hammer (*martelo*), though purists swear by floppy leeks and smelly garlic plants.

As you might expect, these head-spinning attacks of *amor* cause much flirtatious giggling, squealing and chasing in the maze of medieval lanes that spill down to the riverfront. Though the exact origins of the festa are veiled in mystery, *tripeiros* (Porto residents) will tell you that it is rooted in pagan festivals to celebrate the summer solstice and bountiful harvests. Bountiful certainly sums up the streets on 23 June, which teem with hammer-wielding locals of all ages, scoffing grilled sardines, drinking *vinho*, dancing like there is no tomorrow and letting Chinese lanterns drift into the night sky.

Douro Azul   Boating

(Map p102; 📞223 402 500; www.douroazul. com; 6-bridges cruise adult/child €10/5; ⊙9.30am-6.30pm) Douro Azul is the largest of several outfits that offer cruises in ersatz *barcos rabelos*, the colourful boats that were once used to transport port wine from the vineyards. Cruises last 45 to 55 minutes and depart at least hourly on summer days. You can board at Cais de Ribeira, or across the river at Cais de Gaia.

Porto Walkers   Walking

(Map p102; ☑918 291 519; www.portowalkers. pt; Praça da Liberdade, Avenida dos Aliados) Peppered with anecdotes and personality, these young and fun guided walking tours are a great intro to Porto, at 10.45am and 3.30pm daily. The tours are free (well, the guides work for tips, so give what you can). Simply turn up at the meeting point on Praça da Liberdade and look out for the guide in the red T-shirt.

The company also runs a number of other themed walks, including a four-hour port-wine tour (€18), which begins at 3pm every day except Monday next to Ponte de Dom Luís I, and a daily pub crawl, which begins at 11pm on Praça dos Leões.

Kopke   Wine

(Map p102; ☑223 746 660; www.sogevinus. com; Avenida Diogo Leite 312; tastings by the glass from €2; ☺10am-7pm May-Oct, to 6pm Nov-Apr) Founded in 1638, Kopke is the oldest brand on the hill, but its lodge is not open to the public, which is why you should stop here for the smooth caramelised bite of a seriously good aged tawny. The 10-year is tasty; the 20-year is spectacular. Port-wine tastings can be matched with Arcádia chocolates or organic olive oil.

Sogevinus   Wine

(Map p102; ☑223 746 660; www.sogevinus. com; Av Ramos Pinto 280; tastings by the glass €1.30-22.50; ☺10am-7pm May-Oct, to 6pm Nov-Apr) Sogevinus is the port-wine holding company that owns the Kopke, Cálem, Barros, Gilberts and Burmester labels. This shop stocks a wide array of its ports, around 30 of which can be tasted by the glass.

Ramos Pinto   Wine

(Map p102; ☑936 809 283; www.ramospinto.pt; Av Ramos Pinto 400; tours incl tasting €6; ☺10am-6pm May-Oct, reduced hours Nov-Apr) Right on the riverfront, you can visit the rather grand

Ramos Pinto and take a look at its historic offices and ageing cellars. The basic 40-minute tour includes a visit to the museum plus a two-port tasting of a white and tawny. Tours are offered in several languages.

Quinta do Noval   Wine

(Map p102; ☑223 770 282; www.quintadonoval. com; Avenida Diogo Leite 256; tastings by the glass €2.50-25; ☺10.30am-7.30pm Jun-Sep, 10am-5.30pm Oct-May) Dating back to 1715, Quinta do Noval is one of Porto's most historic cellars, with its ports and wines hailing from the vineyards on a small estate in the Douro Valley.

Instituto dos Vinhos do Douro e do Porto   Wine

(Map p102; www.ivdp.pt; Rua Ferreira Borges 27; wine tasting €5; ☺11am-7pm Mon-Fri) When area vintners apply for the certification that ultimately christens their casks with the term 'Port', they bring vials to the labs set in this attractive relic just uphill from the river. The labs are off limits to visitors, but you're welcome to explore the lobby exhibits, and the attached wine shop offers tastings.

ViniPortugal   Wine

(Map p102; www.viniportugal.pt/ogivalrooms; Palácio da Bolsa, Rua Ferreira Borges; ☺11am-7pm Tue-Sat) Housed in the grand Palácio da Bolsa, ViniPortugal's tasting room is the perfect way to brush up on your knowledge of Portuguese wines (including those produced in the nearby Douro). An enocard costing €2 is your ticket to tasting two to four wines from a selection of 12 chosen from different regions of the country. The friendly, clued-up staff will talk you through them.

🎧 TOURS

eFun GPS Tours   Tours

(Map p102; ☑220 923 270; www.efungpstours. com; Rua Cândido dos Reis 55) One of the most fun and ecofriendly ways to zip about town is in a nippy Renault Twizy with efun GPS tours on itineraries such as the 1½-hour By the River tour (€38), taking in riverfront attractions from Ponte da Arrábida to the fishing village of Afurada.

Ramos Pinto cellars

The 1½-hour Secret Streets tour (€38) rambles through the historic centre, the 2½-hour Essential tour (€51) takes in both sides of the river, while the 3½-hour Full Experience tour (€63) goes all the way to the Atlantic and Foz do Douro. All tours include a cellar visit. The company also arranges three- to four-hour walking tours, from a romp of the historic centre (€19) to a tapas and port-wine tour and *azulejos* tour, both €29.

Other Side   Tours
(Map p102; ☑916 500 170; www.theotherside. pt; Rua Souto 67; ☺9am-8pm) Well-informed, congenial guides reveal their city on half-day walking tours of hidden Porto (€19), *petisco* (tapas) trails (€25), and e-bike tours of Porto and Foz (€29). They also venture further afield with full-day trips to the Douro's vineyards (€85) and to Guimarães and Braga (€69).

Be My Guest   Walking
(☑938 417 850; www.bemyguestinporto.com; 3hr tours €20) To get better acquainted with Porto, sign up for one of Be My Guest's

terrific themed walking tours of the city, skipping from an insider's peek at *azulejos* to belle époque architecture. Run by a passionate trio of guides – Nuno, Sabina and Fred – it also arranges four-hour cookery workshops (€30) and wine-tasting tours (€25). Meeting points vary.

Living Tours   Tours
(Map p102; ☑228 320 992; www.livingtours. pt; Rua Mouzinho da Silveira 352-4; ☺9am-8pm Apr-Oct, to 6pm Nov-Mar) A great range of sightseeing options are on offer at this friendly agency, from half-day city tours (€35) to fado tours with dinner (€65) and day trips to the Douro and Minho (€95).

Blue Dragon Tours   Tours
(Map p102; ☑222 022 375; www.bluedragon. pt; Avenida Gustavo Eiffel 280; tours from €15) This reputable outfit runs classic three-hour bike tours (from €15), which begin on Avenida dos Aliados and take in major sights such as the Sé and Mercado do Bolhão. It also offers several half-day walking tours, including Jewish Porto (from €15) and a foodie tour (from €39), as well

as three-hour Segway tours (from €55). Prices depend on group sizes.

🔒 SHOPPING

Besides the bog-standard Portuguese souvenirs – cork, cockerels, you name it – the best thing you can possibly take home from Gaia is port wine. Stock up at one of its excellent *garrafeiras* (wine shops) or lodges. Many can arrange shipping for larger orders.

Armazém   Crafts, Vintage

(Map p102; Rua da Miragaia 93; ⊙11.30am-8pm) Bang on trend with Porto's thirst for new creative spaces is the hipsterish Armazém, located in a converted warehouse down by the river. A gallery, cafe and store all under one roof, with an open fire burning at its centre, it sells a pinch of everything – vintage garb, antiques, vinyl, artwork, ceramics and funky Portuguese-designed Mexxca bags and fashion.

Tradições   Gifts & Souvenirs

(Map p102; Rua das Flores 238; ⊙10am-7pm) For Portuguese souvenirs, Tradições is the real deal. In this sweet, friendly shop,

the owner knows the story behind every item – from bags beautifully fashioned from Alentejo cork to Algarvian *flôr de sal* (hand-harvested sea salt), Lousã honey to Lazuli *azulejos*.

Oliva & Co   Food

(Map p102; www.olivaeco.com; Rua Ferreira Borges 60; ⊙10am-7pm Mon-Fri, to 8pm Sat) Everything you ever wanted to know about Portuguese olive oil becomes clear at this experiential store, which maps out the country's six PDO regions producing the extra-virgin stuff. Besides superb oils and olives, you'll find biscuits, chocolate and soaps made with olive oil. Try before you buy or join one of the in-depth tastings in collaboration with Taste Porto.

43 Branco   Arts & Crafts

(Map p102; Rua das Flores 43; ⊙11am-7pm Mon-Sat) One-of-a-kind Portuguese crafts, fashion and interior design take centre stage at this new concept store, which brings a breath of fresh creativity to Rua das Flores. Here you'll find everything from filigree, gem-studded Maria Branco jewellery to funky sardine pencil cases,

From left: Rua Santa Catarina; Livraria Lello (p106); Shop display of port; Area around São Bento train station (p105)

Porto-inspired Lubo T-shirts and beautifully packaged Bonjardim soaps.

A Pérola Do Bolhão — Food & Drinks
(Map p102; Rua Formosa 279; ⏰9.30am-7.30pm Mon-Sat) Founded in 1917, this delicatessen sports Porto's most striking art nouveau facade and is stacked high with sausages and cheeses, olives, dried fruits and nuts, wine and port.

águas furtadas — Arts, Fashion
(Map p102; www.aguasfurtadasdesign.blogspot.co.uk; Rua de Miguel Bombarda 285; ⏰10am-8pm Mon-Sat, 1-7pm Sun) This boutique is a treasure-trove of funky Portuguese fashion, design, crafts and accessories, including born-again Barcelos cockerels in candy-bright colours and exquisitely illustrated pieces by influential Porto-based graphic designer Benedita Feijó.

Workshops Pop Up — Arts & Crafts
(Map p102; ☎966 974 119; www.workshops-popup.com; Rua do Almada 275; ⏰1-7.30pm Mon-Fri, 10am-7.30pm Sat) Bringing a new lease of life to a restored smithy, this store is the brainchild of Nuno and Rita.

It harbours an eclectic mix of pop-ups selling everything from original ceramics to vintage fashion, accessories and prettily wrapped Bonjardim soaps. It also runs English-speaking cookery workshops (followed by a meal with wine) for €30, or €42 including a market visit.

Touriga — Wine
(Map p102; ☎225 108 435; Rua da Fábrica 32; ⏰10am-1pm & 2.30-8pm Tue-Sat) Run with passion and precision by David Ferreira, this fabulous wine shop is a trove of well- and lesser-known ports and wines – many from small producers. Stop by for a wine or port-wine tasting (€3 to €12) or book ahead for the incredibly informative port-wine class (€25). Shipping can be arranged.

Coração Alecrim — Arts & Crafts
(Map p102; www.coracaoalecrim.com; Travessa de Cedofeita 28; ⏰noon-8pm Mon-Sat) 'Green, indie, vintage' is the strapline of this enticing store, accessed through a striking doorway painted with woodland animals (crickets chirrup a welcome as you enter). It stocks high-quality handmade Portuguese products, from pure wool

blankets and beanies to one-off *azulejos,* shell coasters and beautiful ceramics.

A Vida Portuguesa   Gifts & Souvenirs

(Map p102; www.avidaportuguesa.com; Rua Galeria de Paris 20; ◷10am-8pm Mon-Sat, 11am-7pm Sun) This lovely store in an old fabric shop showcases a medley of stylishly repackaged vintage Portuguese products – classic toys, old-fashioned soaps and retro journals, plus those emblematic ceramic Bordallo Pinheiro *andorinhas* (swallows).

Porto Wine House   Food & Drinks

(Map p102; www.portowinehouse.com; Rua Cândido dos Reis 4-10; ◷9am-7pm) Stock up on fine whites, rubies and tawnies here, as well as *conservas* (tinned fish), preserves and other goodies. Ships worldwide.

🍴 EATING

Porto's food scene has gone through the roof in recent years. Hot at the moment are *petiscos* (small Portuguese plates, ideal for sharing), lazy weekend brunches, creative vegetarian buffet-style restaurants with bags of charm and imaginative riffs on hand-me-down recipes and old-school taverns championing slow food. And don't forget the temptation of local cafes and patisseries around nearly every corner.

Yeatman   Gastronomy €€€

(☏220 133 100; www.the-yeatman-hotel.com; Rua do Choupelo 88; tasting menus €90/145; ◷7.30-11pm) With its polished service, elegant setting and dazzling views over river and city, the Michelin-starred restaurant at the five-star Yeatman hotel is sheer class. Chef Ricardo Costa puts his imaginative spin on seasonal ingredients from lobster to pheasant – all skilfully cooked, served with flair and expertly matched with wines from the 1000-bottle cellar that is among the country's best.

DOP   Gastronomy €€€

(Map p102; ☏222 014 313; www.ruipaula. com; Largo de São Domingos 18; menus €20-56; ◷7-11pm Mon, 12.30-3pm & 7-11pm Tue-Sat; 🛜) Housed in the Palácio das Artes, DOP is one of Porto's most stylish addresses, with its high ceilings and slick, monochrome

Book bar and restaurant

interior. Much-feted chef Rui Paula puts a creative, seasonal twist on outstanding ingredients, with dish after delicate, flavour-packed dish skipping from octopus carpaccio to cod with lobster rice. The three-course lunch is terrific value at €20.

Flor dos Congregados   Portuguese €€

(Map p102; ✆222 002 822; www.flordos congregados.pt; Travessa dos Congregados 11; mains €8-16; ☺7-10pm Mon, 10am-10pm Tue-Sat) Tucked away down a narrow alley, this softly lit, family-run restaurant brims with stone-walled, wood-beamed, art-slung nooks. The frequently changing blackboard menu goes with the seasons.

Everything from veal to sea bream is cooked and seasoned to a T. The must-try 'Terylene' slow-cooked marinated pork sandwich goes superbly with a glass of sparkling Tinto Bruto red.

Pedro Lemos   Gastronomy €€€

(✆220 115 986; www.pedrolemos.net; Rua do Padre Luís Cabral 974; tasting menus €80-120; ☺12.30-3pm & 7.30-11pm Tue-Sun) One of Porto's two Michelin-starred restaurants, Pedro Lemos is sheer delight. With a love of seasonally sourced produce and robust flavours, the eponymous chef creates culinary fireworks using first-class ingredients from land and sea – be it ultra-fresh Atlantic bivalves or Alentejano black pork cooked to smoky deliciousness with wild mushrooms. Choose between the subtly lit, cosy-chic dining room or the roof terrace.

Belos Aires   Argentine €€

(Map p102; ✆223 195 661; www.facebook. com/belosairesrestaurante; Rua de Belomonte 104; mains €12-20; ☺8-11.30am & 7pm-midnight Mon-Sat; ⚘) At the heart of this intimate part-Argentine, part-Portuguese restaurant is Mauricio, a chef with an insatiable passion for his homeland, and a big personality revealed as you watch him dashing around in the open kitchen. The market-fresh menu changes frequently, but you'll always find superb steaks and to-die-for *empanadas* (savoury turnovers). Save an inch for the chocolate brownie with *dulce de leche*.

Mercearia das Flores   Deli €

(Rua das Flores 110; petiscos €2.50-7.50; ☺9am-8pm Mon-Thu, 10am-10pm Fri & Sat, 1-8pm Sun; ⚘) This rustic-chic delicatessen/food store serves all-day *petiscos* made with organic regional products on the three tables and two counters of its bright and airy interior. You can also order wines by the glass, tea from the Azores and locally brewed Sovina beer. Try the spicy sardines and salad on dark, sweet *broa* cornbread.

All In Porto   Portuguese €€

(Map p102; ✆220 993 829; www.facebook. com/allinporto; Rua Arquitecto Nicolau Nasoni 17; petiscos €7-22; ☺10am-midnight) Wine barrel tables, lanterns and funky Porto murals create a hip, laid-back space for sampling a stellar selection of Portuguese wines and nicely prepared *petiscos*. These range from flame-grilled *chouriço* (spicy sausage) to spicy sardine roe, cheeses and *conservas* (canned fish). Quiet enough for conversing, it's also a chilled spot to begin or end an evening over drinks.

Book   Portuguese €€

(Map p102; ✆917 953 387; www.restaurante book.pt; Rua de Aviz 10; mains €16-23; ☺noon-3pm & 7.30pm-2am) One of Porto's hottest tables, this place has a library theme and buzzes with a mix of well-heeled locals and tourists. The decor is a blend of industrial and classic, and dishes are modern takes on Portuguese mainstays, such as duck breast with sweet potato and port wine or creamy rice with prawns, lime and coriander. Service can be slow. Book ahead.

Camafeu   Modern Portuguese €€

(Map p102; ✆937 493 557; www.facebook. com/camafeu83; Praça de Carlos Alberto 83; mains €12-19; ☺6-11pm Tue-Thu, 6.30pm-midnight Fri & Sat; ⚘) Visiting Camafeu, which overlooks Praça Carlos Alberto, is like eating in a friend's stylish 1st-floor apartment. There's room for just a handful of lucky diners in the chandelier-lit salon, which boasts French windows, antique furnishings and a polished wooden floor. Dishes such as slow-cooked pork cheek with *alheira* (a light, garlicky sausage of poultry or game), hazelnut and mushroom crumble and green asparagus are prepared with love and served with flair.

Leitaria da Quinta do Paço Bakery, Cafe €

(Map p102; www.leitariadaquintadopaco.com; Praça Guilherme Gomes Fernandes 47; éclairs €1.10; ⏲8.45am-8pm Mon-Thu, to 9pm Fri & Sat) Since 1920, this cafe-patisserie has given a pinch of Paris to Porto with its delectable sweet and savoury éclairs, which are now justifiably famous. Sit in the slick interior or on the plaza terrace for a *cimbalinho* (espresso) and feather-light, cream-filled éclairs in flavours from classic lemon to the more unusual blue cheese, apple and fennel or chocolate and port wine.

Miss'Opo Portuguese €€

(Map p102; ☎222 082 179; www.missopo.com; Rua dos Caldeireiros 100; petiscos €2-9; ⏲8pm-midnight Tue-Sun) Don't miss dinner at this cool guest house in the maze of alleyways up from the Ribeira, with a stylishly rough-around-the-edges look and delicious small plates being churned out of the tiny kitchen. Reserve ahead, especially on weekends. There are six lovely apartments (up to three people €75 to €120, up to six people €145 to €200) upstairs, featuring blond wood and kitchenettes.

Tapabento Tapas €€

(Map p102; ☎912 881 272, 222 034 115; www.tapabento.com; Rua da Madeira 222; tapas & sharing plates €4-16, mains €18-21; ⏲7pm-midnight Tue, noon-midnight Wed-Thu, to 2am Fri & Sat) There's a good buzz at split-level Tapabento, discreetly tucked behind São Bento train station. Stone walls, bright prints and cheek-by-jowl tables set the scene for outstanding tapas and Douro wines. Sharing is the way to go – be it fresh oysters with shallot vinaigrette, razor clams with garlic and coriander or Azores cheese with rocket and walnuts.

Save room for imaginative desserts such as peanut foam and chestnut mousse with saffron.

Tascö Portuguese €€

(Map p102; ☎222 010 763, 919 803 323; www.soldoutarena.com; Rua do Almada 151A; petiscos €4.50-10.50; ⏲noon-1am) Tascö's slick, banquette-lined interior is playfully peppered with personality in the form of a tree-shaped bookcase and a huge blackboard for scrawling messages. Super-friendly staff keep the good vibes and *petiscos* coming – lip-smacking little dishes of *rojões* (pork cooked in garlic, wine and cumin), *morcela* (black pudding), octopus, and the like, paired with craft beers, wines and ports.

Casa Agrícola Portuguese €€€

(www.casa-agricola.com; Rua do Bom Sucesso 241; mains €17-29; ⏲12.30-3pm & 8-10.30pm Mon-Sat) Abutting a chapel, this beautifully restored, 18th-century rural house is a splash of historic charm in an otherwise modern neighbourhood. The 1st-floor restaurant exudes old-world sophistication, with its polished-wood floor, bistro seating and chandeliers. It's an intimate choice for Portuguese flavours such as monkfish *cataplana* (stew). The more informal cafe bar downstairs has a happy hour from 4pm to 8pm.

Casinha Boutique Café Cafe €

(☎934 021 001; www.casinhaboutique.com; Avenida da Boavista 854; mains €4.50-12; ⏲9am-midnight Mon-Sat, 10am-10pm Sun; 📶) All pretty pastel shades and hidden garden alcoves, this cafe lodged in a restored 19th-century townhouse is as cute as a button. The food impresses, too, with wholesome, locally sourced ingredients going into freshly prepared sandwiches, quiches, salads, crepes and totally divine desserts. There's also a deli for takeaway Portuguese olive oils, wines, preserves and more.

Cantinho do Avillez Gastronomy €€

(Map p102; ☎223 227 879; www.cantinhodoavillez.pt; Rua Mouzinho da Silveira 166; mains €17-22.50; ⏲12.30-3pm & 7pm-midnight Mon-Fri, 12.30pm-midnight Sat & Sun) Rock star chef José Avillez' latest venture is a welcome fixture on Porto's gastro scene. A bright, contemporary bistro with a retro spin, Cantinho keeps the mood casual and buzzy. On the menu are seasonal Portuguese dishes with a dash of imagination: from flaked *bacalhau* with melt-in-the-mouth 'exploding' olives to giant red shrimps from the Algarve with Thai spices.

Cantina 32   Portuguese €€

(Map p102; 222 039 069; www.cantina32. com; Rua das Flores 32; petiscos €5-15; 12.30-2.30pm & 7.30-11pm;) Industrial-chic meets boho at this delightfully laid-back haunt, with its walls of polished concrete, mismatched crockery and vintage knick-knacks. The menu is just as informal – *petiscos* such as *pica-pau* steak (bite-sized pieces of steak in a garlic-white-wine sauce), quail egg croquettes, and cheesecake served in a flower pot reveal a pinch of creativity.

Da Terra   Vegetarian €

(Map p102; 223 199 257; www.daterra.pt; Rua Mouzinho da Silveira 249; buffet €9.90; noon-3.30pm & 7.30-11pm;) Porto's shift towards lighter, super-healthy food is reflected in the buffet served at Da Terra. This popular,

contemporary bistro puts its own spin on vegetarian and vegan food – from creative salads to Thai-style veggies and tagines. It also does a fine line in fresh-pressed juices and desserts. The website posts details of upcoming workshops and cookery courses.

Essência   Vegetarian €

(228 301 813; www.essenciarestaurante vegetariano.com; Rua de Pedro Hispano 1190; 2-/3-course veg €7/9, nonveg €8/10; 12.30-3pm & 8-10.30pm Mon-Thu, 12.30-3pm & 8pm-midnight Fri & Sat;) This bright, modern brasserie is famous Porto-wide for its generous vegetarian (and nonvegetarian!) menus, stretching from wholesome soups and salads to curries, pasta dishes and *feijoada* (pork and bean casserole). There's a terrace for warm-weather dining.

Cafeína   Modern European €€

(226 108 059; www.cafeina.pt; Rua do Padrão 100; mains €17-19; 12.30-6pm & 7.30pm-12.30am Sun-Thu, to 1.30am Fri & Sat;) Hidden coyly away from the seafront, Cafeína has a touch of class, with soft light casting a flattering glow across its moss-green

Mercearia das Flores (p115)

Dining by the Rio Douro

walls, crisp tablecloths, lustrous wood floors and bookcases. The food is best described as modern European, and is as simple as stuffed squid with saffron purée or rack of lamb in a herb and lemon crust, expertly matched with Portuguese wines.

Sardinha Alfândega Portuguese €€

(Map p102; ☑931 724 508; www.facebook. com/sardinhadalfandega; Rua Sobre-o-Douro 1A; lunch €7.50, mains €8-14; ☉noon-11pm) Lodged in a wing of a former convent, this wood-floored restaurant keeps it contemporary with monochrome hues, mod lighting and blown-up food prints. Affording cracking views of the Douro, the terrace is a great spot for drinks before dinner. Fresh fish is the star of the menu, from crispy squid to fillet of Atlantic wreckfish.

A Sandeira Sandwiches €

(Map p102; ☑223 216 471; Rua dos Caldeireiros 85; mains €4.50, lunch menu €5; ☉11am-3pm Mon-Wed, to midnight Thu-Sat; ☎) Charming, boho-flavoured and lit by fairy lights, A Sandeira is a great bolt-hole for an inexpensive lunch. Chipper staff bring to the table creative salads such as smoked ham, rocket, avocado and walnuts, and Porto's best sandwiches (olive, feta, tomato and basil, for instance). The lunch menu including soup, a salad or sandwich and a drink is a steal.

BUGO Art Burgers Burgers €

(Map p102; ☑226 062 179; www.bugo.com. pt; Rua Miguel Bombarda 598; burgers €7-13.50; ☉noon-3pm & 7.30-11pm Mon-Fri, 12.30-4pm & 7.30pm-midnight Sat) ☏ Spilling out onto gallery-lined Rua de Miguel Bombarda, this bright, happening bistro promises to elevate burgers to an art form. It delivers with brilliantly fresh burgers ranging from Black Angus, salmon or lentil options to oriental-style numbers – using mostly organic and free-range produce. The staff are chirpy, the mood is upbeat and the chocolate cake with berry coulis is divine.

Taberna de Santo António Portuguese €

(Map p102; ☑222 055 306; Rua das Virtudes 32; mains €5-10; ☉8am-2am Tue-Fri, 9am-2am Sat & Sun) This family-run tavern prides itself on serving up good honest Portuguese grub with a smile. It dishes up generous helpings of codfish, grilled sardines and *cozido* (meat and vegetable stew) to the lunchtime crowds. It's a friendly TV-and-tiles place in the traditional Portuguese mould, with pavement seating on warm days.

🍸 DRINKING & NIGHTLIFE

While Porto isn't going to steal the clubbing crown any time soon, *tripeiros* (Porto residents) love to get their groove on, especially in the Galerias, with its speakeasy-style bars and the party spilling out onto the streets. With just enough urban edge to keep the scene fresh-faced, a night out here can easily jump from indie clubs to refined rooftop bars.

Prova   Wine Bar
(Map p102; www.prova.com.pt; Rua Ferreira Borges 86; ⏰4pm-2am Wed-Mon; 📶) Diogo, the passionate owner, explains the finer nuances of Portuguese wine at this chic, stone-walled bar, where relaxed jazz plays. Stop by for a two-glass tasting (€5), or sample wines by the glass – including beefy Douros, full-bodied Dãos and crisp Alentejo whites. These marry well with sharing plates of local hams and cheeses (€14). Diogo's port tonics are legendary.

Aduela   Bar
(Map p102; Rua das Oliveiras 36; ⏰3pm-2am Mon, 1pm-2am Tue-Sat, 2pm-midnight Sun) Retro and hip but not self-consciously so, chilled Aduela bathes in the nostalgic orange glow of its glass lights, which illuminate the green walls and mishmash of vintage furnishings. Once a sewing machine warehouse, today it's where friends gather to converse over wine and appetising *petiscos* (€3 to €8).

Museu d'Avó   Bar
(Map p102; Travessa de Cedofeita 54; ⏰8pm-4am Mon-Sat) The name translates as 'Grandmother's Museum' and indeed it's a gorgeous rambling attic of a bar, crammed

with cabinets, old clocks, *azulejos* and gramophones, with curios hanging from its rafters. Lanterns and candles illuminate young *tripeiros* locked in animated conversation as the house beats spin. If you get the late-night munchies, it also whips up tasty *petiscos* (€2 to €8).

Wine Box   Wine Bar
(Map p102; www.thewineboxporto.com; Rua dos Mercadores 72; ⏰1.30pm-midnight Thu-Tue; 📶) Wine cases turn the interior into quite a feature at this slinky, black-walled bar. The friendly staff will guide you through the 137 (at the last count) wines on the menu, most of which are available by the glass. They go nicely with tapas such as padrón peppers and clams in a herby sauce.

Vinologia   Wine Bar
(Map p102; www.vinologia.pt; Rua de São João 28-30; ⏰11am-midnight) This cosy wine bar is an excellent place to sample the fine quaffs of Porto, with over 200 different ports on offer. If you fall in love with a certain wine, you can usually buy a whole bottle (or even send a case home).

Café Majestic   Cafe
(Map p102; www.cafemajestic.com; Rua Santa Catarina 112; ⏰9.30am-midnight Mon-Sat) Yes, we know, it's pricey and rammed with tourists brandishing selfie sticks, but you should at least have a drink at Café Majestic just so you can gawp at its beaux arts interior, awash with prancing cherubs, opulently gilded woodwork and gold-braided waiters. Skip the so-so food and just go for coffee. There's a pavement terrace for sunny-day people-watching.

Zenith Lounge Bar   Lounge
(Rua de Serralves 124; ⏰10am-2am Tue-Sat May-Oct; 📶) All of Porto spreads photogenically at your feet from this uber-hip rooftop lounge, which perches on the 15th floor of the HF Ipanema Park. Centred on a pool, the strikingly lit lounge attracts a good-looking, cocktail-sipping crowd, with regular live music, guest DJs and party nights in summer.

Marés Vivas

Over a weekend in mid-July, Afurada dusts off its party clothes to host the Marés Vivas, welcoming big rock and pop names to the stage. Headliners in recent years have included James Bay, Elton John, James, Tom Odell, Beth Orton and Foy Vance.

Elton John performing at Marés Vivas
DIOGO BAPTISTA / ALAMY STOCK PHOTO ©

Wall   Bar
(Map p102; www.facebook.com/thewallbar.
baixa; Rua de Cândido dos Reis 90; ⊙5pm-4am
Mon-Sat, 9pm-4am Sun) With backlit walls
featuring a 3D cubist artwork of spirit
bottles, high ceilings and a funky world
map of names, the Wall has a dash of the
urban sophisticate about it. Mingle with an
effortlessly cool crowd enjoying the chilled
DJ beats and expertly mixed cocktails
(it boasts a mean mojito).

Pinguim Café   Bar
(Map p102; www.pinguimcafe.blogspot.co.uk;
Rua de Belomonte 65; ⊙9pm-4am Mon-Fri, 10pm-
4am Sat & Sun) A little bubble of bohemian
warmth in the heart of Porto, Pinguim attracts an alternative crowd. Stone walls and
dim light create a cosy, intimate backdrop
for plays, film screenings, poetry readings,
rotating exhibitions of local art, and G&T
sipping. It's full to the rafters at weekends.

Rota do Chá   Teahouse
(Map p102; www.rotadocha.pt; Rua Miguel
Bombarda 457; tea €2.50; ⊙11am-8pm Mon-Thu,
to midnight Fri & Sat) This proudly bohemian
cafe has a verdant but rustic back garden

where students and the gallery crowd sit
around low tables sampling from an enormous 300-plus tea menu divided by region.
Tasty snacks include quiches, muffins,
scones and toast. It also serves weekend
brunches and weekday lunch specials (€7).

Terraplana   Cafe
(Avenida Rodrigues de Freitas 287; ⊙11am-mid-
night Tue-Thu, to 2am Fri & Sat, 5pm-midnight
Sun) Totally relaxed and cool without
trying, Terraplana takes you through from
late-morning coffee to evening cocktails
(around €7.50 a pop). Granite and tiles set
the backdrop for the house special, the Terraplana Cafe, with coffee liqueur, vodka and
an espresso shot. Or try the Living Dead
Margarita, with a ginger and chilli kick.

Era Uma Vez No Paris   Bar
(Map p102; Rua Galeria de Paris 106; ⊙11am-
2am Mon-Thu, to 4am Fri & Sat) A little flicker
of bohemian Parisian flair in the heart of
Porto, Era Uma Vez No Paris time warps
you back to the more decadent 1920s. Its
ruby-red walls, retro furnishings and frilly
lampshades spin a warm, intimate cocoon
for coffee by day and drinks by night. DJs
keep the mood mellow with indie rock and
funk beats.

Café Candelabro   Cafe
(Map p102; Rua da Conceição 3; ⊙10.30am-
2am Mon-Fri, 2pm-2am Sat, 2.30pm-midnight Sun)
Cool cafe bar in a former bookstore, with a
boho crowd and a retro vibe featuring black-
and-white mosaic tile floors, bookcases with
old books and magazines, and big windows
opening out to the street. It gets busy, with
blasting techno on weekend nights.

Café Au Lait   Bar
(Map p102; www.facebook.com/aulait.cafe;
Rua Galeria de Paris 44; ⊙9.30pm-4am Mon-Sat)
Housed in a former textile warehouse, this
narrow, intimate bar now stitches together
a lively and unpretentious artistic crowd.
Beside cocktails, there are snacks and
salads, including vegetarian grub. DJs and
occasional gigs amp up the vibe and add to
the good cheer.

Casa da Música

⭐ ENTERTAINMENT

FC Porto
Football

(www.fcporto.pt) The Estádio do Dragão is home to Primeira Liga heroes FC Porto. It's northeast of the centre, just off the VCI ring road (metro stop Estádio do Dragão).

Casa da Música
Concert Venue

(House of Music; ☑220 120 220; www.casada musica.com; Avenida da Boavista 604; ☺box office 9.30am-7pm Mon-Sat, to 6pm Sun) Grand and minimalist, sophisticated yet populist, Porto's cultural behemoth boasts a shoebox-style concert hall at its heart, meticulously engineered to accommodate everything from jazz duets to Beethoven's Ninth.

The hall holds concerts most nights of the year, from classical and blues to fado and electronica, with occasional summer concerts staged outdoors in the adjoining plaza.

Restaurante O Fado
Fado

(Map p102; ☑222 026 937; www.ofado.com; Largo de São João Novo 16; ☺8.30pm-1am Mon-Sat) Porto has no fado tradition of its own, but you can enjoy the Lisbon or Coimbra version of 'Portugal blues' into the wee hours at Restaurante O Fado. It's a tad touristy, but the fado is good. Mains will set you back €23.50 to €30.

Hot Five Jazz & Blues Club
Jazz

(Map p102; ☑934 328 583; www.hotfive.pt; Largo Actor Dias 51; ☺10pm-3am Wed-Sat) True to its name, this spot hosts live jazz and blues as well as the occasional acoustic, folk or all-out jam session. It's a modern but intimate space, with seating at small round tables, both fronting the stage and on an upper balcony. Concerts often start later than scheduled.

Teatro Municipal Rivoli
Theatre

(Map p102; ☑223 392 200; www.teatro municipaldoporto.pt; Praça Dom João I; ♿) This art deco theatre is one of the linchpins of Porto's evolving cultural scene. It traverses the whole spectrum from theatre to music, contemporary circus, cinema, dance and marionette productions.

ZACARIAS PEREIRA DA MATA / SHUTTERSTOCK ©

Boavista FC   Football

(www.boavistafc.pt; Rua 1º de Janeiro, Estádio do Bessa Século) FC Porto's worthy cross-town rival, Boavista FC, has as its home turf the Estádio do Bessa, which lies just off Avenida da Boavista. Check the local editions of *Jornal de Notícias* for upcoming matches.

Maus Hábitos   Performing Arts

(Map p102; www.maushabitos.com; 4th fl, Rua Passos Manuel 178; ⊗noon-midnight Tue & Sun, to 2am Wed & Thu, to 4am Fri & Sat) Maus Hábitos or 'Bad Habits' is an arty, nicely chilled haunt hosting a culturally ambitious agenda. Changing exhibitions and imaginative installations adorn the walls, while live bands and DJs work the small stage.

Fado in Porto   Fado

(Map p102; www.calem.pt; Avenida Diogo Leite 344; €17.50; ⊗6.30pm Tue-Sun) Lisbon and Coimbra may be the spiritual home of fado, Portugal's unique brand of melancholic folk music with guitar accompaniment, but you'll find decent performances over a glass of port or two at the Cálem cellars every evening.

ℹ️ GETTING THERE & AWAY

AIR

Situated around 19km northwest of the city centre, the gleaming, ultra-modern **Francisco de Sá Carneiro Airport** (☑229 432 400; 4470-558 Maia) operates direct flights to major international hubs including London, Brussels, Madrid, Frankfurt and Toronto.

TAP (www.flytap.com) has multiple daily flights to/from Lisbon. There are also low-cost carriers, such as easyJet (www.easyjet.com) and Ryanair (www.ryanair.com), with nonstop services to London, Madrid, Paris, Frankfurt, Amsterdam and Brussels.

BUS

As in many Portuguese cities, bus services in Porto are regrettably dispersed, with no central bus terminal. The good news is that there are frequent services to just about everywhere in northern Portugal, as well as express services to Coimbra, Lisbon and points south.

Renex (Map p102; www.renex.pt; Rua Campo Mártires de Pátria 37) is the choice for Lisbon (€20, 3½ hours), with the most direct routes

Ana Moura fado performance

and eight to 12 departures daily, including one continuing on to the Algarve. Renex also has frequent services to Braga (€6, 1¼ hours). Buses depart from Campo Mártires da Patria 37.

Rede Expressos (Map p102; ☑ 222 006 954; www. rede-expressos.pt; Rua Alexandre Herculano 366) has services to the entire country from the smoggy **Paragem Atlântico terminal** (Map p102).

There are Eurolines (www.eurolines.com) departures from Interface Casa da Música (Rua Capitão Henrique Calvão). Northern Portugal's own international carrier, **Internorte** (www.inter norte.pt; Praça da Galiza 96), departs from the same terminal. Most travel agencies can book outbound buses with either operator.

TRAIN

Porto is the principal rail hub for northern Portugal. Long-distance services start at **Campanhã** (Rua Monte da Estação) station, 3km east of the centre.

Direct IC destinations from Porto include Lisbon (2nd class €24.30, 3¼ hours, hourly).

Most *urbano*, regional and interregional (IR) trains depart from the stunning indoor-outdoor São Bento station, though all these lines also pass through Campanhã.

For destinations on the Braga, Guimarães and Aveiro lines, or up the Douro Valley as far as Marco de Canaveses, take one of the frequent *urbano* trains.

GETTING AROUND

Metro Porto's compact, six-line metro network runs from 6am to 1am daily. It's handy for zipping between neighbourhoods and getting to/from the airport and beaches north of the city. A map is available at http://en.metrodoporto.pt.

Tram Porto's vintage trams are transport at its atmospheric best. There are three lines: 1 running along the river from the historic centre to Foz, 18 between Massarelos and Carmo, and 22 doing a loop through the centre from Carmo to Batalha/Guindais.

 Transport Tickets & Passes

For maximum convenience, Porto's transport system offers the rechargeable **Andante Card** (www.linhandante. com), allowing smooth movement between tram, metro, funicular and many bus lines.

The card itself costs only €0.60 and can be recharged for one year. Once you've purchased the card, charge it with travel credit according to which zones you will be travelling in.

Purchase credit at metro ticket machines and staffed TIP booths at central hubs such as Casa da Música and Trindade, as well as the STCP office, the funicular, the electric tram museum and a scattering of other authorised sales points.

Your time begins from when you first enter the vehicle or platform: just wave the card in front of a validation machine marked 'Andante'.

Each trip allows you to move between methods of transport without additional cost.

Bus Central hubs of Porto's extensive bus system include the Jardim da Cordoaria, Praça da Liberdade and São Bento station.

Taxi To cross town expect to pay between €5 and €8. There's a 20% surcharge at night. There are taxi ranks throughout the centre.

THE ALGARVE

The Algarve at a Glance...

The alluring coast of the Algarve receives much exposure for its breathtaking cliffs, golden beaches, scalloped bays and sandy islands. But 'S' (for sun, surf and sand) is only one letter in the Algarvian alphabet; other initials stand for activities, beach bars, castles (both sand and real), diving, entertainment, fun...

Portugal's premier holiday destination sold its soul to tourism in the '60s and never really looked back. Behind sections of the south coast's beachscape loom brash resorts. However, the west coast is another story – one more about nature. The enchanting inner Algarve boasts pretty castle towns and historic villages and the wonderful Via Algarviana hiking trail.

The Algarve in One Week

Heading east to west, a week is enough to visit the major locations along the coast, including **Tavira**, **Ilha de Tavira**, **Faro**, **Albufeira**, **Portimão** and **Lagos**, taking a few side trips to places such as Olhão, Silves and Loulé en route.

The Algarve in Two Weeks

Two weeks allows you sufficient time to make a full exploration of the Algarve's coast of sun, sand and surf, from the wonderful Ilha da **Tavira** in the east to the dramatic **Ponta de Sagres** in the west, as well as delve deep into the region's lesser-known hinterland of historic towns, cork orchards and dramatic hiking trails.

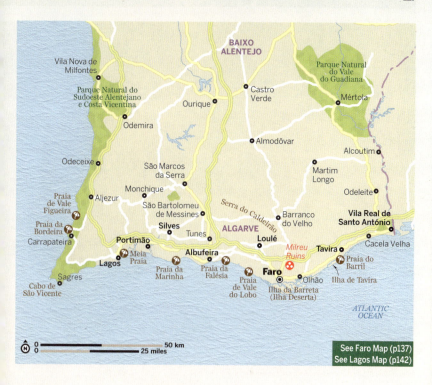

See Faro Map (p137)
See Lagos Map (p142)

Arriving in the Algarve

Faro National bus and train connections, as well as the airport, well-served from many cities in Europe.

Lagos National bus connections.

Portimão Bus connections to Lisbon and beyond.

Sleeping

The Algarve has the full range of accommodation options you would expect to find in a resort-packed region, from five-star plushness to backpacker hostels. Rates can almost double or even triple in July and especially August and a bed can be almost impossible to come by in the busiest resorts. From September to June there are some amazing deals to be had.

With so many places to stay in Praia da Rocha, few choose to sleep over in Portimão, though if you do there are a couple of decent options. The town could also be a good choice in July and August, when the beach towns are hopelessly booked out.

Praia da Marinha

BLICKWINKEL / ALAMY STOCK PHOTOS ©

Beaches

The top reason the vast majority of tourists visit the Algarve, the region's 150km of soft golden sand is one Portugal's undisputed highlights.

The Algarve's extraordinary coastline – stretching for over 150km along the Atlantic Ocean – is incredibly diverse and offers an abundance of enticing choices.

Geography of the Coast

The Algarve's coastline has everything from small, secluded coves to wide stretches of rugged, dune-backed shores, and from simple rock-backed nooks with calm waters (great for kids) to rugged coasts with huge swells.

The coast's varied geography changes dramatically along its length and makes for some quirky beachscapes. From Vila Real de Santo António to the tiny village of Cacela Velha, the beaches are a dune system. The central coast sees kilometres of limestone cliffs – think eroded rock towers and plenty of nooks and caves.

Great For...

☑ **Don't Miss**

There are many less-frequented beaches on the Algarve's underrated west coast.

Praia de Dona Ana

IGNACIO PALACIOS / GETTY IMAGES ©

The increasingly rocky coast from Lagos to Sagres culminates in the wind-scoured grandeur of the Cabo de São Vicente (p239). Here, dramatic black cliffs, bordered by beautiful sandy stretches, head north along the Parque Natural do Sudoeste Alentejano e Costa Vicentina (Costa Vicentina Natural Park). This stretch is made for serious surfers.

Top Ten Beaches

Our (highly subjective) picks include the following stretches of sand.

Odeceixe Only just in the Algarve, this Atlantic beach has a river on one side and the ocean on the other.

Praia da Falésia A posh 'resort' beach between Quarteira and Albufeira backed by high ochre-hued cliffs.

Praia da Marinha Great snorkelling, with a novel entry via a long staircase – just east of Carvoeiro.

Meia Praia Lagos' beach is a vast, popular and scenic place, with options for water sports.

Praia do Barril Crown jewel of Ilha de Tavira, with an anchor cemetery.

Ilha da Barreta (Ilha Deserta) South of Faro, this beach island is accessed by boat through nature-filled lagoons.

Praia de Vale Figueira Near Salema, this is a long stretch of wild, little-frequented coast.

Praia da Bordeira Untamed beauty (with surfing) – near Carrapateira on the west coast.

Praia de Dona Ana & Camilo Enchanting, golden rock formations near Lagos.

Praia de Vale do Lobo West of Faro, this beach has all the tourist services within reach and on tap.

Water Sports

Getting into, onto and occasionally above the water is what it's all about along the coast of the Algarve, whether that be surfing, diving, boat trips, kayaking or wildlife spotting. And have no fear, there are plenty of outfits in every resort waiting to help you do it.

Loulé market

Inland Algarve

The Algarve isn't all about the coast – head inland to discover historic towns, spas and a superb hiking trail. Explore by car to reveal the Algarve's remoter, less-inhabited side.

Great For...

☑ Don't Miss

Unwinding at the spa in Monchique after hiking in the surrounding hills.

Via Algarviana

Covering some of the most beautiful scenery in the Algarve, the 300km **Via Algarviana** (www.viaalgarviana.org) walking trail crosses the breadth of Portugal from Alcoutim to Cabo de São Vicente, taking in the wooded hillsides of the Serras de Caldeirão and Monchique. It takes about 14 days to walk the trail. Though the route is not yet fully marked, new maps are accurate. The best times to hike the trail are between March and October – things can get damp and chilly outside of this period. For more information, visit www.viaalgarviana. org (run by the environmental group Almargem) or www.algarveway.com (a private website run by enthusiasts). The official Via Algarviana route booklet is available from the Algarve Tourist Association's offices.

Roman mosaic, Milreu

ⓘ Need to Know

Transport links are threadbare away from the coast so you'll need your own car.

✕ Take a Break

Inland Algarve's most characterful cafe is **Pastelaria Rosa** (Largo do Município; pastries €1.50-3; ⊘7.30am-10pm Mon-Sat; 🛜)

★ Top Tip

Anywhere in inland Algarve can be tackled as a day trip from the coast.

the town and around. It's built around an 18m-deep Moorish well with a spiral staircase heading into the depths.

Roman Ruins at Milreu

Set in beautiful countryside north of Faro are the impressive ruins of a **Roman villa** (€2; ⊘9.30am-1pm & 2-6.30pm Tue-Sun May-Sep, 9am-1pm & 2-5.30pm Tue-Sun Oct-Apr). The villa, inhabited from the 1st century AD, has the characteristic peristyle form, with a gallery of columns around a courtyard. The highlight is the temple, the fish mosaics and former central pool of which suggest that it was devoted to a water cult.

Loulé

One of the Algarve's largest inland towns, and only 16km northwest of Faro, Loulé (lo-lay) has an attractive old quarter and Moorish castle ruins, and its history goes back to the Romans. A few of Loulé's artisan traditions still survive; crafty folk toil away making wicker baskets and at copperworks and embroidery in hole-in-the-wall workshops about town. The town's most impressive piece of architectural heritage is its art-nouveau market, a 1908 revivalist neo-Arab confection with four oriental-looking cupolas at the four corners and Moorish features picked out in raspberry red against cream walls.

Silves

Some 15km north of Portimão, Silves is an attractive town of jumbling orange rooftops and winding streets scattered over a hillside above the Rio Arade. It boasts one of the best-preserved castles in the Algarve, a russet-coloured, Lego-like structure affording enjoyable views over the town. Just below the castle is the **Sé** (Rua da Sé; €1; ⊘9am-12.30pm & 2-5pm Mon-Fri year round, 9am-1pm Sat Jun-Aug) (cathedral), built in 1189 on the site of an earlier mosque. In many ways, this is the Algarve's most impressive cathedral, with a substantially unaltered Gothic interior. The town's other unmissable is the **Museu Municipal de Arqueologia** (📞282 444 838; Rua das Portas de Loulé; adult/under 10yr €2.10/free, joint ticket with Castelo €3.90; ⊘10am-6pm), a modern museum displaying fascinating finds from

Parque Natural da Ria Formosa

MARCIN KRZYZAK / SHUTTERSTOCK ©

Parque Natural da Ria Formosa

With its international airport, engaging Faro is the gateway to the Algarve. Once you have explored the town, a boat trip to the Parque Natural da Ria Formosa awaits.

Great For...

☑ Don't Miss

Take your binoculars along for a spot of birdwatching.

Parque Natural da Ria Formosa

The **Ria Formosa Natural Park** (www.icnf. pt) is mostly a lagoon system stretching for 60km along the Algarve coastline and encompassing 18,000 hectares, from west of Faro to the tiny village of Cacela Velha. It encloses a vast area of *sapal* (marsh), *salinas* (salt pans), creeks and dune islands. To the west there are several freshwater lakes, including those at Ludo and Quinta do Lago; the marshes are an important area for migrating birds. The park provides some of the most stunning natural vistas in the Algarve and is a must for anyone staying in the area. Birdwatchers are drawn to the park due to the huge variety of wetland birds here, along with ducks, shorebirds, gulls and terns. This is a favourite nesting place of the little tern and a rare purple gallinule.

Salicornia plant

HS FLORAL / ALAMY STOCK PHOTO ©

❶ Need to Know

Boat trips out into the Parque Natural da Ria Formosa run year-round and cost around €25.

✕ Take a Break

The only place to eat in the Parque Natural da Ria Formosa is **Estaminé** (☏ 917 811 856; www.animaris.pt; Ilha da Barreta; mains €9-15; ⊙ 10.30am-7pm Jun-Sep, 11am-5.30pm Oct-May) ✐

★ Top Tip

Take a picnic, water, binoculars, swimwear and waterproofs if the weather looks iffy.

Getting into the Park

Boats leave from Faro waterfront with several tour companies offering trips. **Animaris** (Map p137; ☏ 918 779 155, 917 811 856; www.animaris.pt) runs excursions to Ilha da Barreta (Ilha Deserta). Boats (€10 to €15 return) leave from southeast of the marina, in front of the Cidade Velha (Old Town) walls. There's a ticket kiosk by the marina. The same company runs 1½-hour year-round boat trips (€25) through Parque Natural da Ria Formosa. Boats leave from the pier next to Arco da Porta Nova. Animaris also runs ecofriendly restaurant Estaminé on Ilha da Barreta, and it is the only company to operate year-round, providing stable employment for locals, another reason to go with it. **Formosamar** (Map p137; ☏ 918 720 002; www.formosamar. com; Clube Naval, Faro Marina) ✐ genuinely

embraces and promotes environmentally responsible tourism. Among the excellent tours it provides are two-hour birdwatching trips around the Parque Natural da Ria Formosa (€25), dolphin watching (€45), cycling (€37), and a two-hour small-boat trip that penetrates some of the narrower lagoon channels (€25). All trips have a minimum number of participants (usually two or three). It has departures from Olhão and Tavira, too, and various ticket offices around the Faro waterfront.

Exploring On Your Own

You don't have to go with a group to explore the Ria Formosa Natural Park. The **Lands** (Map p137; ☏ 914 539 511; www.lands.pt; Clube Naval, Faro Marina) ✐ agency rents out kayaks (€30 for two hours) for you to explore Ria Formosa on your own. Staff can give advice on where you should head and the rest is up to you. Some previous kayaking experience might be a good idea, but it's not essential.

Tavira

Tavira &
Ilha de Tavira

Set prettily on either side of the meandering Rio Gilão, Tavira is arguably the Algarve's most charming town. A hilltop castle and an old Roman bridge are the main draws.

Great For...

☑ Don't Miss

The elaborate, Islamic-era Tavira vase in the Núcleo Islâmico.

Tavira

Tavira's ruined **castelo** (Largo Abu-Otmane; ⏱8am-5pm Mon-Fri, 9am-7pm Sat & Sun, to 5pm winter) FREE rises high and mighty above the town. Possibly dating back to Neolithic times, the structure was rebuilt by Phoenicians and later taken over by the Moors; most of what now stands is a 17th-century reconstruction. The interior holds a pleasantly exotic botanic garden, and the octagonal tower offers fine views over Tavira. Near the castle rises the Torre da Tavira, formerly the town's water tower (100m) which now houses a camera obscura. A simple but ingenious object, the camera obscura reveals a 360-degree panoramic view of Tavira in real time. Down from the castle, the **Igreja da Misericórdia** (Largo da Misericórdia; ⏱9.30am-1pm & 2-6pm Mon-Sat) is the Algarve's most important

Igreja da Misericórdia

Need To Know
Regular buses and trains run to Faro.

✕ Take a Break
Busy **Pastelaria Tavirense** (Rua Dr Marcelino Franco 17; pastries €0.50-3; ☉8am-midnight; ❄🛜) is a convenient spot for a quick sandwich, cake and coffee stop.

★ Top Tip
Sample some daytime fado at the excellent Fado Com História near the castle.

Renaissance monument, with a magnificent carved, arched doorway. Down by the river on busy Praça da República be sure to pop into the **Núcleo Islâmico** (Praça da República 5; adult/child €2/1, with Palácio da Galeria €3/1.50; ☉10am-12.30pm & 3-6pm mid-Jun–mid-Sep, 10am-4.30pm Tue-Sat mid-Sep–mid-Jun), a 21st-century museum exhibiting impressive Islamic pieces discovered in various excavations around the old town. Nearby is the **Ponte Romana**, the town's Roman bridge.

Ilha de Tavira
Sandy islands (all part of the Parque Natural da Ria Formosa) stretch along the coast from Cacela Velha to just west of Faro, and this is one of the finest. Made up of dunes, gently shelving sand and a strip of woodland, this is the Algarve at its best, a real hideaway only reachable by boat. Beach time and swimming are obvious attractions, and you can even enjoy a camping holiday on the island. The huge beach at Ilha de Tavira's eastern end, opposite Tavira, has water sports, a campground and cafe-restaurants. Reached by ferry from Quatro Águas, 2km from Tavira, the island usually feels wonderfully remote and empty, but during July and August things get busy. A kilometre west of the jetty is an unofficial nudist area called Praia do Homen Nu, popular with elderly German tourists.

Getting to the Ilha de Tavira
Ferries make the five-minute hop to the island (€1.80 return) from Quatro Águas, 2km southeast of Tavira.

In addition to the local ferry, **Sequa Tours** (☎966 615 071; www.sequatours.com/watertaxiservice.html) water taxi operates 24 hours a day from July to mid-September, and until midnight from May to June. The fare from Quatro Águas-Tavira to the island is around €18 for five people.

A bus goes to Quatro Águas from the Tavira bus station from July to mid-September (eight daily). A taxi costs around €5.

Faro

HISTORY

After hosting the Phoenicians and Carthaginians, Faro boomed as the Roman port Ossonoba. During the Moorish occupation it became the cultured capital of an 11th-century principality.

Afonso III took the town in 1249 – making it the last major Portuguese town to be recaptured from the Moors – and walled it.

Portugal's first printed works – books in Hebrew made by a Jewish printer – came from Faro in 1487.

A city from 1540, Faro had a brief golden age that ground to a halt in 1596, during Spanish rule. Troops under the Earl of Essex, en route to England from Spain in 1597, plundered the city and carried off hundreds of priceless theological works from the bishop's palace, now part of the Bodleian Library in Oxford.

Battered Faro was rebuilt, only to be shattered by an earthquake in 1722 and then almost flattened in 1755. Most of what you see today was built post-quake, though the historic centre largely survived. In 1834 Faro became the Algarve's capital.

◎ SIGHTS

Sé   Cathedral

(Map p137; www.paroquiasedefaro.org; Largo da Sé; adult/child €3.50/free; ☉10am-6.30pm Mon-Fri, 9.30am-1pm Sat Jun-Aug, slightly shorter hours Sep-May) The centrepiece of the Cidade Velha, the sé was completed in 1251 but heavily damaged in the 1755 earthquake. What you see now is a variety of Renaissance, Gothic and baroque features. Climb the tower for lovely views across the walled town and estuary islands. The cathedral also houses the **Museu Capitular**, with an assortment of chalices, priestly vestments and grisly relics (including both forearms of St Boniface), and a small 18th-century shrine built of bones.

The blocky, castle-like cathedral occupies what was probably the site of a Roman temple, then a Visigoth cathedral and then a Moorish mosque. Only the tower gate and several chapels remain of the original Romanesque-Gothic exterior – the rest was obliterated in 1755. The interior has very elaborate baroque side altarpieces, and the altar itself is flanked by matching vaulted Gothic chapels. The baroque organ is worth noting.

Igreja de Nossa Senhora do Carmo & Capela dos Ossos   Church

(Map p137; Largo do Carmo; €3.50; ☉10am-6.30pm Mon-Fri, 9.30am-1pm Sat, last admission 1hr before closing, mass 7pm Mon-Fri, 6pm Sat, 10am Sun) This twin-towered baroque church was completed in 1719 under João V. The spectacular facade was completed after the 1755 earthquake. Brazilian gold paid for it, and the interior is gilded to the extreme. The numerous cherubs seem comparatively serious and sober, no doubt contemplating the ghoulish attraction behind the church: the 19th-century Capela dos Ossos, built from the bones and skulls of over 1000 monks as a blackly reverent reminder of earthly impermanence. It's quite a sight.

Museu Regional do Algarve   Museum

(Map p137; ☏289 827 610; Praça da Liberdade; adult/concession €1.50/1; ☉10am-1.30pm & 2.30-6pm Mon-Fri) Three of the four halls at this worthwhile museum house exhibitions on rural life in the Algarve. This includes mock-ups of 19th-century shops and rooms, a real fishing boat, some impressively woven creations in wicker, bamboo and palm leaves, and lots of rag rugs and fishing nets. The fourth hall is always given over to a temporary show on a folksy local theme.

✪ ACTIVITIES

Praia de Faro   Beach

(Ilha de Faro) The town's beach, with its miles of sweeping sand, a number of windsurfing operators and a handful of cafes, is on the Ilha de Faro, 10km away. It's crammed in

Faro

⊙ Sights

✈ Activities, Courses & Tours

🍴 Eating

🍷 Drinking & Nightlife

July and August. Take bus 14 or 16 from opposite the bus station (half-hourly in summer, via the airport).

San Lorenzo   Golf

(☎289 396 522; www.sanlorenzogolfcourse.com; Vale do Lobo; green fees €110-140) Just west of Faro, this is one of the Algarve's finest courses and enjoys a stunning ocean-side setting.

🍴 EATING

Faro's restaurants are big on seafood, though there's also plenty for those who like their food without fins and tentacles. Faro's big, daily *mercado municipal* (municipal market) is in Largo Mercado.

A Venda   Portuguese €€

(Map p137; Rua Do Compromisso 60; mains €6-15; ⊙noon-11pm Tue-Sat) Sit down to a plate of honest, homestyle Portuguese food like *avó* (granny) used to make at this trendily retro backstreet place everyone's talking about. 'The Shop' has an ancient tiled floor, mismatched furniture and antique glass display cases, plus a loyal following that comes for the food and the occasional session of live music.

Chefe Branco   Portuguese €

(Rua de Loulé 9; mains €4.50-13.50; ⊙noon-11pm) A fabulous local spot with appealing street-side seating and a slightly tacky but cosy interior. The delightful staff serves honest, homestyle fare including rabbit, goat and seafood dishes. The half portions are the biggest this side of the Rio Tejo. Finish with an excellent Algarvian dessert.

Gengibre e Canela   Vegetarian €

(Map p137; Travessa da Mota 10; buffet €7.50; ⊙noon-3pm Mon-Sat, groups only evenings; 🛜🎵) Give the taste buds a break from meat and fish dishes and veg out (literally) at this Zen-like restaurant. The buffet changes daily; there may be vegetable lasagne, vegetarian *feijoada* (bean casserole)

and tofu dishes, but there's only the occasional curry. Wine and desserts are extra.

Faz Gostos   Portuguese, French €€

(Map p137; 📱289 878 422; www.fazgostos. com; Rua do Castelo 13; mains €13-19.50; ⊙noon-3pm & 7-11pm Mon-Fri, 7-11pm Sat; 🛜) Elegantly housed in the old town, this restaurant offers high-class French-influenced Portuguese cuisine in a spacious, comfortably handsome dining area. There's plenty of game, fish and meat on offer with rich and seductive sauces, and a few set menus are available.

Restaurante Madeirense   Madeiran €€

(Map p137; 📱967 168 140; Rua 1 Dezembro 28; mains €8-17; ⊙noon-10.30pm Tue-Sun) For an exotic take on Portuguese cuisine, this small Madeiran restaurant bangs down plates loaded with specialities you'll only get on the Island of Eternal Spring. *Espada* (scabbard fish), *bolo de caco* (potato bread) and *pudim de maracuja* (maracuja pudding) are just some of the treats on offer; round things off with a

Igreja de Nossa Senhora do Carmo (p136)

poncha (sugar-cane liqueur) or sweet Madeira wine.

The interior is bedecked with Madeiran knick-knacks and the tables are dressed with the striking national folk cloth of Madeira (red with multicoloured stripes). Staff are friendly, but only the cook is actually Madeiran.

Gardy Patisserie €

(Map p137; Rua de Santo António 16; pastries €0.50-4; ⊙8.30am-7.30pm Mon-Sat; ⊛) This is the place to head for your patisserie fix, which can be taken under brick vaulting or in the grandly columned space behind. It has a wide variety of homemade specialities but is slow to get going at breakfast time.

🍷 DRINKING & NIGHTLIFE

Bar Chessenta Bar

(Map p137; Rua do Prior 24; ⊙4pm-4am Mon-Thu, 8.30pm-4am Fri-Sun; ⊛) A miracle of split-levelling has managed to fit two floors, toilets and a stage for live music into this tiny space. Right in the heart of Faro's bar zone, the Chessenta is bohemian and simple, with a Che Guevara theme.

Columbus Bar Bar

(Map p137; www.barcolumbus.pt; Praça Dom Francisco Gomes 13; ⊙noon-4am; ⊛) Definitely the place to be, this popular central place has a street-side terrace in the heart of town and an attractive brick-vaulted interior. The bar staff does a fine job mixing cocktails, and there's a pleasing range of spirits. Gets lively from around 11pm.

O Castelo Bar

(Map p137; Rua do Castelo 11; ⊙10.30am-4am Wed-Mon winter, from 10am summer; ⊛) O Castelo is all things to all people: bar, restaurant, club and performance space. Start your day here with a coffee, grab a light meal for lunch or take in sunset over a cocktail. In summer the outside morphs into a party space, and there are regular fado (traditional song) nights. Its location atop the historic old-town walls is superb.

📖 Faro Jewish Heritage Centre

The last vestiges of the first post-Inquisition Jewish presence in Portugal are found at the extraordinary Jewish cemetery, which has 76 beautiful marble gravestones. The small site also has a tiny museum and recreated synagogue (complete with a reconstructed wedding). Knowledgeable caretaker António starts you off with a long-winded DVD, then gives a detailed, interesting tour. You'll find the place tucked behind the football stadium – look for the cypresses – 1km from the centre.

Jewish cemetery, Faro
ALEX SEGRE / ALAMY STOCK PHOTO ©

ℹ INFORMATION

Turismo (Map p137; www.visitalgarve.pt; Rua da Misericórdia 8; ⊙9am-1pm & 2-6pm) Busy but efficient office with friendly staff.

ℹ GETTING THERE & AWAY

AIR

TAP (Air Portugal; ☎707 205 700; www.flytap. com) has multiple daily Lisbon–Faro flights (40 minutes). There's an office at the airport. Internationally there are many flights a day to/from regional airports across the UK and Germany.

For flight enquiries call the **airport** (p301).

BUS

Buses arrive at and depart from **Eva bus station** (Map p137; ☎289 899 760; www.eva-bus.com; Av da República 5). **Eva** (☎289 899 760; www. eva-bus.com) services run to Seville in Spain

  Where to Stay in Faro

Faro has it all, from four-star comfort to crash-pad *residenciais*. Outside high season, prices can more than halve. The vast majority of hotels and guest houses are in the city centre.

ANIAD / SHUTTERSTOCK ©

(€20, 3½ hours, four daily) via Huelva (€16, 2½ hours).

Renex (Map p137; ☑289 812 980; www.renex. pt; Avenida da República 106), located opposite the bus terminal, has express coaches to Lisbon (€20, five hours, at least hourly).

TRAIN

There are three direct trains from Lisbon daily (€21.20 to €22.20, 3¾ hours); 1st-class fares are slightly higher. You can also get to Porto (€41.70, six to eight hours, four daily), sometimes changing at Lisbon. The trans-Algarve line runs through Faro on its way between Vila Real de Santo António and Lagos.

GETTING AROUND

Próximo (Map p137; ☑289 899 700; www. proximo.pt) city buses 14 and 16 run to the bus station (€2.22, 20 minutes, half-hourly June to August, slightly less frequently in low season). From here it's an easy stroll to the centre.

A taxi into town costs around €13 (20% more after 10pm and on weekends), plus around €2 for each luggage item.

Lagos

HISTORY

Phoenicians and Greeks set up shop at this port (which later became Roman Lacobriga) at the mouth of the muddy Rio Bensafrim. Afonso III recaptured it from the Moors in 1241. In 1415 a giant fleet set sail from Lagos under the command of the 21-year-old Prince Henry the Navigator to seize Ceuta in Morocco, thereby setting the stage for the Age of Discoveries.

The shipyards of Lagos built and launched Prince Henry's caravels, and Henry split his time between his trading company here and his navigation school at Sagres. Local boy Gil Eanes left Lagos in 1434 as commander of the first ship to round West Africa's Cape Bojador. Others continued to bring back information about the African coast, along with ivory, gold and slaves. Lagos has the dubious distinction of having hosted (in 1444) the first sale of Africans as slaves to Europeans, and the town grew into a slave-trading centre.

It was also from Lagos in 1578 that Dom Sebastião, along with the cream of the Portuguese nobility and an army of Portuguese, Spanish, Dutch and German buccaneers, left on a disastrous crusade to Christianise North Africa, which ended in a debacle at Alcácer-Quibir in Morocco. Sir Francis Drake inflicted heavy damage on Lagos a few years later, in 1587.

Lagos was the Algarve's high-profile capital from 1576 until 1755, when the earthquake flattened it.

SIGHTS

As far as touristy towns go, Lagos *(lah-goosh)* has got the lot. It lies along the bank of the Rio Bensafrim, with 16th-century walls enclosing the old town's pretty, cobbled lanes and picturesque piazzas and churches. Beyond these lies a modern but not overly unattractive sprawl. The town's good restaurants and the range of fabulous nearby beaches add to the allure. With every activity under the sun on offer, plus a pumping nightlife, it's not surprising that people of all ages are drawn here.

Aside from its hedonistic appeal, Lagos has historical clout, having launched many naval excursions during Portugal's extraordinary Age of Discoveries.

Igreja de Santo António   Church
(Map p142; Rua General Alberto da Silveira; adult/child incl museum €3/1.50; ☉10am-12.30pm & 2-5.30pm Tue-Sun) This little church, bursting with gilded, carved wood, is a stupendous baroque extravaganza. Beaming cherubs and ripening grapes are much in evidence. The dome and *azulejo* (hand-painted tile) panels were installed during repairs after the 1755 earthquake. Enter the church from the adjacent Museu Municipal (p141).

Museu Municipal   Museum
(Map p142; ☑282 762 301; Rua General Alberto da Silveira; adult/concession €3/1.50; ☉10am-12.30pm & 2-5.30pm Tue-Sun) Lagos' town museum, an old-fashioned but lovably curious collection, holds a bit of everything: swords and pistols, landscapes and portraits, minerals and crystals, coins, china, miniature furniture, Roman mosaics, African artefacts, stone tools, model boats, and an intriguing model of an imaginary Portuguese town. The museum is also the entry point for the baroque Igreja de Santo António (p141).

Ponta da Piedade   Viewpoint
(Point of Piety) Protruding south from Lagos, Ponta da Piedade is a dramatic wedge of headland. Three windswept kilometres out of town, the point is well worth visiting for its contorted, polychrome sandstone cliffs and towers, complete with lighthouse and, in spring, hundreds of nesting egrets. The surrounding area is brilliant with wild orchids in spring. On a clear day you can see east to Carvoeiro and west to Sagres. The only way to reach it is by car or on foot.

🏊 ACTIVITIES
Meia Praia   Beach
(Map p142) Meia Praia, the vast expanse of sand to the east of town, has outlets offering sailboard rental and waterskiing

Ponta da Piedade

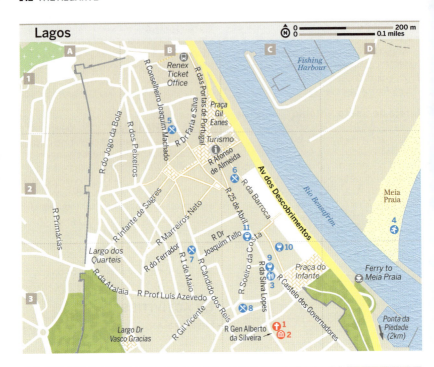

Lagos

Lagos

⦿ Sights
1 Igreja de Santo António C3
2 Museu Municipal C3

✪ Activities, Courses & Tours
3 Lagos Surf Center C3
4 Meia Praia D2

✪ Eating
5 A Forja B1

6 Arribalé C2
7 Café Gombá B3
8 Dom Vinho II C3

⦿ Drinking & Nightlife
9 Bon Vivant C3
10 Stevie Ray's Blues Jazz Bar C3
11 Taberna de Lagos C2

lessons, plus several laid-back restaurants and beach bars. An informal **boat service** (Map p142; €0.50; ☺Apr-Oct) shuttles back and forth from the waterfront in Lagos.

Tiffany's   Horse Riding
(☏282 697 395; www.teamtiffanys.com; Vale Grifo, Almádena; ☺9am-dusk) Seven kilometres west of Lagos, this outfit charges €33 for an hour's horse riding. Other options include a three-hour trip (€85) and an all-day forest trip that includes a luxury picnic (€140).

Lagos Surf Center   Surfing
(Map p142; ☏282 764 734; www.lagossurf-center.com; Rua da Silva Lopes 31; 1-/3-/5-day courses €55/150/225) Will help you catch a wave and head to where there are suitable swells. Children must be accompanied by a family member over 14 years of age. It also rents out wetsuits (€5 per day) and boards (€15 to €25) and offers beach kayaking and paddle-boarding trips.

Blue Ocean — Diving
(☑964 665 667; www.blue-ocean-divers.de) For those who want to go diving or snorkelling. Offers a half-day discovery experience (€30), a full-day dive (€90) and a Divemaster PADI scuba course (€590). It also offers kayak safaris (half-/full day €30/45, children under 12 half price).

TOURS

Dizzy Dolphins — Boating
(☑938 305 000; www.dizzydolphin.com) Run by a former BBC wildlife-documentary producer, this small outfit offers excellent 90-minute summer dolphin-spotting trips on a rigid inflatable.

Axessextreme — Kayaking
(☑919 114 649; www.axessextreme.com; 3hr tour €25) Offers recommended sea-kayaking trips in the Algarve as well as mountain biking and surfing.

EATING

A Forja — Portuguese €€
(Map p142; ☑282 768 588; Rua dos Ferreiros 17; mains €8-17.50; ☺noon-3pm & 6.30-10pm Sun-Fri) Like an Italian trattoria, this buzzing *adega tipica* pulls in the crowds – locals, tourists and expats – for its hearty, top-quality traditional food served in a bustling environment at great prices. Plates of the day are always reliable, as are the simply prepared fish dishes.

Arribalé — Portuguese €€
(Map p142; ☑918 556 618; www.arribale.com; Rua da Barroca 40; mains €9.50-19.50, tapas around €5; ☺7pm-midnight Tue-Sat) Tucked away on an atmospheric street, this super-compact place offers a short, simple menu of mostly salads and grilled meat, though it also does a vegetarian dish of the day. The owners are friendly, quality is high, and there's an appealing, homey vibe. There aren't many tables, so it's worth booking.

Café Gombá — Cafe €
(Map p142; ☑282 762 188; Rua Cândido dos Reis 56; ☺8am-7pm Mon-Sat year round, Sun mid-Jun–mid-Sep; ☀) Although around since 1964, this traditional cafe-bakery with 21st-century decor looks more like it opened in 2014. Elderly locals hang out here for the best cakes, coffees and sandwiches in town, and it's correspondingly cheap.

Dom Vinho II — International €€
(Map p142; Rua Lançarote de Freitas 18; mains €8.50-24; ☺12.30pm-1.30am Mon-Sat, 7pm-1.30am Sun; ☎) Removed from the main-street bustle where its parent restaurant stands, this elegant upstairs dining area boasts solid dark-wood furniture and a refined feel. Service is truly excellent, and there's a top list of vintage wines. The long menu features dishes unusual for Portugal, such lamb in mint sauce and spaghetti bolognese. Limited availability after 11pm.

DRINKING & NIGHTLIFE

Dozens of bars – party palaces and local beer stops – litter the streets of Lagos, with some of the Algarve's most diverse and most clichéd drinking holes on hand. These draw plenty of surfers, backpackers and younger party animals. They are generally open until the wee hours of the morning, and a few are open during the day.

Meia Praia has some beachfront gems just seconds from sun, swimming and sand, some with weekend live music.

Bon Vivant — Bar
(Map p142; www.facebook.com/bonvivant. lagos; Rua 25 de Abril 105; ☺2pm-4am; ☎) This long-standing central bar is far classier than some of the nearby options, takes some care over its mainly R&B music and makes an effort to keep patrons entertained. Spread across several levels with various terraces, Bon Vivant shakes up some great cocktails and is pretty hot once it gets going (usually late). Look out for the bartenders' juggling feats.

View towards Meia Praia (p141), Lagos

Bahia Beach Bar   Bar
(www.bahiabeachbar.eu; Meia Praia; ☺10am-late May-Oct, to 6pm Nov-Apr) An essential hang-out on Meia Praia beach, with live music at weekends.

Linda's Bar   Bar
(www.lindabeachbar.pt; São Roque, Meia Praia; ☺10am-11pm Thu-Tue summer, 11am-6pm Thu-Tue winter; 🛜) A madly popular beach hang-out, with fab food, good salads, cocktails and tunes.

Stevie Ray's Blues Jazz Bar   Bar
(Map p142; www.stevie-rays.com; Rua da Senhora da Graça 9; ☺Tue-Sat 9pm-6am; 🛜) This intimate two-level candlelit joint is the best live-music bar in town, attracting a smart-casual older crowd. At weekends it has live blues, jazz and oldies. Admission is free, but a €5 minimum consumption is applied.

Taberna de Lagos   Bar
(Map p142; www.tabernalagos.pt; Rua Dr Joaquim Tello 1; ☺noon-2am; 🛜) Boasting a stylish space and brooding electronic music in a historic central building, this airy and atmospheric bar and restaurant attracts a somewhat savvier bar-goer than the typical Lagos drinking den (higher cocktail prices also keep some punters away). It has live fado on Monday night.

ℹ️ INFORMATION

Turismo (Map p142; ☏282 763 031; www.visital-garve.pt; Praça Gil Eanes; ☺9am-7pm Jul & Aug, to 6pm Easter-Jun & Sep, to 5pm Oct-Easter) The very helpful staff offers excellent maps and leaflets.

ℹ️ GETTING THERE & AWAY

BUS
Renex operates an express service from Lagos to Lisbon (€20); tickets are available from the **Renex ticket office** (Map p142; ☏282 768 932, 282 768 931; Rua das Portas de Portugal 101). Buses also go to Seville (via Huelva) in Spain (€21, 5½ hours, two to three times daily Monday to Friday, more frequently in summer).

TRAIN

Lagos is at the western end of the Algarve line. Trains go daily to Lisbon (all requiring a change at Tunes; €22.70, four hours, five daily).

Portimão

HISTORY

Portimão was an important trading link for Phoenicians, Greeks and Carthaginians (Hannibal is said to have visited). The Romans called it Portos Magnus and it was fought over by Moors and Christians. In 1189 Dom Sancho I and a band of crusaders sailed up the Rio Arade from here to besiege Silves. Almost destroyed in the 1755 earthquake, it regained its maritime importance in the 19th century. It became the region's fishing and canning centre before this, too, declined.

Where to Stay in Lagos

Accommodation options are extensive in Lagos, with more places out on Meia Praia and on Praia da Dona Ana. Rooms are pricier and scarcer from July to mid-September. Locals sometimes meet buses to tout their private homes – check where the property in question is before committing or head to the tourist office for a list of officially approved individuals.

ALVARO GERMAN VILELA / SHUTTERSTOCK ©

SIGHTS

Bustling Portimão is the western Algarve's main commercial centre and the second-most-populous city in the Algarve. Those expecting a gritty port town will be disappointed/relieved – the centre is a small, friendly hub with a pleasant waterfront, an assortment of outdoor cafes, and sizzling fish restaurants in the old quarter and quayside. You can also arrange a boat trip up the Rio Arade. Most people only pass through en route to Praia da Rocha.

Museu de Portimão   Museum

(www.museudeportimao.pt; Rua Dom Carlos I; adult/child €3/free, 10am-2pm Sat free; ☺2.30-6pm Tue, 10am-6pm Wed-Sun Sep-Jul, 7.30-11pm Tue, 3-11pm Wed-Sun Aug) The ultra-modern, award-winning Museu de Portimão, housed in a 19th-century fish cannery, is one excellent reason to visit Portimão. The museum focuses on three areas: archaeology, underwater finds and, the most fascinating, a recreation of the fish cannery (mackerel and sardines). You can see former production lines, complete with

sound effects – clanking and grinding and the like. An excellent video (in Portuguese) of the fishing industry reveals each step in the process, from netting the shoals to packaging.

Igreja Matriz   Church

(Rua Coutinho; ☺10.30am-12.30pm & 3-7pm Mon-Sat, 10am-1pm & 5-7pm Sun) The town's parish church stands on high ground to the north of the centre and features a 14th-century Gothic portal – all that remains of the original structure after the 1755 earthquake. Inside there are some interesting *azulejos* and lots of neoclassical and neo-baroque gilding.

🏊 ACTIVITIES

Penina Golf Resort   Golf

(☎282 420 200; www.penina.com; 2 players from €110) Between Lagos and Portimão, this is the original Algarve golf course and, for a championship course, offers comparatively affordable green fees.

 Praia da Rocha

Five minutes' drive from Portimão, Praia da Rocha has one of the Algarve's best beaches, backed by ochre-red cliffs and the small 16th-century Fortaleza da Santa Catarina.

Behind the beach looms the town; this has long known the hand of development, with high-rise condos and luxury hotels sprouting along the cliffside, and a row of restaurants, bars and clubs packed along the main thoroughfare. If you look hard beyond the concrete facade, Praia da Rocha has several vestiges of an elegant past, including some 19th-century mansions, which are now atmospheric guest houses.

There's also the sleek Marina de Portimão, painted autumnal colours (to match the cliffs), and a well-known casino where you can fritter away your holiday money.

ALAN COPSON / GETTY IMAGES ©

Santa Bernarda — Boating
(☎967 023 840; www.santa-bernarda.com; adult/child from €35/20) Santa Bernarda runs trips visiting the caves and coast on a 23m wooden sailing ship with wheelchair access and a pirate theme. The full-day trip includes a beach barbecue and time to swim.

🍴 EATING

Carvi — Seafood €€
(☎282 417 912; Rua Direita 34; mains €8-14.50; ⊗noon-midnight Wed-Mon) Famous hereabouts for its seafood, Carvi is a short walk down Rua Direita from the *turismo*. Service isn't always as warm as it could be, but the quality of the food, served at communal rows of tables dressed in white linen, makes up for it. There's also a very long wine list.

Casa da Isabel — Patisserie €
(Rua Direita 61; pastries €1-5; ⊗9am-midnight Jul & Aug, to 8pm Sep-Jun; 🖥) This delightfully elegant little tearoom is housed in a cute, tile-fronted mansion and churns out a mouth-watering array of desserts, of a type traditionally invented and made by nuns in convents. Although it serves a range of teas and infusions, most prefer coffee to go with their tooth-rotters.

Clube Naval do Portimão — Portuguese €€
(Restaurante do Cais; ☎282 432 325; Zona Ribeirinha; mains €13.50-17; ⊗noon-3pm & 7-11pm Tue-Sun; 🖥) Near the municipal museum on the waterfront, the Naval Club has a fancy upstairs restaurant with unsurpassed views over the water. Go for the fish of the day, tuna steaks, or skewers. The downstairs cafe is great for a coffee or beer waterside.

🎭 ENTERTAINMENT

Bar Marginália — Live Music
(Rua Arco Maravilhas; ⊗9pm-2am Tue & Wed, to 3am Thu, to 4am Fri & Sat; 🖥) This charismatic backstreet bar is one of Portimão's best locations for live music, with weekend concerts (normally on the heavier side of the spectrum), plus Thursday karaoke sessions.

ℹ️ INFORMATION

Turismo Municipal (☎282 402 487; www.cm-portimao.pt; Plaza 1 de Dezembro; ⊗9.30am-5.30pm Mon-Fri) Portimão's information office

SABINE LUBENOW / GETTY IMAGES ©

Museu de Portimão (p145), Portimão

is housed in the wonderful Teatro Municipal de Portimão ('Tempo').

ⓘ GETTING THERE & AWAY

BUS

Eva buses leave from near the petrol station along the riverside on Avenida Guanaré. Services include the following:

Cabo São Vicente €6.35, 1½ hours, one daily.

Faro €5.50,1¾ hours, seven daily.

Lagos €4, 35 minutes, hourly.

Lisbon €20, 3¼ hours, six daily.

TRAIN

Eight daily trains connect Portimão with Tunes (€2.95, 45 minutes). Change at Tunes for Lisbon.

Olhão

A short hop east of Faro, Olhão (pronounced *ol-yowng*) is the Algarve's biggest fishing port, with an active waterfront and pretty, bustling lanes in its old quarters.

There aren't many sights, but the flat-roofed, Moorish-influenced neighbourhoods and North African feel make it a pleasant place to wander. The town's fish restaurants draw the crowds, as does the morning fish and vegetable market on Avenida 5 de Outubro, best visited on Saturday.

Olhão is also a springboard for Parque Natural da Ria Formosa's sandy islands, Culatra and Armona, plus the park's environmental centre at Quinta de Marim. For fans of Portuguese football, until recently this small town had the Algarve's only Primeira Liga team – Olhanense.

◉ SIGHTS

Mercados Municipais   Market
(Avenida 5 de Outubro; ⊙7am-2pm Mon-Sat)
By the water, these two noble centenarian red-brick buildings are excellent examples of industrial architecture and house picturesque traditional fruit and fish markets

Where to Stay in Portimão

With so many places to stay in Praia da Rocha, few choose to sleep over in Portimão, though if you do there are a couple of decent options. The town could also be a good choice in July and August, when the beach towns are hopelessly booked out.

that are worth a look at any time but are especially appealing on a Saturday morning. A string of simple seafood eateries and cafes makes them an atmospheric spot for a bite with water views.

Quinta de Marim   Nature Reserve
(www.icnf.pt; ⊘8am-8pm Mon-Fri, 10am-8pm Sat & Sun Apr-Oct, 9am-noon & 2-5pm daily Nov-Mar) Three kilometres east of Olhão is the beautiful 60-hectare Centro Educação Ambiental de Marim (commonly known as Quinta de Marim). A 3km trail takes you through various ecosystems – dunes, salt marshes, pine woodlands – as well as to a wildlife rescue centre and a historic water mill. Chameleons are among the local species of interest. The Parque Natural da Ria Formosa headquarters and interpretation centre is also here.

To get here, take a municipal bus to the campground (200m before the visitor centre).

✕ EATING

Tasca o Galo   Portuguese €€

(Rua a Gazeta de Olhão 7; mains €8-16; ⊙5pm-midnight Mon-Sat) In a converted merchant's store in an alley just back from the seafront, this tiny 22-seat affair serves a brief menu of homemade dishes including *cataplana* (seafood stew) and cuttlefish. Begin with a simple €2 starter of award-winning olive oil and bread while you admire the mishmash of furniture, colourful Portuguese tablecloths and light, breezy dining room. Friendly Portuguese-Swedish owners.

Tacho à Mesa   Portuguese €€

(☏289 096 734; Rua Lavadouros 46; mains €8-15; ⊙11am-3pm Mon-Sat, 7.30-10.30pm Tue-Sat; 🛜) The white, modern interior in this spot set back from the main drag, Avenida da República, plays host to some excellent traditional cooking accompanied by a cordial welcome. With fresh produce purchased twice a day, it produces a great *cataplana*, super-juicy *bochechas de porco* (pork cheeks) and other Algarvian-Alentejan delights.

Sabores do Churrasco Barbecue €€

(www.saboresdochurrasco.pt; Avenida 5 de Outubro 162; buffet €10-16; ⊙noon-4pm & 7pm-midnight;) On offer here is an authentic-as-they-come Brazilian *churrasqueira*, and an incredible all-you-can-eat carnivorous extravaganza – five kinds of grilled meat or, for an even greater protein injection, 12 kinds in one sitting.

ℹ️ GETTING THERE & AWAY

Eva express buses run to Lisbon (€20, 3¾ hours, four to five daily), as do Renex services. Buses run frequently to/from Faro (€3.25, 20 minutes). Regular trains run to Faro (€1.40, 10 minutes, hourly) and east to Fuzeta (€1.40, 10 minutes) and Tavira (€2.35, 30 minutes).

Six kilometres west of Lagos, the small resort of Luz – fronted by a sandy beach that's ideal for families – is packed with Brits. Most accommodation is prebooked by those on a package deal. Luz is a convenient side trip from Lagos.

From left: Mediterranean Chameleon, Parque Natural da Ria Formosa; Faro church; Praia da Luz

SEBASTIAN WASEK / GETTY IMAGES ©

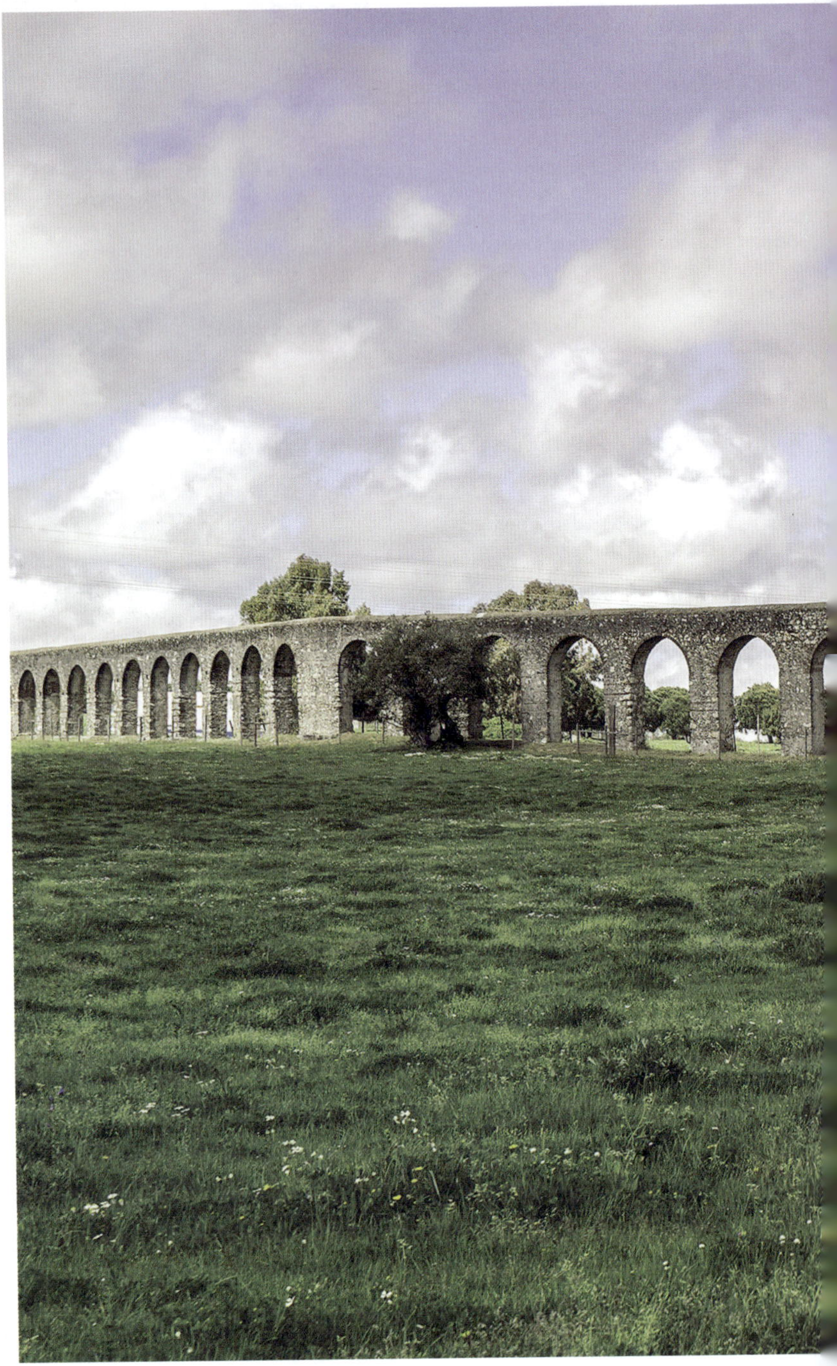

ÉVORA

Évora at a Glance...

One of Portugal's most beautifully preserved medieval towns, Évora is enchanting. Inside the 14th-century walls, Évora's narrow, winding lanes lead to striking architectural works: an elaborate medieval cathedral and cloisters; the cinematic columns of the Templo Romano (near the intriguing Roman baths); and a picturesque town square, once the site of some rather gruesome episodes courtesy of the Inquisition. Aside from its historic and aesthetic virtues, Évora is also a lively university town, and its many characterful restaurants and cafes serve up hearty Alentejan cuisine. Outside of town, Neolithic monuments and rustic wineries make for fine day trips.

Évora in Two Days

Your first day in Évora should be spent taking in the town's architectural gems such as the **Igreja de São Francisco** (p154) and the **Templo Romano** (p155). Spend day two exploring the **Sé** (p154) and the **Museu do Évora** (p156). Round off both days with some delicious Alentejan fare in one of the town's celebrated **restaurants** (p160).

Évora in Four Days

On day three get out of town to see the **megaliths** that dot the surrounding landscapes west of Évora (p159). These Neolithic remains date back 5000 to 7500 years but you'll need a car to find them. You could spend day four seeking out **local wineries** (p157)or seeing some of the town's less well-known sites such as the **Museu do Évora** (p173).

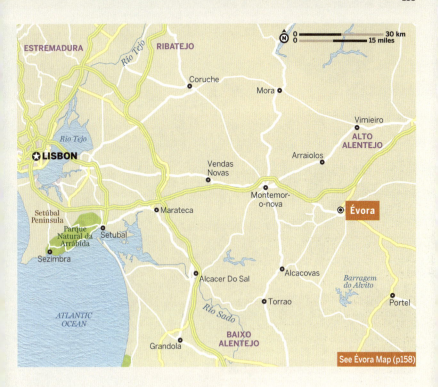

Arriving in Évora

Bus station Handles long-distance coach services to towns and cities across southern Portugal and beyond.

Train station Services to Lisbon and a couple of cities on the Algarve coast depart from here.

Sleeping

Most of Évora's best accommodation is within the town walls where about a fifth of the population also lives. From outside the walls it can be a trek to the sights of the city centre.

The Sé, Évora's fortress-like cathedral

©MANUEL PHOTOGRAPHY - PORTUGAL / GETTY IMAGES ©

Évora's Architectural Treasures

Few cities in Portugal boast the wealth and diversity of architecture that Évora does. An almost uninterrupted ring of defensive town walls contains Roman and medieval sites aplenty.

Great For...

☑ Don't Miss

You can walk 8.5km along Évora's 16th-century aqueduct – ask the tourist office for details.

Medieval Gems

Évora's best-known church is the **Igreja de São Francisco** (Map p158; Praça 1 de Maio), a tall and huge Manueline-Gothic structure, completed around 1510 and dedicated to St Francis. Legend has it that the Portuguese playwright Gil Vicente is buried here.

Guarded by a pair of rose granite towers, Évora's fortress-like medieval cathedral, the **Sé** (Map p158; Largo do Marquês de Marialva; €1.50, with cloister & towers €3.50, with museum €4.50; ⊗9am-5pm), has fabulous cloisters and a museum jam-packed with ecclesiastical treasures. It was begun around 1186, during the reign of Sancho I, Afonso Henriques' son, and was completed about 60 years later; there was probably a mosque here before. The flags of Vasco da Gama's ships were blessed here in 1497.

Bones and skulls in the walls of Capela dos Ossos

MICHELE FALZONE / ALAMY STOCK PHOTO ©

about the deity to which it was dedicated, and some archaeologists believe it may have been dedicated to Julius Caesar.

Inside the entrance hall of the *câmara municipal* are more Roman vestiges, only discovered in 1987. These impressive Roman baths, which include a *laconicum* (heated room for steam baths) with a superbly preserved 9m-diameter circular pool, would have been the largest public building in Roman Évora. The complex also includes an open-air swimming pool, discovered in 1994.

The small, fabulous **Igreja de São João** (Church of St John the Evangelist; Map p158; €7; ⏰10am-12.30pm & 2-5pm Tue-Sun), which faces the Templo Romano, was founded in 1485 by one Rodrigo Afonso de Melo, count of Olivença and the first governor of Portuguese Tangier, to serve as his family's pantheon. It is still privately owned, by the Duques de Cadaval, and notably well kept.

Roman Ruins

Once part of the Roman Forum, the remains of **Templo Romano** (Temple of Diana; Map p158; Largo do Conde de Vila Flor), dating from the 2nd or early 3rd century, are a heady slice of drama right in town. It's among the best-preserved Roman monuments in Portugal, and probably on the Iberian Peninsula. Though it's commonly referred to as the Temple of Diana, there's no consensus

Capela dos Ossos

One of Évora's most popular sights is also one of its most chilling. The walls and columns of this mesmerising *memento mori* (reminder of death) are lined with the bones and skulls of some 5000 people. This was the solution found by three 17th-century Franciscan monks for the overflowing graveyards of churches and monasteries.

Other Sites

Northwest of the centre is the 16th-century **Aqueduto da Água de Prata** (Aqueduct of Silver Water; Map p158), designed by Francisco de Arruda (better known for Lisbon's Tower of Belém) to bring clean water to Évora. The 17th-century facade of the **Palácio Cadaval** (Palace of Cadaval; Map p158; incl Igreja de São João €7; ⏰10am-12.30pm & 2-5pm Tue-Sun) hides a much older palace and castle which served as a royal residence.

SIGHTS

Praça do Giraldo   Plaza

(Map p158) The city's main square has
seen some potent moments in Portuguese
history, including the 1483 execution of
Fernando, Duke of Bragança; the public
burning of victims of the Inquisition in the
16th century; and fiery debates on agrarian
reform in the 1970s. Nowadays it's still the
city's focus, host to less dramatic activities
such as sitting in the sun and coffee
drinking.

The narrow lanes to the southwest were
once Évora's *judiaria* (Jewish quarter). To
the northeast, Rua 5 de Outubro, climbing
to the *Sé*, is lined with handsome town-
houses wearing wrought-iron balconies,
while side alleys pass beneath Moorish-
style arches.

> *The cloistered courtyard
> reveals Islamic, Roman and
> medieval remains*

Museu do Évora   Museum

(Map p158; ☑ 266 730 480; Largo do Conde
de Vila Flor; adult/child €3/free; ☺ 9.30am-
5.30pm Tue-Sun) Adjacent to the cathedral,
in what used to be the archbishop's palace
(built in the 16th century), is this elegant
museum. The cloistered courtyard reveals
Islamic, Roman and medieval remains.
In polished rooms upstairs are former
Episcopal furnishings and a gallery of
Flemish paintings. Most memorable is *Life
of the Virgin,* a 13-panel series originally
part of the cathedral's altarpiece, created
by anonymous Flemish artists working in
Portugal around 1500.

Jardim Público   Gardens

(Map p158; ☺ 8am-9pm May-Aug, to 7pm Mar,
Apr, Sep & Oct, to 5.30pm Nov-Feb) For a lovely
tranquil stroll, head to the light-dappled
public gardens (with a small outdoor cafe)
south of the Igreja de São Francisco. Inside
the walls of the 16th-century Palácio de
Dom Manuel is the **Galeria das Damas**
(Ladies' Gallery; Map p10; Palácio de Dom
Manuel; ☺ 10am-noon & 2-6pm Mon-Fri, 2-6pm
Sat) **FREE**), an indecisive hybrid of Gothic,

Praça do Giraldo

Manueline, neo-Moorish and Renaissance styles. It's open when there are (frequent) temporary art exhibitions.

From the town walls you can see, a few blocks to the southeast, the crenellated, pointy-topped Arabian Gothic profile of the **Ermida de São Brás** (Chapel of St Blaise; Map p158; Avenida Dr Barahona).

Fórum Eugénio de Almeida   Museum

(Map p158; www.fundacaoeugeniodealmeida.pt; Largo do Conde de Vila Flor; adult/child €4/free, Sun free; ☺10am-6pm Tue-Sun) In a building that once housed the Holy Office of Inquisition, this centre of arts and culture hosts some of Évora's most thought-provoking art exhibitions throughout the year. Also part of the foundation is the Casas Pintadas, a small collection of outdoor murals.

Convento dos Lóios Notable Building

(Map p158; Largo do Conde de Vila-Flor) The former Convento dos Lóios, to the right of Igreja de São João, has elegant Gothic cloisters topped by a Renaissance gallery. A national monument, the convent was converted into a top-end *pousada* (inn) in 1965. If you want to wander around, wear your wealthy-guest expression – or have dinner at its upmarket restaurant.

Coleção de Carruagens   Museum

(Carriage Collection; Map p158; Largo Dr Mário Chicò 4; €1, Sun before 12.30pm free; ☺10am-12.30pm & 1.30-6pm Tue-Sun) Part of the Eugénio de Almeida Foundation, this pint-sized museum houses an intriguing collection of old carriages. It's hidden away behind the *Sé*, and is largely overlooked by most visitors.

Casas Pintadas   Historic Site

(Map p158; €1; ☺10am-6pm Tue-Sun) Painted on the garden walls of an open vaulted gallery are a series of unusual 16th-century murals that were once part of a noble's residence. Recently restored, these paintings depict creatures real and imagined, such as birds, hares, foxes, a basilisk, a mermaid and a harpy. Access is via the Fórum Eugénio de Almeida.

The Wine Route

Wines here, particularly the reds, are fat, rich and fruity. But tasting them is much more fun than reading about them, so drop in on some wineries. The **Rota dos Vinhos do Alentejo** (Wine Route of the Alentejo) splits the region into three separate areas – the Serra de São Mamede (dark reds, full bodied, red fruit hints); Historic (smooth reds, fruity whites) around Évora, Estremoz, Borba and Monsaraz; and the Rio Guadiana (scented whites, spicy reds). Some wineries also have accommodation options.

You'll see brown signs all over the place announcing that you are on the wine trail, and you can pick up the booklet that lists wineries and their details at any local tourist office. Otherwise visit the helpful **Rota dos Vinhos do Alentejo** (p159) headquarters.

Alentejo vineyard

ACTIVITIES

Cartuxa Winery   Wine

(☎266 748 383; www.cartuxa.pt; Estrada da Soeira; from €5; ☺tours 10.30am, 11.30am, 3pm & 4.30pm) For a taste of history, this is a fun visit – Cartuxa is one of the oldest wineries in Alentejo. Run by the well-known local philanthropic foundation Eugenio De Almeida, it produces some good wines at all prices, along with olive oils and other products. You must reserve a tour (strictly at the times given); prices start at €5 and

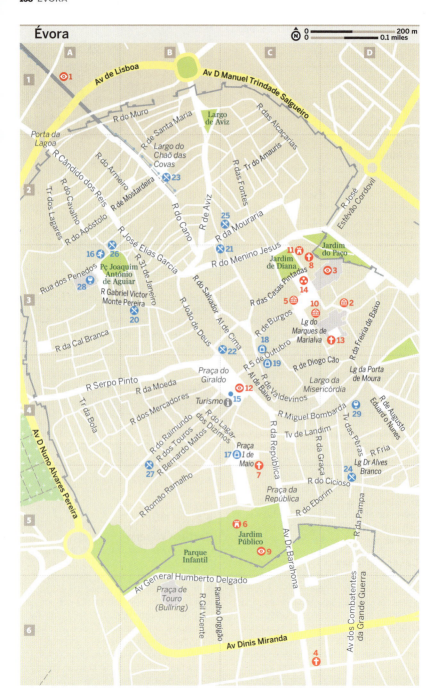

Évora

0 — 200 m
0 — 0.1 miles

Évora

then vary according to how many wines you want to taste.

The winery is located about 2km northwest of the old city walls.

Rota dos Vinhos do Alentejo   Wine
(Wine Route of the Alentejo; Map p158; ☑266 746 498; www.vinhosdoalentejo.pt; Praça Joaquim António de Aguiar 20-21; ☺2-7pm Mon, 11am-7pm Tue-Fri, 10am-1pm Sat) Head here to sample some of the great wines of the Alentejo. Every Monday new wines are on offer, with more than 70 wineries represented. Tastings of the dozen varieties on hand are free (try them all!). Bottles will set you back anywhere from €3.50 to €9.

TOURS

Rota do Fresco   Cultural
(☑284 475 413; www.rotadofresco.com; per person €25) Offers fascinating cultural tours led by an art historian to local baroque sites filled with frescos and *azulejos* (hand-painted tiles). Reservations required.

Ebora Megalithica   Tours
(☑964 808 337; www.eboramegalithica.com; per person €25, maximum 7 people; ☺tours 10am & 2.30pm Mon-Sat) If you're interested in the megaliths – Almendres, Zambujeiro and

the Menir dos Almendres – this three-hour tour is a must. Young archaeologist enthusiast Mário makes the megalithic sites accessible in every sense, providing their where, what, why and how. He succeeds in making the experience an educational yet relaxed one.

Agia   Walking
(Map p158; ☑963 702 392; www.alentejo guides.com; adult/under 12yr €15/free, minimum 2 people; ☺10am) Agia offers daily two-hour guided walking tours of Évora, departing from outside the *turismo* (tourist office) on Praça do Giraldo.

⊖ SHOPPING

Feiras no Largo   Market
(Map p158; Praça 1 de Maio; ☺8am-2pm Sat & Sun) Each weekend sees the Feiras no Largo, one of four different markets held in the city. Expect antiquities, used books and collectables, art and *artesanatos* (handicrafts shops).

Gente da Minha Terra   Food, Gifts & Souvenirs
(Map p158; www.gentedaminhaterra.pt; Rua 5 de Outubro 39; ☺10am-7pm) On a boutique-lined street leading off the main plaza,

 Évora's History

The Celtic settlement of Ebora had been established here before the Romans arrived in 59 BC and made it a military outpost, and eventually an important centre of Roman Iberia.

After a depressing spell under the Visigoths, the town got its groove back as a centre of trade under the Moors. In AD 1165 Évora's Muslim rulers were hoodwinked by a rogue Portuguese Christian knight known as Giraldo Sem Pavor (Gerald the Fearless). The well-embellished story goes like this: Giraldo single-handedly stormed one of the town's watchtowers by climbing up a ladder of spears driven into the walls. From there he distracted municipal sentries while his companions effortlessly took the town.

Évora's golden age was from the 14th to 16th centuries, when it was favoured by the Alentejo's own House of Avis, as well as by scholars and artists. Declared an archbishopric in 1540, it got its own Jesuit university in 1559.

When Cardinal-King Dom Henrique, last of the Avis line, died in 1580 and Spain seized the throne, the royal court left Évora and the town began wasting away. The Marquês de Pombal's closure of the university in 1759 was the last straw. As is often the case, it was this decline that led to the preservation of so much of the town's architecture. French forces plundered Évora and massacred its defenders in 1808.

Templo Romano (p155)
JACQUESVANDINTEREN / GETTY IMAGES ©

this is a great one-stop shop for gifts. The shelves are packed with quality olive oils, *azulejos*, textiles, ceramics and pretty packages of tinned sardines and other preserves.

Montsobro   Homewares

(Map p158; www.montsobro.com; Rua 5 de Outubro 66; ⊙10am-6pm Mon-Sat) One of many shops along Rua 5 de Outubro, this was the first – and is still one of the best – that sells cork products.

EATING

Salsa Verde   Vegetarian €

(Map p158; ☏266 743 210; www.salsa-verde.org; Rua do Raimundo 93A; small plate €4.95 or per kg €14.40; ⊙noon-3pm & 7-9.30pm Mon-Fri, noon-3pm Sat; 🛜🍴) Vegetarians (and Portuguese pigs) will be thankful for this veggie-popping paradise. Pedro, the owner, gives a wonderful twist to traditional Alentejan dishes such as the famous bread dish, *migas,* prepared with mushrooms. Low-playing bossa nova and a cheerful airy design make a fine complement to the dishes – all made from fresh, locally sourced products (organic when possible).

Chão das Covas   Portuguese €

(Map p158; ☏266 706 294; www.facebook.com/chaodascovascafe; Largo do Chão das Covas; sharing plates €4.50-6, mains €7-10; ⊙11am-3pm & 5.30-11pm Tue-Sun) Tucked away on a small plaza beside the aqueduct, this friendly, boxcar-sized eatery serves up tasty home-cooked Alentejan classics that change by day, as well as good-value *petiscos* (sharing plates) like fried squid, roasted peppers, cheese platters and the like. It's a fine place to linger, with a barrel-vaulted ceiling, B&W photos of Évora and terrace seating on warm days.

Pastelaria Conventual
Pão de Rala   Bakery €

(Map p158; Rua do Cicioso 47; pastries €1.20-3; ⊙7.30am-8pm; 🛜) The *azulejo*-covered walls (complete with a bakery scene) and low-playing fado create a fine setting for nibbling on heavenly pastries and convent cakes, all made on the premises. Don't miss the *pão de rala* (an egg yolk, sugar, lemon zest and almond cake) – it's sweet stuff and wonderfully sinful.

Café Arcada   Cafe €

(www.facebook.com/Cafe.Arcada.Evora; Praça do Giraldo 10; mains €7-10; 🕗8am-9.30pm Sun-Thu, to 10.30pm Fri & Sat) This busy, barn-sized cafe is an Évora institution serving coffee, crêpes and cakes. You can sit at an outdoor table on the lovely plaza.

Botequim da Mouraria   Portuguese €€

(Map p158; 📞266 746 775; Rua da Mouraria 16A; mains €14-17; 🕗12.30-3pm & 7-10pm Mon-Fri, noon-3pm Sat) Poke around the old Moorish quarter to find some of Évora's finest food and wine – gastronomes believe this is Évora's culinary shrine. Owner Domingos will expertly guide you through the menu, which also features an excellent

Low-playing bossa nova and a cheerful airy design

variety of wines from the Alentejo. There are no reservations and just nine stools at a counter. It is extremely popular and lines are long. To have any chance of getting a seat, arrive before it opens.

Adega do Alentejano   Portuguese €€

(Map p158; 📞266 744 447; Rua Gabriel Victor Monte Pereira 21; mains €8-13; 🕗noon-3pm & 7-10pm Mon-Sat) Red-and-white checked tablecloths, rustic decor and garrulous host named Carlos set the stage for a fun, casual night of Alentejo fare that won't break the bank. Start off with the rich *sopa de tomate* (tomato soup) served with sausages (good for sharing), then move on to hearty pork or codfish dishes. House wine comes straight from the barrel.

Almendres megalith

Carne de porco à alentejana (braised pork with baby clams)

Restaurante
O Fialho   Portuguese €€
(Map p158; ☏266 703 079; http://restauran-
tefialho.pai.pt; Travessa dos Mascarenhas 16;
mains €14.50-18; ☉noon-3pm & 7-10pm Tue-Sun)
An icon of Évora's culinary scene, O Fialho
has been wowing diners since 1945 – as
evidenced by the photos of visiting digni-
taries lining the walls. Amid wood panelling
and white tablecloths, professional wait
staff serve up first-rate Alentejan cuisine.
The appetisers steal the show, along with
the extensive wine list.

Quarta Feira   Portuguese €€€
(Map p158; ☏266 707 530; Rua do Inverno
16; dinner per person incl appetisers, wine &
dessert €25; ☉12.30-2.30pm & 7.30-9.30pm
Tue-Sat) Don't bother asking for the menu
since there's just one dish on offer at this
jovial eatery tucked away in the Moorish
quarter. Luckily it's a stunner: slow-cooked
black pork so tender it falls off the bone,
plus freshly baked bread, cured ham (and
other appetisers), dessert and ever-flowing
glasses of wine – all served for one set
price.

Arched ceilings, checked tablecloths
and the warm smile of owner-chef Zé Dias
(indeed, that's his likeness on the wine
label) make this place a favourite with
out-of-towners.

🍷 DRINKING & NIGHTLIFE
Art Cafe   Cafe
(Rua Serpa Pinto 6; ☉11am-midnight Tue-Sat, to
9pm Sun & Mon) Set in the cloisters of the old
Palácio Barrocal, this bohemian cafe and
drinking spot has outdoor tables, hipster
wait staff and ambient electronic grooves.
The outdoor tables beneath are a fine
spot to unwind with a sangria after a day
exploring. Tasty veg-friendly snacks too
(*gazpacho, tostas,* lasagna).

Bar do Teatro   Bar
(Map p158; www.facebook.com/bardoteatroga-
rciaderezende; Praça Joaquim António de Aguiar;
☉4pm-2am) Next to the theatre, this small,

inviting bar has high ceilings and old-world decor that welcomes a friendly mixed crowd. The music tends towards lounge and electronica.

Kitsch Underground Lounge
Cocktail Bar

(Map p158; Rua Miguel Bombarda 56A; ☺10pm-3am Tue-Sat) Kitsch draws a young friendly crowd to a two-room space on Rua Miguel Bombarda (a street with a few other bars nearby). DJs spin ambient grooves – deep house, electro jazz – while the bobbing crowd sips sweet cocktails. It's fairly dead until after midnight.

ℹ INFORMATION

There are several banks with ATMs on and around Praça do Giraldo, including **Caixa de Crédito Agrícola**.

Turismo (Map p158; ☎266 777 071; www.cm-evora.pt; Praça do Giraldo 73; ☺9am-7pm Apr-Oct, to 6pm Nov-Mar) is a helpful, central tourist office, which offers a great town map.

ℹ GETTING THERE & AWAY

TRAIN
The **Évora station** (☎266 742 336) is outside the walls, 600m south of the *jardim público.* There are daily trains to/from Lisbon (€12.20, 1½ hours, four daily). Trains also go to/from Lagos (€26.30, 4½ to five hours, three daily) and Faro (€25.30, four to five hours, two daily).

BUS
The bus station is located a short distance west of the walled centre. Services:

Coimbra €18.50, 4½ hours, four daily.

Faro €17.50, four hours, three daily.

🍴 Food of the Alentejo

Warning to vegetarians: pork will confront you at every repast in the Alentejo. Bread also figures heavily; you'll find it in gazpacho or *açorda.* During hunting season, *perdiz* (partridge), *lebre* (hare) and *javali* (wild boar) are the go. The Alentejo also has surf-and-turf blends such as *carne de porco à alentejana* (braised pork with baby clams).

Chouriço (spicy sausage)
CAMILLA WATSON / GETTY IMAGES ©

Lisbon €12.50, 1½ to two hours, hourly.

ℹ GETTING AROUND

Evora Adventure Bike (☎969 095 880, 266 702 326; Travessa do Barão 18; half-day/4 days €8/40; ☺9am-9pm) Half-day and multi-day bike rental.

Taxis (☎266 734 734) congregate in Praça do Giraldo. On weekdays expect to pay about €6 from the train station to Praça do Giraldo.

RIO DOURO VALLEY

Rio Douro Valley at a Glance...

One of the world's oldest demarcated wine regions, the Douro Valley showcases steep terrace vineyards carved into mountains, granite bluffs, and whitewashed quintas (estates) and 18th-century wine cellars that draw in visitors from around the world. Come for the ports and wines, winding scenic roads, postcard-pretty villages and excellent regional restaurants.

The valley also hosts Portugal's most scenic train ride, the Linha do Douro running from Porto to Pocinho, a distance of 160km. The Douro can also be seen from cruise ships that ply its waters, stopping off along the way for wine-tasting sessions at the many producers en route.

Rio Douro Valley in a Week

How long it takes you to tackle the Douro Valley depends on what mode of transport you use. By car, around a week is the ideal length of the trip. Hire a car in Porto and head up the valley, overnighting in Peso da Régua and Pinhão en route. You can manage the same itinerary in the same time frame by train.

Rio Douro Valley in a Week or More

A week gives you the time for some real slow travel, sampling myriad wines as you go. The only problem with this is driving a hire car afterwards! Designate a driver and head up the valley from Porto. By train you may not be able to reach some of the more remote wineries.

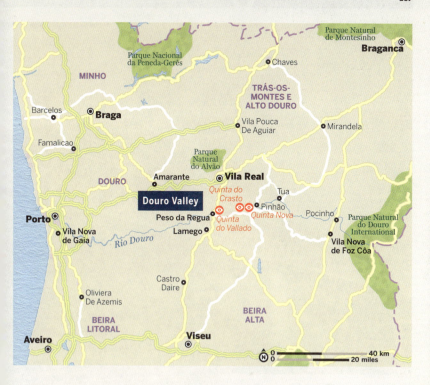

Arriving in the Rio Douro Valley

São Bento/Campanhã train station
Trains leave these stations for Peso da Régua where you change for the Douro Valley. At least five trains run all the way from Porto to Pocinho.

N108/222 These two roads follow the valley.

Sleeping

The Douro is a popular destination meaning all of the towns in the valley offer accommodation of most types. Book well ahead in summer and possibly autumn, too. The Douro can be visited as a day trip from Porto, so consider options there, too.

There are lodgings all along the valley, from town-based hotels to rural stays at tiny wineries. Booking ahead in the summer months is essential, though at other times of the year you could just turn up or book on the day through tourist offices and booking websites.

Douro Valley's steam train

RICHARD SEMIK / ALAMY STOCK PHOTO ©

Wines, Trains & the River Douro

One of the most attractive and popular tourist routes in Iberia, the road and rail journey through the Douro Valley is unmissable for fans of wine, trains and stunning landscapes.

Great For...

☑ Don't Miss

A wine-tasting session at Quinta do Vallado (☎254 323 147; www.quintado vallado.com), a winery dating from 1716.

Wines of the Douro

The Douro has been a demarcated wine region since 1756, and the reds and whites that emerge every autumn from the stunning valley in which they are produced holds Portugal's highest wine classification – Denominação de Origem Controlada (DOC). The Douro is best known for its port, but its table wines are equally as celebrated. It's thought grapes have been grown here since Roman times. Port made an appearance in the mid-18th century but it wasn't until the late 20th century that serious table wines were made for export. Countless lodges offer tastings. In 2001 the valley was declared a Unesco World Cultural Heritage Site, not only recognising the valley as a great wine-producing region, but also placing it firmly on the tourist map.

Local wine tasting

GETTY IMAGES ©

ℹ **Need to Know**

Trains from Porto run five times daily; journey time: three hours 30 minutes. Fare: €13 each way.

✕ **Take a Break**

DOC (p173) is regarded as the best restaurant in the Douro Valley.

★ **Top Tip**

An excellent website to consult before heading into the Douro Valley is www. dourovalley.eu. This gives the lowdown on wineries, the railway, cruises and many other aspects of touring in the region.

Cruise & Car

In addition to the train, cruise ships are another popular way of seeing the valley. Cruises leave from Porto and terminate at the Spanish border. Cycling is also becoming a favourite way to travel, though intoxicating Douro wine and pedalling may seem an odd mix. Some of the old railway lines in the valley have been converted into cycle trails.

Great Train Journey

Without doubt Portugal's greatest rail journey, the 160km long line from Porto to Pocinho is a wonder of 19th-century engineering. The line opened in 1887 and once ran all the way from the Atlantic to the Spanish border. Branch lines once wriggled their way up side valleys to remote villages, but these were closed with the arrival of the petrol engine. This left just the main route with its 20 tunnels, 34 stations and 30 bridges. For a real 19th-century experience, try to catch one of the special steam services that run between Régua and Tua on summer weekends. (You can do the return train journey in a day if pressed for time.)

The Douro Valley

Wine lovers have their work cut out for them on a leisurely journey through the Douro Valley, Portugal's premier wine country; not only is it one of the world's oldest demarcated wine regions, it's also dazzling – steep terraced vineyards rise sharply from the banks of the Douro River and whitewashed *quintas* (estates) perch high up in the hills. Visitors are just as wowed by these dramatic vistas as they are by the area's viticulture, which has been turning out some of Portugal's premier wines for centuries.

Start Porto
Distance 325km
Duration One week

3 Riverside **Peso da Régua** is set in the heart of vineyard country. Stop off for a tasting at nearby Quinta do Vallado (p168), a winery since 1716.

1 Any self-respecting wine tour will begin in Porto (p89), gateway to the world's most famous port-wine region.

2 Across the river is **Vila Nova de Gaia** (p96), where you can sample countless varieties at its many port-wine lodges. Graham's has a small museum.

4 A short detour south of the river, **Lamego** (p174) is known for its fine sparkling wine.

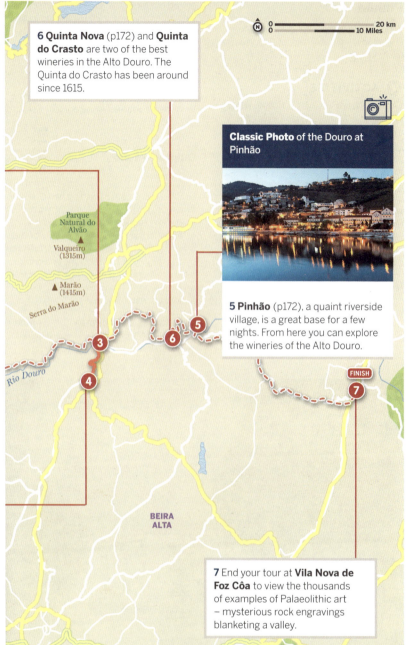

6 Quinta Nova (p172) and **Quinta do Crasto** are two of the best wineries in the Alto Douro. The Quinta do Crasto has been around since 1615.

0   20 km
0   10 Miles

Classic Photo of the Douro at Pinhão

5 Pinhão (p172), a quaint riverside village, is a great base for a few nights. From here you can explore the wineries of the Alto Douro.

Parque Natural do Alvão

Valqueiro (1315m)

Marão (1415m)

Serra do Marão

Rio Douro

FINISH

BEIRA ALTA

7 End your tour at **Vila Nova de Foz Côa** to view the thousands of examples of Palaeolithic art – mysterious rock engravings blanketing a valley.

Pinhão

Wine tasting in the local *quintas* (estates) is what visiting this village of 1000 souls is all about.

❸ ACTIVITIES

Quinta Nova   Hiking, Winery

(☎254 730 430; www.quintanova.com; Covas do Douro; wine tours €7, tastings €8-48; ⊙tours 11am, 12.45pm, 3.30pm, 4.45pm) Set on a stunning ridge, surrounded by luscious, ancient vineyards, overlooking the deep green Douro River with mountains layered in the distance, the Quinta Nova estate is well worth an in-depth exploration. The three hiking and biking trails (the longest is 2½ hours) are the best in the region.

To get here, head 9km west of Pinhão, along the north bank of the Douro (EN322-2).

Quinta do Bomfim   Wine

(☎254 730 350; www.symington.com/news/quinta-do-bomfim; tours €7.50, incl tasting €10; ⊙10.30am-7pm daily Apr-Oct, 9.30am-5.30pm Tue-Sun Nov-Mar) Symington's swank *quinta* showcases a small museum inside a re-stored old winery. Guided tours (in several languages) include a visit to the old lodge dating back to 1896 where young wine is still aged in old wooden vats. The tour ends in the gorgeous tasting room with a terrace featuring beautiful vistas of the Douro, where wines are available by the glass.

The vineyard walks offer a great chance to immerse yourself in the ancient vineyard terraces (€5 with a map, hat and a bottle of water).

Quinta do Tedo   Wine

(☎254 789 165; www.quintadotedo.com; Folgosa; tours incl tasting €8; ⊙10am-7pm) Blessed with sublime real estate carved by two rivers – the Douro and the Tedo – this American-French-Portuguese–owned 14-hectare estate offers short 20-minute tours of the winery (which is certified organic), followed by a tasting of port, table wine and organic olive oil. There are also certified hiking trails on the property that are especially wonderful for bird watching.

Quinta das Carvalhas   Wine

(☎254 738 050; carvalhas@realcompanhiavelha.pt; tours bus/jeep €12.50/35) This *quinta*

Quinta Nova

excels at their 'vintage' tours, guided by the in-house agriculturalist, who takes you on a two-hour jeep tour around the gorgeous vineyards and to the top of the estate's ridge (book ahead). The cheaper alternative is with a bus that picks people up from the train station (10am, noon, 3pm & 5pm), with a tasting of three wines at the end. It also offers walks around the vineyards (€10) and picnics in amazing on-site ruins (€45).

EATING

DOC   Portuguese €€€

(✆254 858 123; www.ruipaula.com; Estrada Nacional 222, Folgosa; mains €27.50-29; ⏰12.30-3.30pm & 7.30-11pm) Architect Miguel Saraiva's ode to clean-lined, glass-walled minimalism, DOC is headed up by Portuguese star chef Rui Paula. Its terrace peering out across the river is a stunning backdrop. Dishes give a pinch of imagination to seasonal, regional flavours, from fish *açordas* (stews) to game and wild mushrooms – all of which are paired with carefully selected wines from the cellar.

The restaurant is in Folgosa, midway between Peso da Régua and Pinhão, on the south side of the river.

Veladouro   Portuguese €€

(✆254 738 166; Rua da Praia 3; mains €7-15; ⏰10am-midnight) Simple but tasty Portuguese food, such as wood-grilled meats and fish, is served inside this quaint schist building or outside under a canopy of vines. From the train station, turn left and go along the main road for 150m, then left again under a railway bridge and right at the river.

❶ GETTING THERE & AWAY

Regional trains go to and from Peso da Régua (€2.75, 25 minutes, five daily), where you can catch an onward train to Porto.

It's best to have your own wheels if you want to explore the area independently, as some of the best spots are not accessible by public transport.

Douro-a-Vela Boat Trips

One of the sweetest thrills in the area demands that you simply lie back and cruise upriver into the heart of the Alto Douro aboard a sailboat. Catch the boat from the Folgosa do Douro pier, just outside DOC restaurant. The price listed is based on a six-person minimum (or pay €180 for two). Book ahead.

Peso da Régua

◎ SIGHTS

Museu do Douro   Museum

(www.museudodouro.pt; Rua Marquês de Pombal; adult/concession €6/3; ⏰10am-6pm) It's not all about the wine. Sometimes it's about contemporary canvases, impressionist landscapes, old leather-bound texts, vintage port-wine posters and the remains of an old flat-bottomed port hauler. You'll find it all in a gorgeous converted riverside warehouse, with a restaurant and bar on-site. The gift shop, stocked with wine, handmade soaps and some terrific silver, is brilliant.

✪ ACTIVITIES

Steam Train to Tua   Rail

(Comboio Vapor; www.cp.pt; one-way €4; ⏰Jun-Oct) While the gorgeous Linha da Tua line remains out of service, you can still ride in this lovingly restored steam train, which travels four times daily along the Douro from Régua to Tua, making a 20-minute stop in Pinhão.

Tomaz do Douro   Cruise

(✆222 082 286; www.tomazdodouro.pt; cruises from €10) Tomaz do Douro offers a set of different cruises along the Douro, with different departure points.

⊗ EATING

A couple of traditional taverns that dish out good-value lunch menus and an inventive restaurant serving updated Portuguese classics make Régua a decent place to eat.

Festa de Nossa Senhora dos Remédios

Lamego's biggest party runs for several weeks from late August to mid-September. In an afternoon procession on 8 September, ox-drawn carts rattle through the streets carrying *tableaux vivants* (religious scenes represented by costumed people), and devotees slowly ascend the stairway on their knees. Less pious events in the run-up include rock concerts, folk dancing, car racing, parades and at least one all-night party.

Taberna do Jéréré   Portuguese €€

(Rua Marquês de Pombal 38; mains €9-16; ⊙noon-3pm & 7-11pm Mon-Sat, noon-3pm Sun) Excellent Portuguese dishes, including *bacalhau á Jéréré* (dried salt-cod with shrimp, mushroom and spinach), served in a tastefully rustic dining room with a beamed ceiling and granite floors. Great-value lunch specials.

Castas e Pratos   Portuguese €€€

(☑254 323 290; www.castaspratos.com; Avenida José Vasques Osório; mains €20-30; ⊙10.30am-11pm) The coolest dining room in town is set in a restored wood-and-stone railyard warehouse with exposed original timbers. You can order grilled *alheira* (a light, garlicky sausage of poultry or game) or octopus salad from the tapas bar downstairs, or have the locally caught cod in an almond crust with Lamego ham or kid goat in port with fava beans in the mezzanine.

ⓘ INFORMATION

Turismo (☑254 312 846; www.cm-pesoregua.pt; Avenida do Douro; ⊙9.30am-12.30pm & 2-6.30pm Mon-Sat) The new high-tech *turismo* office facing the Douro River supplies information about the town and the region, including the accommodation options and vineyards in the area.

ⓘ GETTING THERE & AWAY

Transdev buses run regularly to/from Lamego (€2.30, 20 minutes), and Tâmega/Rodonorte

has five daily departures to Vila Real (€6, 30 minutes).

There are around 13 trains daily from Porto (€10, two hours); some continue up the valley to Pinhão (€2.80, 25 minutes, five daily). Around five trains depart daily for Tua (€4; 40 minutes). If you've taken a train this far and suddenly realise you need a car to visit the vineyards, your best bet is **Europcar** (☑254 321 146; www.europcar.com; Avenida João Franco; rental per day from €82).

Lamego

◎ SIGHTS

Museu de Lamego   Museum

(Largo de Camões; adult/student €3/1.50; ⊙10am-6pm Tue-Sun) Occupying a grand, 18th-century Episcopal palace, the Museu de Lamego is one of Portugal's finest regional museums. The collection features five entrancing works by renowned 16th-century Portuguese painter Vasco Fernandes (Grão Vasco), richly worked Brussels tapestries from the same period, and an extraordinarily diverse collection of heavily gilded 17th-century chapels rescued in their entirety from the long-gone Convento das Chagas.

Igreja de Nossa Senhora dos Remédios   Church

(7.30am-8pm May-Sep, to 6pm Oct-Apr) One of the country's most important pilgrimage sites, this twin-towered 18th-century church has a trim blue-and-white stucco interior with a sky-blue rococo ceiling and a gilded altar. The church, however, is quite overshadowed by the zigzagging monumental stairway that leads up to it. The 600-plus steps are resplendent with *azulejos* (hand-painted tiles), urns, fountains and statues, adding up to one of the greatest works in Portuguese rococo style.

It's a dramatic sight at any time, but the action peaks in late summer when thousands of devotees arrive and ascend the steps in search of miracles during the Festa de Nossa Senhora dos Remédios. Most offerings are made at the rear altar where Mother Mary reigns supreme. If you can't face the climb by foot, a road (turn off 1km out on the Viseu road) winds up the hill for about 3km before reaching the top.

Sé
Cathedral

(Largo da Sé; ⏲9am-1pm & 3-6.30pm) Older than Portugal itself, Lamego's striking *sé* (cathedral) has been declared a national monument. There is little left of the 12th-century original except the base of its square belfry. The rest of the structure, including the brilliantly carved Gothic triple portal, dates mostly from the 16th and 18th centuries. Arresting biblical frescoes and the high choir stalls are the work of 18th-century Italian baroque architect Nicolau Nasoni, who left his mark all over Porto. With luck you will find the door open to the peaceful 16th-century cloisters, located just around the corner.

⊗ EATING

Like most regions that produce good wines, Lamego delivers food to match. Its *fumeiros* (smoked meats) are justly famous and can be found in one of several wonderful gourmet food shops on Rua de Olaria. Hit the **mercado municipal** (Avenida 5 de Outubro; ⏲7.30am-6pm Mon-Fri, to 5pm Sat) early for fresh fruit and veggies if you're packing a picnic.

Manjar do Douro
Portuguese €€

(☎254 611 285; Avenida Dr Alfredo de Sousa 43; mains €6-16; ⏲8am-midnight) Well-known traditional restaurant frequented by business folk at lunchtime and dishing out well-prepared Portuguese mainstays.

Trás da Sé
Portuguese €

(☎254 614 075; Largo da Sé; mains €5-6; ⏲noon-10pm) Congratulations to the chef line the walls at this *adega*-style (wine tavern) place, where the atmosphere is friendly, the menu short and simple, the food good and the *vinho maduro* (matured wine) list long.

Pastelaria Scala
Cafe €

(Avenida Visconde Guedes Teixeira 31; pastries €1-2; ⏲8am-10pm) The charming wooden booths and tables are almost always crammed with locals who descend for great coffee and even better pastries.

Igreja de Nossa Senhora dos Remédios

Ponte de São Gonçalo

ℹ INFORMATION

Turismo (254 099 000; www.cm-lamego.pt; Rua Regimento de Infantaria 9; ⊙10am-7.30pm) This fantastic tourist office is full of solid suggestions from warm, knowledgeable, English-speaking staff.

ℹ GETTING THERE & AWAY

The most appealing route to Lamego from anywhere in the Douro Valley is by train to Peso da Régua and by bus or taxi from there. A taxi from Régua costs about €15 to €20.

From Lamego's bus station, Joalto/EAVT and Rede Expressos are the only operators. Buses travel hourly to Peso da Régua (€2.30, 30 minutes) and daily to Viseu (€8.90, 1¼ hours) and Lisbon (€18.50, 5¾ hours). The Lisbon bus also passes through Vila Real (€6, one hour) and Chaves (€11.40, 2¼ hours). **Copy Print** (254 619 447; Avenida Visconde Guedes Teixeira; ⊙8am-8pm), a newsagent beside the *turismo*, sells tickets for these services.

Self-drivers take note: parking can be tight in Lamego.

Amarante

◉ SIGHTS

Museu Amadeo de Souza-Cardoso   Museum

(Alameda Teixeira de Pascoaes; adult/child €1/ free; ⊙10am-12.30pm & 2-6pm Tue-Sun Jun-Sep, 9.30am-12.30pm & 2-5.30pm Oct-May) Hidden in one of the Mosteiro de São Gonçalo's cloisters is this delightfully eclectic collection of modernist and contemporary art, a pleasant surprise in a town of this size. The museum is named after Amarante's favourite son, artist Amadeo Souza-Cardoso (1889–1918) – one of the best-known Portuguese artists of the 20th century, who abandoned naturalism for home-grown versions of impressionism and cubism. The museum is full of his sketches, cartoons, portraits and abstracts.

Ponte de São Gonçalo   Bridge

A symbol of the town's heroic defence against the French (marked by a plaque at the southeastern end), the granite Ponte de São Gonçalo is Amarante's visual centrepiece. The original bridge, allegedly built at Gonçalo's urging in the 13th century, collapsed in a flood in 1763; this one was completed in 1790.

Mosteiro de
São Gonçalo　　　　　Monastery
(⊘9am-7pm Jun-Sep, to 5.30pm Oct-May) Founded in 1543 by João III, the Mosteiro de São Gonçalo and **Igreja de São Gonçalo** weren't completed until 1620. Above the church's photogenic, Italian Renaissance side portal is an arcaded gallery, 30m high, with 17th-century statues of Dom João and the other kings who ruled while the monastery was under construction: Sebastião, Henrique and Felipe I.

The bell tower was added in the 18th century. The best view of the royal statues is from the steep lane just west of the church entrance. Within the lofty interior is an impressive gilded baroque altar, pulpits, an organ casing held up by fishtailed giants, and Gonçalo's tomb in a tiny chapel (to the left of the altar). Tradition has it that those in search of a partner will have their wish granted within a year if they touch the statue above his tomb. Sure enough, its limestone toes, fingers and face have been all but rubbed away by hopefuls.

✪ ACTIVITIES

Rio Tâmega　　　Boating, Walking
(boat hire per 30min/1hr €5/10; ⊘boat hire 9am-8pm) For an idyllic river stroll, take the cobbled path along the north bank. A good picnic or daydreaming spot is the rocky outcropping overlooking the rapids 400m east of the bridge. You can also potter about the peaceful Rio Tâmega in a paddle or row boat; boat hire is available along the riverbank.

✪ EATING

Adega Regional
Quelha　　　　　Portuguese €€
(☑255 425 786; Rua de Olivença; mains €5-14.50; ⊘11.30am-2pm & 7-10pm Mon-Thu, 11.30am-10pm Fri-Sun) One of several low-key *adegas* proffering Amarante's fine smoked meats and cheese, Adega Quelha is a good place

Portuguese
St Valentine

Amarante enjoys some small degree of national fame for being the hometown of São Gonçalo, Portugal's St Valentine. He is the target for lonely hearts who make pilgrimages here in the hope of finding true love.

to sample the local delicacies among locals. Grab a bite and a jug of red wine at the bar, or sit down to a simple but filling meal.

Zé da Calçada　　　Portuguese €€
(☑255 426 814; Rua 31 de Janeiro 83; mains €8-12; ⊘noon-10pm) Excellent northern cuisine served in an elegant country-style dining room or on a veranda with idyllic views of the Moistero and the bridge. Top picks here include duck rice and grilled goat. Weekday lunch specials are great value.

Confeitaria da Ponte　　　Bakery €
(☑255 432 034; Rua 31 de Janeiro 186; pastries €1.10-1.50; ⊘8.30am-8.30pm) Boasting a peaceful, shaded terrace overlooking the bridge, this traditional bakery has the best ambience for enjoying Amarante's famous pastries and eggy custards.

❶ INFORMATION

Turismo (☑255 420 246; www.amarante.pt/turismo; Alameda Teixeira de Pascoaes; ⊘9am-5.30pm Mon-Fri) Next to the museum, in the former cloisters of São Gonçalo. It offers city maps, but very little English is spoken.

❶ GETTING THERE & AWAY

At the small but busy **Estação Quemado** (www.rodonorte.pt; Rua Antonio Carneiro), buses stop at least five times daily from Porto (€6.40, one hour) en route to Vila Real (€6.30, 40 minutes) and Bragança (€12, 2¾ hours). There are also daily buses to Braga (€7.80, 1½ hours) and Lisbon (€18, 4¼ hours).

BRAGA

Braga at a Glance...

Portugal's third-largest city is an elegant town laced with ancient narrow lanes closed to vehicles, strewn with plazas and a splendid array of baroque churches. The constant chiming of bells is a reminder of Braga's age-old devotion to the spiritual world. Its religious festivals – particularly the elaborately staged Semana Santa (Holy Week) – are famous throughout Portugal. But don't come expecting piety alone: Braga's upscale old centre is packed with lively cafes and trim boutiques, some excellent restaurants and low-key bars catering to students. In fact, it's such a young city that in 2012 it was pronounced the European Youth Capital.

Braga in Two Days

On day one head straight for Braga's remarkable **cathedral** (p182), the city's must-see. After lunch take in some of the city's other, smaller churches before finishing off the day with dinner at Casa de Pasto das Carvalheiras or Anjo Verde. Day two could be spent exploring the **Museu dos Biscainhos** (p184) and shopping in the bustling city centre.

Braga in Four Days

Make sure one of the days you are here is a Thursday so you can make it to the sprawling **Feira de Barcelos** (p188) market, 22km west of Braga. On day four make a pilgrimage to **Bom Jesus do Monte** (p184), a church 5km east of the city. In the evening join Braga's students for a few cold ones in one of the city's great bars.

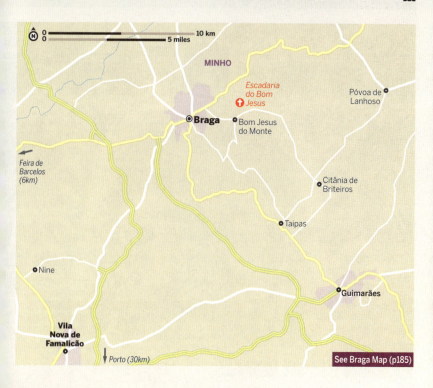

N
0 ___ 10 km
0 ___ 5 miles

MINHO

Escadaria do Bom Jesus

Póvoa de Lanhoso

Braga

Bom Jesus do Monte

Feira de Barcelos (6km)

Citânia de Briteiros

Taipas

Nine

Guimarães

Vila Nova de Famalicão

Porto (30km)

See Braga Map (p185)

Arriving in Braga

Bus station Braga has a centralised station that serves as a major regional hub.

Train station Handles commuter trains to Porto and AP services.

Sleeping

Reservations are essential during Semana Santa (Easter) and possibly at the height of summer. Braga has a wide range of accommodation from backpacker hostels to luxury guesthouses though most hotels fall into the lower to mid-range category. The tourist office can help with bookings.

The vast majority of Braga's accommodation options are located in the city centre, a short walk from most of the sights, restaurants and shopping. For the quietest night's snooze, choose hotels and guest houses around the Sé. Around the immediate historical centre you might find yourself on a busy road.

Detail of Braga cathedral's elaborate interior

Braga's Cathedral

Top billing in Braga goes to its cathedral, the Sé, whose asymmetrical towers block one end of a picturesque city-centre street. A working church, it is the seat of the Archdiocese of Braga.

Braga's extraordinary cathedral (Sé), the oldest in Portugal, was begun when the archdiocese was restored in 1070 and completed in the following century. It's a wonderfully rambling complex made up of differing styles, and architecture buffs could spend half a day happily distinguishing the Romanesque bones from Manueline musculature and baroque frippery. Allow at least three hours to see everything.

Great For...

☑ Don't Miss

Chapel of Piety (Capela da Piedade) a beautiful 16th-century Renaissance tomb.

The Cathedral

The Sé's original Romanesque style is the most interesting and survives in the cathedral's overall shape, the southern entrance and the marvellous west portal, which is carved with scenes from the medieval legend of Reynard the Fox (now sheltered inside a Gothic porch). The most appealing external features are the filigree Manueline

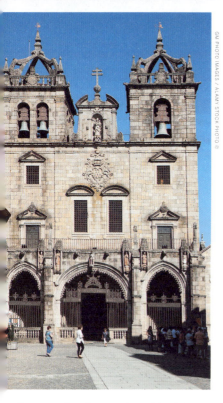

❶ Need to Know

Rua Dom Paio Mendes; www.se-braga.pt;
⊘9am-7pm high season, 9am-6.30pm low
season.

✕ Take a Break

Caldo Entornado (p187) is a great place
to grab some lunch.

★ Top Tip

Come for Sunday mass (11.30am) to
hear the Sé's organ in action.

of the Virgin suckling Christ, attributed
to 16th-century French sculptor Nicolas
Chanterène. Another remarkable highlight
is the iron cross that was used in 1500 to
celebrate the very first Mass in Brazil.

Choir

To visit the choir, visitors must purchase
a separate ticket and join a guided tour
(some guides speak English), which gives
an up-close look at the mesmerising organs
and gilded choir stalls. Visitors will then
be led downstairs and into the cathedral's
showpiece Capela dos Reis (Kings' Chapel),
home to the tombs of Henri of Burgundy
and Dona Teresa, parents of the first king of
Portugal, Afonso Henriques. You'll also visit
the *azulejo*-covered Capela de São Geraldo
(dating from the 12th century but reworked
over the years) and the 14th-century
Capela da Glória, whose interior was painted in unrepentantly Moorish geometric
motifs in the 16th century.

towers and roof – an early work by João
de Castilho, who went on to build Lisbon's
illustrious Mosteiro dos Jerónimos.

You can enter the cathedral through the
west portal or via a courtyard and cloister
that's lined with Gothic chapels on the
north side. The church itself features a fine
Manueline carved altarpiece, a tall chapel
with *azulejos* (hand-painted tiles) telling the
story of Braga's first bishop (São Pedro de
Rates), and fantastic twin baroque organs
(held up by formidable satyrs and mermen).

Treasury

Connected to the church is the treasury,
housing a goldmine of ecclesiastical booty,
including the lovely Nossa Senhora do Leite

HISTORY

Founded by Romans, Braga was settled in the 1st century BC, named Bracara Augusta and made capital of the Roman province of Gallaecia. Braga's position at the intersection of five Roman roads helped it grow fat on trade, but it fell to the Suevi around AD 410, and was sacked by the Visigoths 60 years later. The Visigoths' conversion to Christianity in the 6th century and the founding of an archbishopric in the next century put the town atop the Iberian Peninsula's ecclesiastical pecking order.

The Moors moved in around 715, sparking a long-running tug of war that ended when Fernando I, king of Castilla y León, definitively reconquered the city in 1040. The archbishopric was restored in 1070, though prelates bickered with their Spanish counterparts for the next 500 years over who was Primate of All Spain. The pope finally ruled in Braga's favour, though the city's resulting good fortune began to wane in the 18th century when a newly anointed Lisbon archdiocese stole much of its thunder.

Not surprisingly, it was from conservative Braga that António de Oliveira Salazar, with his unique blend of Catholicism and fascism, gave the speech that launched his 1926 coup, introducing Portugal to half a century of dictatorship.

◎ SIGHTS

GNRation   Cultural Centre

(Map p185; www.gnration.pt; Praça Conde de Agrolongo 123; ⊘9.30am-6.30pm Mon-Fri, 2.30-6.30pm Sat) FREE Braga's newest cultural centre lives inside an 18th-century building that once housed police headquarters. Enter through the modern entrance with a glass sliding door and you're inside an incubator of the city's creative industry, with concerts, film screenings, workshops and theatre performances.

Museu dos Biscainhos   Museum

(Map p185; Rua dos Biscainhos; adult/student €2/1, first Sun of the month free; ⊘9.30am-12.45pm & 2-5.30pm Tue-Sun) An 18th-century aristocrat's palace is home to the enthusias-

tic municipal museum, with a nice collection of Roman relics and 17th- to 19th-century pottery and furnishings. The palace itself is the reason to come, with its polychrome, chestnut-panelled ceilings and 18th-century *azulejos* depicting hunting scenes. The ground floor is paved with deeply ribbed flagstones on which carriages would have once rattled through to the stables.

Centro Interpretativo das Memórias da Misericórdia de Braga   Museum

(Map p185; Rua do Raio 400; ⊘10am-1pm & 2.30-6.30pm Tue-Sat) FREE Braga's newest museum is housed inside Palácio do Raio, the extroverted work by André Soares, its rococo face covered in *azulejos*. The gorgeous interiors, also filled with *azulejos,* showcase works of sacred art, textiles, paintings, sculptures, jewellery and pottery, all bearing witness to 500 years of the building's history.

Check out the collection of old medical instruments (weighing scales, pharmacy vials, tincture bottles); the building housed São Marcos hospital from 1884.

Escadaria do Bom Jesus   Christian Site

At Bom Jesus do Monte, a hilltop pilgrimage site 5km from Braga, there is an extraordinary stairway, with allegorical fountains, chapels and a superb view. City bus 2 runs frequently from Braga to the site, where you can climb the steps (pilgrims sometimes do this on their knees) or ascend by funicular (one way €1.20).

Fonte do Ídolo   Ruins

(Idol Spring; Map p185; Rua do Raio; adult/student €1.85/0.95; ⊘9am-1pm & 2-6pm Tue-Fri, 10am-5pm Sat & Mon) This spring, a Roman ruin opened to the public, is set underneath a mod lobby. An essential community water source, it was carved into a fountain during pre-Roman times by Celicus Fronto, an immigrant from the city-state of Arcobriga. One carving is of a toga-clad pilgrim thought to be holding the horn of plenty. There's an introductory video, too.

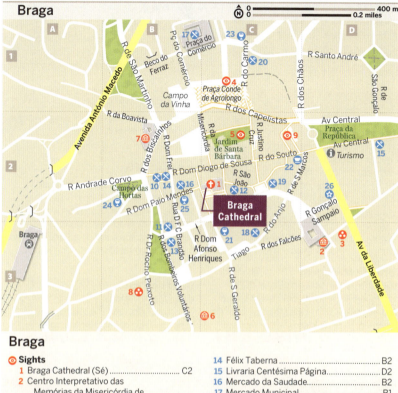

Braga

◎ Sights

⊗ Eating

◉ Drinking & Nightlife

◉ Entertainment

Jardim de Santa Bárbara   Gardens

(Map p185; Rua Justino Cruz) FREE This 17th-century square has narrow paths picking their way through a sea of flowers and topiary. On sunny days the adjacent pedestrianised streets fill with buskers and cafe tables.

Termas Romanas do Alto Cividade   Ruins

(Map p185; Rua Dr Rocha Peixoto; adult/student €1.85/0.95; ⊘9am-1pm & 2-6pm Tue-Fri, 10am-5pm Sat & Mon) These ruins of an extensive bathing complex – with an attached theatre – dating from the 2nd century

AD, were probably abandoned in the 5th century. See the seven-minute introductory video in English or Portuguese.

Museu Dom Diogo de Sousa Museum

(Map p185; Rua dos Bombeiros Voluntários; adult/student €3/1.50, Sun free; ⊗9.30am-6pm Tue-Sun May-Sep, 9.30am-5.30pm Tue-Sun Oct-Apr) The archaeological museum houses a nicely displayed collection of fragments from Braga's earliest days. The four rooms feature pieces from Palaeolithic times (arrowheads, funerary objects and ceramics) through the days of Roman rule and on up to the period dominated by the Suevi-Visigoth kingdom (5th through 7th centuries).

The most fascinating pieces are the huge *miliários* (milestones), carved with Latin inscriptions, that marked the Roman roads.

Torre de Menagem Landmark

(Map p185; Largo Terreiro do Castelo) FREE The square-shaped, crenellated tower behind the cafes on Praça da República is the walled-up Torre de Menagem, which is all that survives of a fortified medieval palace.

TOURS

Tourists' Affairs Tours

(☑253 253 169; www.thetouristsaffairs.com) This excellent tour agency run by a pair of young enthusiastic locals, an architect and an archaeologist, specialises in all things Minho. Their focus is on tailor-made à la carte tours of Minho and beyond, but they also do free walking tours of Braga – call a day ahead to reserve a spot.

EATING

The boisterous **mercado municipal** (Map p185; Praça do Comércio; ⊗8am-3pm Mon-Fri, 6am-1pm Sat) buzzes on weekdays and Saturday mornings, and is ideal for self-caterers. You can also hit one of several fruit-and-vegetable shops along Rua de São Marcos.

Casa de Pasto das Carvalheiras Fusion €€

(Map p185; ☑253 046 244; Rua Dom Afonso Henriques 8; mains €4.50-14; ⊗noon-3pm & 7pm-midnight) This funky eatery with lots of

Escadaria do Bom Jesus (p184)

colourful details and a long bar serves up flavourful fusion food served as *pratinhos* (small plates). The menus change weekly and feature dishes like salmon ceviche, *alheira* (a light, garlicky sausage of poultry or game) rolls with turnip sprouts and black octopus polenta. Weekday lunch menus are a great deal (€8 or €12, depending on the number of dishes you order).

Anjo Verde — Vegetarian €

(Map p185; Largo da Praça Velha 21; mains €7.50-8.60; noon-3pm & 7.30-10.30pm Mon-Sat;) Braga's vegetarian offering serves generous, elegantly presented plates in a lovely, airy dining room. Vegetarian lasagne, risotto and vegetable tarts are among the choices. Mains can be bland, but the spiced chocolate tart is a superstar.

Brac — Portuguese €€

(Map p185; 253 610 225; Campo das Carvalheiras; snacks €3-9, mains €13-17; 11am-midnight Mon-Sat) Braga's gourmet hotspot offers tasty *petiscos* (tapas) at the backlit bar and more elaborate dishes like prawn curry and roasted black pork in the swank dining room with stone columns and exposed stone walls. Happy hour is every night from 5.30pm to 7pm.

Taberna Velhos Tempos — Portuguese €

(Map p185; 253 214 368; Rua do Carmo 7; mains €7.50-11; noon-2.30pm & 8-10.30pm Mon-Sat) A rustic tavern with wooden beams, lots of bric-a-brac and a menu of tasty mainstays. Try the *bacalhau com nata* (baked codfish) or duck rice. The portions are huge so order only half sizes.

Spirito Cupcakes & Coffee — Ice Cream €

(Map p185; Largo São João do Souto 19; cup €2-3.50, cone €2-4; 1.30-7pm Mon-Thu, 1.30-7pm & 9pm-midnight Fri & Sat) Don't miss the artisanal gelato at this always-buzzing shop, where lines form out the door for a cup or cone of oatmeal-, cookie- or bubblegum-flavoured ice creams. There are great cupcakes and coffees, too.

Praça da República

The cafes and restaurants on this broad plaza are a pleasant place to start or finish your day. An especially mellow atmosphere descends in the evening, when coloured lights spring up and people of all ages congregate to enjoy the night air.

The square-shaped, crenellated tower behind the cafes is the walled-up Torre de Menagem, which is all that survives of a fortified medieval palace.

Retro Kitchen — Portuguese €

(Map p185; 253 267 023; Rua do Anjo 96; mains €8.50-12; noon-2.30pm & 8-10.30pm Mon & Wed-Sat) A vintage theme runs through this funky, laid-back restaurant featuring tasty daily specials and a display of eclectic retro items curated by the friendly owner couple. The lunch menu is a steal at €6.

Félix Taberna — Portuguese €€

(Map p185; 253 617 701; Largo da Praça Velha 18-19; mains €10.75-16.75; noon-3pm & 7pm-1am Mon-Fri, 7pm-1am Sat) Savour terrific Portuguese dishes in this attractive country-style tavern with two cosy dining rooms showcasing lots of bric-a-brac. The menu is small but dishes are delicious, including breaded sardines, duck rice and codfish *à minha moda*.

Livraria Centésima Página — Cafe €

(Map p185; Avenida Central 118-120; snacks €2.60-4.90; 9am-7.30pm Mon-Sat) Tucked inside Centésima Página, an absolutely splendid bookshop with foreign-language titles, this charming cafe serves a rotating selection of tasty quiches along with salads and desserts, and has outdoor tables in the pleasantly rustic garden. Their lunch specials are a steal.

Caldo Entornado — Portuguese €€

(Map p185; 253 065 578; www.caldoentornado. com; Rua São João 8; mains €11-15; noon-3pm

Feira de Barcelos

The largest, oldest and most celebrated of the Minho's markets is the **Feira de Barcelos** (Campo da República, Barcelos; ☺sunrise-sunset Thu), held every Thursday in Barcelos on the banks of the Rio Cávado. Despite attracting travellers, the market retains its rural soul. Villagers hawk everything from scrawny chickens to hand-embroidered linen, and Roma women bellow for business in the clothes section. Snack on sausages and homemade bread as you wander among the brass cowbells, hand-woven baskets and carved ox yokes. Pottery is what most outsiders come to see.

& 7-11pm Tue-Sat, noon-3pm Mon & Sun) Run by a friendly couple, this minimalist eatery with contemporary decor and pine-wood details serves great-value weekday lunches (€8) and a range of well-prepared mains such as cod puff pastries, prawn curries and *picanhas* (rump steaks).

Mercado da Saudade　　　Cafe €

(Map p185; Rua Dom Paio Mendes 59; snacks €2-3.50; ☺11am-8pm Thu, 11am-2am Fri & Sat, 11am-10pm Sun) A colourful little grocery store-cafe, with a few storefront and sidewalk tables, where you can buy a variety of Portuguese products – from cork items, shoes and soaps to edibles such as chocolates and sardines. Its snacks are delicious; try the Portuguese pork sandwich and wash it down with a glass of wine or Sovina, the local handcrafted beer.

DRINKING & NIGHTLIFE

The Minho produces the famous *vinho verde* (green wine – 'green' because it's made from immature grapes, either red or white), *caldo verde* (Galician kale and potato soup), *broa de Milho* (golden corn loaf),

thrifty *sopa seca* (dry soup) and seasonal eel-like lamprey, trout and salmon dishes.

While it's no counterpart to Lisbon or Porto, Braga has a pretty buzzy nightlife, though it's mostly limited to the clutch of cafes and bars in the city centre. The crowd is generally young, as it's a student town.

Barhaus　　　Bar

(Map p185; Rua Dom Gonçalo Pereira 58; ☺3pm-2am Mon-Thu, 3pm-4am Fri & Sat) A popular spot with two indoor bars and a huge open-air patio, which draws a crowd with posh pretensions. DJs spin '80s music on weekends, when there's a €3 cover.

Café A Brasileira　　　Cafe

(Map p185; Largo do Barão de São Marinho 17; ☺7am-8pm Mon-Sat) A Braga classic, this 19th-century cafe is a converging point for old and new generations. Try the *café de saco* (a small shot of filtered coffee).

Convento do Carmo　　　Bar

(Map p185; 📱929 255 229; Travessa do Carmo; ☺9pm-2am Thu, 6pm-6am Fri & Sat) A gorgeous bar-restaurant-performance space housed in a restored convent, with a flowery garden patio featuring a pool. A great place for a glass of wine and a taste of Braga's cultural repertoire – it hosts concerts, exhibits and theatre performances.

Domus Vinum　　　Wine Bar

(Map p185; www.domus-vinum.com; Largo da Nossa Senhora da Boa Luz 12; tapas €4-7; ☺6pm-2am Tue-Sun) With Brazilian beats, a lantern-lit front patio and excellent wines by the glass, Domus Vinum draws a stylish crowd. The Portuguese and Spanish tapas are excellent. It's just west of the old-town entrance portal, Arco da Porta Nova.

Estúdio 22　　　Bar

(Map p185; Rua Dom Paio Mendes 22; ☺6pm-2am Mon-Thu & Sun, 6pm-4am Fri & Sat) Loungey cafe-bar on a bustling strip by the cathedral, great for coffee drinking during the day and sampling the speciality gin and tonics at night to the sound of live bands or DJs spinning funk and bossa.

ENTERTAINMENT

Teatro Circo de Braga   Theatre

(Map p185; ☑253 203 800; www.theatrocirco.
com; Avenida da Liberdade 697) One of the
most dazzling theatres in the country,
inside a grand fin de siècle building, where
you can catch concerts, theatre and dance,
with offerings ranging from the staid to the
truly avant-garde.

INFORMATION

Turismo (Map p185; ☑253 262 550; www.
cm-braga.pt; Avenida da Liberdade 1; ☺9am-7pm
Mon-Fri, 9am-12.30pm & 2-5.30pm Sat & Sun Jun-
Sep, shorter hours in low season) Braga's helpful
tourist office is in an art-deco-style building
facing the fountain.

ℹ GETTING THERE & AROUND

CAR

Because of one-way and pedestrian-only streets,
driving in central Braga is tricky, and most parking incurs a fee. There is a large, fee-charging car
park under Praça da República. You might also
try the side streets east of Avenida da Liberdade.

BUS

Braga has a centralised bus station that serves
as a major regional hub.

Airport Bus (☑253 262 371; www.getbus.eu)
About 10 buses daily do the 50-minute run
between the Porto airport and Braga, in each direction. The one-way fare is €8 (€4 for children),
return is €14 (€8 for children).

Rede Expressos (www.rede-expressos.pt) Has
up to 15 daily buses to Lisbon (€21, 4½ hours).

Transdev Norte/Arriva (☑253 209 401) Has at
least eight buses per day to Barcelos (€2.65, one
hour) and Porto (€4.80, one hour).

TRAIN

Braga is at the end of a branch line from Nine
and also within Porto's *suburbano* network,
which means commuter trains travel every hour
or so from Porto (€3.10, about one hour); don't
waste €32.80 on an Alfa Pendular (AP) train.

Useful AP links include Coimbra (€19.80, 2¼
hours, five to seven daily) and Lisbon (€31, four
hours, two to four daily).

São João do Souto neighbourhood, Braga

MAREK STEPAN / GETTY IMAGES ©

COIMBRA

In this Chapter

Coimbra at a Glance...

The medieval capital of Portugal for over a hundred years and site of the country's greatest university for the past five centuries, Coimbra wears its weighty importance in Portuguese history with dignity. Its atmospheric, historic core cascades down a hillside in a lovely setting on the east bank of the Rio Mondego: it's a multicoloured collage of buildings spanning nearly a millennium.

During the academic year, you'll be sure to feel the university's influence. On a summer evening, the city's old stone walls reverberate with the haunting metallic notes of the guitarra (Portuguese guitar) and the full, deep voices of fado singers.

Coimbra in Two Days

Head straight up through the Old Town to the **Velha Universidade** (p194), Coimbra's famous old university – it is the unrivalled highlight of any visit. Spend the rest of the day exploring the historical centre. Day two could be spent dipping in and out of Coimbra's old churches and monasteries and taking in a performance of the city's own version of fado.

Coimbra in Four Days

On day three it's time to get out of the city to explore the wonderful Roman ruins at **Conímbriga** (p199), a short bus ride south. Your fourth day in Coimbra might be spent shopping for the city's distinctive pottery or hanging out with the students in some of the learned bars and clubs.

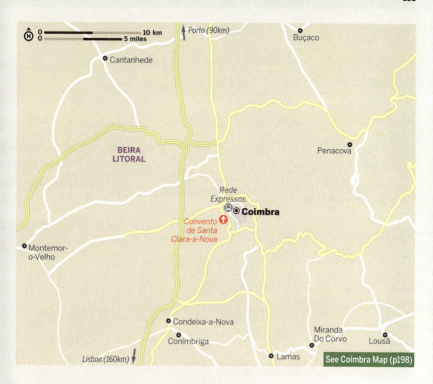

Arriving in Coimbra

Bus station Handles intercity services across Portugal.

Coimbra B station Long-distance trains stop here.

Coimbra A station A more central station that handles local trains.

Sleeping

As one of Portugal's top tourist cities, Coimbra has plenty of places to stay. Most want to bed down in the thick of the Old Town action but there are many other options a short walk or bus ride from the centre.

If you opt for accommodation in the old town, it will be atmospheric, though be aware that parking can be tricky the closer you get to the centre. Thanks to Coimbra's good public transport system, staying out of the city centre is not the hassle you might expect. Student dorms often open their doors to tourists, some year-round.

Biblioteca Joanina

SERGIO AZENHA / ALAMY STOCK PHOTO ©

Velha Universidade

Coimbra's main highlight is without doubt, the university nucleus, consisting of a series of remarkable 16th- to 18th-century buildings, all set within and around the vast Pátio das Escolas (patio or courtyard).

There's a lot to see at the Velha Universidade so you should allow at least two hours. The sights include the Paço das Escolas (Royal Palace), clock tower, Prisão Acadêmica (prison), Capela de São Miguel (chapel) and the highlight of any visit to Coimbra, the Biblioteca Joanina (library).

Biblioteca Joanina

This extraordinary library, a gift from João V in the early 18th century, seems too extravagant and distracting for study, with its rosewood, ebony and jacaranda tables, elaborately frescoed ceilings and gilt chinoiserie bookshelves. Its 60,000 ancient books deal with law, philosophy and theology. A lower floor has more tomes and the Prisão Acadêmica, an erstwhile lock-up for misbehaving students.

Great For...

☑ Don't Miss

The view across Coimbra from the Pátio das Escolas is worth getting the camera out for.

University buildings

TOMASZ STOLZ PHOTOGRAPHY / ALAMY STOCK PHOTO ©

Coimbra A Train Station

Universidade de Coimbra

Rio Mondego

Av Emídio Navarro

R de S João

R José Falcão

Jardim Botânico

🛈 Need to Know

239 242 744; www.uc.pt/en/ informacaopara/visit/paco; adult/student €9/7, tower €1; 9am-7.30pm mid-Mar–Oct, 9.30am-1pm & 2-5.30pm Nov–mid-Mar

✕ Take a Break

Enjoy the view and the great food at central Loggia (p200)

★ Top Tip

Visitors are only allowed into the library in small groups every 20 minutes.

Capela de São Miguel

This extraordinarily beautiful, ornate baroque chapel has a brightly painted ceiling, ornate tilework, Manueline features and a gilded organ. It has been recently renovated. Concerts still take place here on occasion – ask at the *turismo*.

Other Attractions

The Schools Palace, the original Royal Palace, houses the university's iconic *salas* (rooms). Here, important traditional academic ceremonies still take place. To visit the palace, from the courtyard gate take the stairway on the right up to Sala dos Capelos, a former examination room hung with dark portraits of Portugal's kings, and heavy quiltlike decoration. Nearby is the private Examination Room, lined with paintings of the university rectors. The adja-

cent passageway affords visitors excellent city views. In fine weather, you may be permitted to enter the balcony; it's worth doing for fabulous vistas.

Another of the university's symbolic structures in Coimbra, the 18th-century tower – and its clock and bells – regulate academic life. Built between 1728 and 1733 on the premise that there could be no order without a clock, it was nicknamed 'a cabra' ('goat'; or 'bitch' in contemporary lingo), as it rang out to end the day's classes, signifying the curfew (in the days when students had to be home by 7pm or face prison). In fine conditions, you can climb the tower (€1).

Tickets & Tours

Buy your ticket at the university's visitor centre near the Porta Férrea. You can enter and explore on your own (with the exception of the library), or head off with a knowledgable university tour guide on one of three different tours (€12.50 to €20). These take place daily at 11am and 3pm.

HISTORY

The Romans founded a city at Conímbriga, though it was abruptly abandoned in favour of Coimbra's more easily defended heights. The city grew and prospered under the Moors, who were evicted definitively by Christians in 1064. The city served as Portugal's capital from 1139 to 1255, when Afonso III decided he preferred Lisbon.

The Universidade de Coimbra, Portugal's first university (and among the first in Europe), was actually founded in Lisbon by Dom Dinis in 1290 but settled here in 1537. It attracted a steady stream of teachers, artists and intellectuals from across Europe. The 16th century was a particularly heady time thanks to Nicolas Chanterène, Jean de Rouen (João de Ruão) and other French artists who helped create a school of sculpture here that influenced styles all over Portugal.

Today Coimbra's university remains Portugal's most prestigious – and one of its most traditional. Students still attend class in black robes and capes – often adorned with patches signifying course of study, home town or other affiliation – while a rigorously maintained set of rites and practices called the *codigo de praxe* governs all aspects of student life.

SIGHTS

Crowning Coimbra's steep hilltop is the university, around and below which lies a tangle of old town lanes. The new town, locally called 'Baixa', spreads at the foot of the hill and along the Rio Mondego.

Museu Nacional de
Machado de Castro   Museum

(☑239 853 070; www.museumachadocastro.pt; Largo Dr José Rodrigues; adult/child €6/free, cryptoportico only €3, with audio guide €7.50; ⊘2-6pm Tue, 10am-7pm Wed-Sun Apr-Sep, 2-6pm Tue, 10am-6pm Wed-Sun Oct-Mar) This great museum is a highlight of central Portugal. It's built over the Roman forum, the remains of which can be seen and cover several levels. Part of the visit takes you down to the vaulted, spooky and immensely atmospheric galleries of the cryptoportico that allowed the forum to be level on such a hilly site. The artistic collection is wide-ranging and

Museu Nacional de Machado de Castro

superb. The route starts with sculpture, from the architectural (column capitals) through Gothic religious sculpture and so on.

Highlights include a section of the delicate cloister of São João de Almedina and some exquisite alabaster pieces from England. Renaissance masters arriving in Coimbra from other parts of Europe brought their own styles and contributed to the establishment of a distinctive Coimbra tradition. A whole chapel has even been reassembled here. The section downstairs includes impressive 16th-century terra-cotta figures from *Hodart's Last Supper*, while paintings on the higher floors include stunning Flemish panels by Metsys. A collection of gold monstrances, furniture and Moorish-influenced pieces are almost too much by the time you reach them.

Museu da Ciência
Museum

(📞239 854 350; www.museudaciencia.org; Largo Marquês de Pombal; adult/student €5/3.50; 🕙10am-6pm Tue-Sun) This wonderful science museum occupies a centuries-old former monastery converted by Pombal into the university's chemical engineering building. It features intriguing interactive science displays coexisting with 18th-century lab sinks; don't miss the giant glowing globe in a room paved with medieval stones, or the psychedelic insect's-eye view of flowers. Displays are in English/Portuguese. There's also a great cafe with terrace and views down to the new town.

The most extraordinary section, reopened in 2016, is housed in a building opposite (guided visits only). The collection displays 17th- to 19th-century teaching aids of the former physics and zoology study laboratories. Think curiosity cabinets and some of the most simple, ingenious scientific contraptions around (we love the centaur used to measure the direction and velocity of an arrow). Part of the joy, too, is observing the exquisite craftsmanship.

Sé Velha
Cathedral

(Old Cathedral; 📞239 825 273; www.sevelha -coimbra.org; Largo da Sé Velha, Rua do Norte 4; €2.50; 🕙10am-6pm Mon-Sat, 1-6pm Sun)

✳️ Festival das Artes

This two-week festival in June or July brings classical music to the Quinta das Lágrimas, jazz to the riverboats, guest chefs to local restaurants and other forms of merriment to Coimbra's streets.

Quinta das Lágrimas
SAIKO3P / SHUTTERSTOCK ©

Coimbra's stunning 12th-century cathedral is one of Portugal's finest examples of Romanesque architecture. The main portal and facade are exceptionally striking. Its crenellated exterior and narrow, slit-like lower windows serve as reminders of the nation's embattled early days, when the Moors were still a threat. These buildings were designed to be useful as fortresses in times of trouble.

The church was financed by the first king of Portugal, Afonso Henriques. The high, barrel-vaulted nave preserves its main Romanesque features; side altars and well-preserved Gothic tombs of bishops are backed by bright Andalusian tiles. The high gilt retable is in ornate late-Gothic style and depicts the Assumption of Mary. Contrast this with the Renaissance Capela do Santíssimo Sacramento alongside. If you want to visit on a Sunday, note that Mass is at 11am.

Convento de Santa Clara-a-Nova
Convent

(📞239 441 674; www.rainhasantaisabel.org; Calçada de Santa Isabel; cloister €2; 🕙9am-6.45pm Mon-Fri Nov-Feb, 8.30am-7pm Mon-Sat, from 9am Sun Mar-Oct) Begun on higher

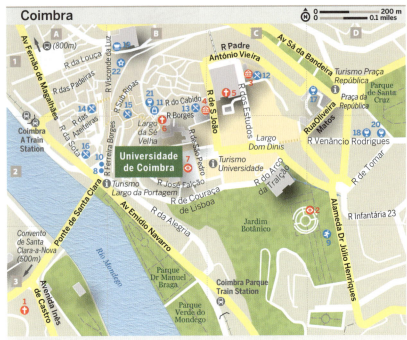

Coimbra

ground in the 17th century to replace its flooded twin, this convent is devoted almost entirely to the saintly Queen Isabel's memory. Aisle panels tell her life story, while her solid-silver casket is enshrined above the altar, and even her clothes hang in the sacristy. Her statue

is the focus of the **Festa da Rainha Santa** (www.rainhasantaisabel.org).

Convento de Santa Clara-a-Velha   Convent
(☏239 801 160; Rua das Parreiras; adult/student €4/2.50; ⊙10am-7pm Tue-Sun Apr-Sep, 10am-

6pm Tue-Sun Oct-Mar) This Gothic convent was founded in 1330 by the saintly Dona Isabel, Dom Dinis' wife; it served as her final resting place until flooding forced her to be moved uphill. The adjacent museum displays archaeological finds and shows two films, one about the nuns who lived here, the other documenting the 20-year renovation that cleared the river ooze that had drowned it since the 17th century.

Jardim Botânico   Gardens

(☑239 855 233; www.uc.pt; ☺9am-8pm Apr-Sep, 9am-5.30pm Oct-Mar) **FREE** A serene place to catch your breath, the lovely university-run botanic garden sits in the shadow of the 16th-century Aqueduto de São Sebastião. Founded by the Marquês de Pombal, the garden combines formal flowerbeds, meandering paths and elegant fountains.

The green-fingered can also visit the lush greenhouses (closed at the time of research) and the adjacent Museu Botânico, while Skygarden (p199) has a series of ziplines here.

Conímbriga Roman Ruins   Ruins

(ruins & museum adult/child €4.50/free; ☺10am-7pm) In the rolling country southwest of Coimbra, Conímbriga boasts Portugal's most extensive Roman ruins, one of the best-preserved sites on the Iberian Peninsula. It tells the poignant tale of a town that, after centuries of security, was split in two by quickly erected walls and then entirely abandoned as the Roman Empire disintegrated.

Elaborate mosaics, heated baths and fountains evoke toga-clad dalliances. Through the middle of this runs a massive defensive wall, built in haste to fend off raids.

Sé Nova   Cathedral

(New Cathedral; ☑239 823 138; www.senova. do.sapo.pt; Largo da Sé Nova; €1; ☺8.30am-6.30pm Mon-Sat, 10am-12.30pm Sun) The large, severe 'new' cathedral, started by the Jesuits in 1598 and completed a century later, dominates the square of the same name

high in the old town. Its sober Renaissance lines contrast with the gilt side panels and ornate baroque altarpiece. Down the side is a gallery of reliquaries featuring bones and worse from minor saints and bishops, including St Francis Xavier, and St Luke (so it is claimed!). Climb to the platform for uplifting city views.

🎿 ACTIVITIES

Skygarden   Zipline

(☑910 230 797; www.skygardenadventure.com; Calçada Martim de Freitas; adult/child €17/13; ☺10am-8pm Tue-Sun Apr-Sep, 10am-5.30pm Tue-Sun Mar & Oct, weekends only Nov & Feb) It's not what you might associate with a historic seat of learning, but for an education of a different kind, you can fly through the lush green of the Jardim Botânico on a 200m valley slide, climb ropes or 'freefall' from an ancient tree.

🔄 TOURS

Go Walks   Walking

(☑910 163 118; www.gowalksportugal.com; Rua do Sargento Mor 4-6; from €12.50) Various themed walking tours – from fado to Jewish Coimbra – run by enthusiastic, knowledgable students who speak good English (French and Spanish also bookable).

Tuk a Day   Tours

(☑964 486 445, 962 826 855; per person €10; ☺9am-1pm & 3-7pm) Travellers love the passionate Sr Amando and his informative, amusing 1¼-hour tours of Coimbra. He speaks many languages (around five at last count) and knows a lot. Minimum three people (or €30). Tours begin at the Portagem.

🔒 SHOPPING

Carlos Tomás   Ceramics

(☑239 812 945; carlostomas_ceramica artesanal@hotmail.com; Largo da Sé Velha 4) Lovely hand-painted ceramics (and more) by Senhor Tomás. Will even do custom-made orders of your own design.

Coimbra Fado

If Lisbon represents the heart of Portuguese fado music, Coimbra is its head. The 19th-century university was male-only so the town's womenfolk, immortalised in song as *tricanas*, were of great interest to the student body. Coimbra fado developed partly as a way of communicating with these heavily chaperoned females, usually in the form of serenades sung under the bedroom window. For this reason, fado is traditionally sung only by men, who must be students or ex-students.

The Coimbra style is considered more lyrical and pure than the Lisbon variety, though it was influenced over the decades by musical traditions from all over Portugal and the Portuguese-speaking world thanks to the varied origins of the student body. It ranges from hauntingly beautiful serenades and lullabies to more boisterous students-out-on-the-piss type of songs. The singer is normally accompanied by a 12-string *guitarra* (Portugese guitar) and perhaps a Spanish (classical) guitar too. Due to the clandestine nature of these bedroom-window concerts, audience appreciation is traditionally indicated by softly coughing rather than clapping.

Guitarra (Portugese guitar)
ARISTIDIS VAFEIADAKIS / ALAMY STOCK PHOTO ©

EATING

The atmospheric narrow streets between Praça do Comércio and Coimbra A train station are full of characterful, older-style Portuguese eateries; just wander down here and smell what's cooking. Many contemporary tapas-style places have opened in the old town (better for vegetarians). There's something to suit all budgets.

Tapas Nas Costas   Tapas €€

(☏239 157 425; www.tapasnascostas.pt; Rua Quebra Costas 19; tapas €3.50-6.60; ⊙noon-midnight Tue-Sat) *The* 'hot spot' about town at the time of research, this sophisticated tapas joint delivers delicious tapas. Decor is stylish, as are the gourmet-style goodies, such as *ovo com alheira de caça e grelos* (sausage with turnip greens and egg; €5.60). What are 'small-to-medium' sized servings for Portuguese are possibly 'normal' for anyone else, so share plates are a satisfying experience.

A good list of wholly Portuguese wines. Reserve ahead.

Cafetaria Museu da Ciência Cafe €

(☏910 575 151; Rua dos Estudos; light meals €4-9; ⊙10am-6.30pm; ☏) Tucked away in a remote part of the top of town, the science museum's cafe offers a large interior warmed by a log fire and an excellent terrace with views over the town below. Its light meals include quiches, salads and juices. It's renowned for its fabulous weekend breakfasts (from 11.30am to 4.30pm; €14.30). Daily plates Monday to Friday cost €6.

Loggia   Portuguese €€

(☏239 853 076; www.loggia.pt; Largo Dr José Rodrigues, Museu Nacional de Machado de Castro; mains €13.50-16; ⊙10am-6pm Tue-Sun, 7.30-10.30pm Wed-Sat) This museum restaurant has one of the town's most enviable locations, with stunning views (thanks to the glass walls) over the cascading roofs of the old city. It's a romantic, candlelit dining scene by night and great value for its confident modern Portuguese mains (the lunchtime €9.50 special is good value).

At other times, it's a venue for coffees or beers in the sunshine. It attracts Coimbra's elegant crowd.

Zé Manel dos Ossos Portuguese €€

(☏239 823 790; Beco do Forno 12; mains €7-15; ⏲noon-3pm & 7.30-10pm Mon-Fri, noon-3pm Sat) Tucked down a nondescript alleyway, this little gem, papered with scholarly doodles and scribbled poems, serves all things cooked off the bone. Come early or be prepared to wait in line. The charismatic service makes dining here an experience.

Restaurante
Zé Neto Portuguese €€

(☏239 826 786; Rua das Azeiteiras 8; mains €9-14; ⏲9am-3pm & 7pm-midnight Mon-Sat) This marvellous family-run place specialises in homemade Portuguese standards, including *cabrito* (kid; half portions €6). Things have been modernised by the elderly owner's daughter who is the chef (until recently her father used to tap out the menu on a vintage typewriter), but thankfully, it hasn't lost its flair for producing great meats.

🍷 DRINKING & NIGHTLIFE

Café Santa Cruz Cafe

(☏239 833 617; www.cafesantacruz.com; Praça 8 de Maio; ⏲7.30am-midnight Mon-Sat) One of Portugal's most atmospheric cafes, where the elderly statesmen meet for their daily cuppas. Santa Cruz is set in a dramatically beautiful high-vaulted former chapel, with stained-glass windows and graceful stone arches. The terrace grants lovely views of Praça 8 de Maio. Don't miss the *crúzios*, award-winning, egg- and almond-based conventual cakes for which the cafe is famous.

You'll pay a bit extra for the atmosphere, but it's worth it. Popular with tourists and locals alike, the cafe also has regular free fado.

AAC Bar Bar

(Bar Associação Académica de Coimbra; www.facebook.com/baraac; Av Sá da Bandeira; ⏲3pm-4am) Join the black-cape-clad students at their student-union bar, where beers are cheap and everyone is welcome. The esplanade out back, with wood decking and a grassy lawn, makes an agreeable refuge.

Outdoor dining in the historic centre

Terrace of a Coimbra bar

Aqui Base Tango   Bar

(http://aquibasetango.com; Rua Venâncio Rodrigues 8; ⊘9pm-4am Tue-Sat) This offbeat house holds one of Coimbra's most enticing bars, a quirky space with extremely original decor and a relaxed, inclusive vibe. Music ranges from jazz to alternative rock and there's always something interesting going on or in the pipeline. Gay friendly, too.

O Moelas   Bar

(☑962 445 275; Rua dos Coutinhos 14; ⊘10pm-4am) A friendly family-run drinking spot for students – cheap drinks for big (and late) nights. Enough said.

Noites Longas   Club

(☑239 835 167; Rua Almeida Garrett 11; ⊘midnight-6am Mon-Sat) This alternative club plays mainly rock and goes loud and very late. It's not subtle but it's a reliable local favourite. Gay friendly.

⊛ ENTERTAINMENT

Coimbra has its own version of fado and catching a performance is a must when in town.

Fado ao Centro   Fado

(☑910 679 838; www.fadoaocentro.com; Rua Quebra Costas 7; show incl drink €10) At the bottom of the old town, this friendly fado centre is a good place to introduce yourself to the genre. There's a performance every evening at 6pm. Shows include plenty of explanation in Portuguese and English about the history of Coimbra fado and the meaning of each song. It's tourist-oriented, but the performers enjoy it and do it well.

You can chat with the performers afterwards over a glass of port (included).

Á Capella   Fado

(☑239 833 985; www.acapella.com.pt; Rua do Corpo de Deus; entry incl drink €10; ⊘shows 9.30pm daily Apr-Oct, Thu-Sun Nov-Mar) A 14th-century chapel turned candlelit cocktail lounge, this place regularly hosts the city's most renowned fado musicians. There's a show every night at 9.30pm (though its opening, or otherwise, can be a bit unpredictable).

Shows cater directly to a tourist crowd, but the atmosphere and music are both superb. The setting is as intimate as the music itself, with heart-rendingly good acoustics.

ℹ️ INFORMATION

The tourist offices (www.turismodecoimbra.pt) at **Largo da Portagem** (📞239 488 120; ⏰9am-6pm Mon-Fri, 9am-1pm & 2-6pm Sat & Sun mid-Sep–mid-Jun, extended hours in summer), **Praça da República** (📞939 010 084; ⏰9am-6.30pm Mon-Fri) and the **Universidade de Coimbra ticket desk** (📞239 834 158; Praça da Porta Férrea; ⏰9am-7.30pm mid-Mar–Oct, 9am-1pm & 2-5.30pm Nov–mid-Mar) all offer good town maps as well as what's-on listings.

ℹ️ GETTING THERE & AWAY

From the rather grim **bus station** (Av Fernão de Magalhães) a 15-minute walk northwest of the centre, **Rede Expressos** (📞239 855 270; www.rede-expressos.pt) runs at least a dozen buses daily to Lisbon (€14.50, 2½ hours) and to Porto (€12, 1½ hours), with almost as many to Braga (€14, 2¾ hours) and to Faro (€27, six to nine hours).

Long-distance trains stop only at **Coimbra B** station, north of the city. Cross the platform for quick, free connections to more-central **Coimbra A** (called just 'Coimbra' on timetables).

Coimbra is linked by regular Alfa Pendular (AP) and *intercidade* (IC) trains to Lisbon (AP/IC €22.80/19.20, 1¾/two hours) and Porto (AP/IC €16.70/13.20, one/1¼ hours).

ℹ️ GETTING AROUND

Between them, buses 27, 28 and 29 run about every half hour from the main bus station and the Coimbra B train station to Praça da República.

Student Party

In the first week of May, Coimbra marks the end of the academic year with Queima das Fitas, a week-long party that serves as the country's biggest and best excuse to get roaring drunk. Literally, the name means 'Burning of the Ribbons', because graduates ritually torch the colour-coded ribbons worn to signify particular courses of study.

In the wee hours of Friday morning, the Queima kicks off with the Serenata Monumental, a hauntingly beautiful midnight fado performance on the steps of the Sé Velha. The agenda continues with sports events, private black-tie balls, nightly concerts at the so-called Queimodromo across the Ponte de Santa Clara, and a beer-soaked Sunday-afternoon parade called the Cortejo dos Grelados that runs from the university down to Largo da Portagem.

In their rush to sponsor the various festivities, Portuguese breweries provide ultracheap beer, which is distributed and drunk in liberal quantities.

Performance of the Serenata Monumental

You can purchase multi-use tickets (three/five/10 trips €2.20/3.15/5.80; day ticket €3.50) at the **SMTUC office** (www.smtuc.pt; Largo do Mercado; ⏰7am-7pm Mon-Fri, 8am-1pm Sat) at the foot of the *elevador*, at official kiosks and also at some *tabacarias* (tobacconists-cum-newsagents). Tickets bought on board cost €1.60 per trip.

AVEIRO

Aveiro at a Glance...

A short distance from Coimbra, Aveiro hugs the edge of the Ria, a shallow coastal lagoon rich in bird life. This could explain the name: Aveiro (uh-vey-roo) may come from the Latin aviarium (place of birds). The town is a prosperous, lively place with a bustling centre based around a busy riverfront.

Aveiro is occasionally dubbed the Venice of Portugal thanks to its high-prowed boats, humpbacked bridges and network of picturesque canals. The moliceiro – the traditional seaweed-harvesting boat – has now been fully converted to tourist use; trips leave regularly, heading out into the lagoon, with boatsmen doubling up as knowledgeable guides.

Aveiro in Two Days

The first thing you'll probably want to do is hop on board a *moliceiro* (p212) for a laid-back tour. Spend the rest of the day exploring the old centre or sampling the town's traditional sweets – *ovos moles*. Spend day two in the town's **museums** (p210), shopping and enjoying Aveiro's traditional **seafood** (p212).

Aveiro in Four Days

Spend day three taking a trip to the **Museu Marítimo de Ílhavo** (p211), 8km south of Aveiro, which looks at Portugal's maritime history. Take a trip to Coimbra (p191) or even Porto (p89) on day four.

Penafiel

Porto ⊙

DOURO   Rio Douro

Peso da Regua

Lamego ⊙

Vila Nova de Gaia

Espinho ⊙

São João de Madeira

Ovar ⊙

BEIRA ALTA

Reserva Natural das Dunas de São Jacinto ⊙ **Aveiro**

⊙ **Viseu**

Águeda

Mangualde

ATLANTIC OCEAN

BEIRA LITORAL

Tondela

Gouveia ⊙

Parque Natural da Serra da Estrela

0   30 km
0   15 miles

Coimbra ⊙

See Aveiro Map (p213)

Arriving in Aveiro

Central bus stop All local and intercity buses arrive and leave from Rua Clube dos Galitos by the river.

Train station Handles regular services to Porto and Coimbra.

Sleeping

Hotels are dotted around the outer edge of the town centre though there are few beds actually in the historical centre. A couple of more upmarket places offer river views. Many tackle Aveiro as a day trip from elsewhere, but if you do turn up unannounced, the best place to head is the tourist office, which can help with bookings.

Moliceiros

ALBERTO LOYO / SHUTTERSTOCK ©

Boat Trips

At the top of every itinerary in Aveiro is a tour on the town's traditional, brightly decorated seaweed-harvesting boats. These relaxing trips head along the river and each boat has a guide on board.

Great For...

☑ Don't Miss
Notice the paintings on the prows of the *moliceiros* – some have very racy themes.

Story of the Moliceiro

Aveiro's *moliceiros* date from the 19th century and were originally used to gather seaweed from the bottom of the canals. This gooey mess was spread out on threshing floors to dry and used as fertiliser on the poor soil which farmers worked around the town. With the development and introduction of chemical fertilisers over the course of the 20th century, the demand for this natural product declined and the boat owners slowly transformed their craft into a tourist attraction. The boats themselves are still made and repaired in the traditional way. As in the olden days, the bow and stern are brightly painted, most often today with some naughty seaside scene, oddly resembling Britain's 'dirty' postcards – you might be glad you don't understand the Portuguese captions and cover kids' eyes

Painted decoration on the prow of a *moliceiro*

❶ Need to Know

Tickets cost €7.50. Boats leave every 30 minutes and tours take 45 minutes.

✕ Take a Break

There are numerous cafes lining the riverfront. A seafood lunch at Maré Cheia (p212) continues the watery theme.

★ Top Tip

All the boat companies (around ten of them) charge the same.

as some of the images decidedly verge on kinky! Each boat seats around 20 to 30 people on benches along both sides, and the ride, powered these days by diesel motor, is smooth.

Boat Trips

There are around ten companies offering *moliceiro* rides, all of them gathered around the bridge over the Canal Central, between the main bus stop and the big Fórum Aveiro shopping mall. Touts try to lure you into their boats, but as all charge the same fare (€7.50), condition of the craft, the friendliness of the boatsmen and extras such as welcome drinks come before cost when choosing which outfit to go with. Tours run around every 30 minutes and the 45-minute cruises explore the town's system of canals. The boatsmen usually

double up as guides and are surprisingly clued up when it comes to Aveiro's history. If you are really fortunate they may even burst into song.

Contact the Aveiro Welcome Center (p215) for a rundown of the companies offering *moliceiro* trips.

The Canals

Describing Aveiro as the 'Portuguese Venice' might be a slight exaggeration, but the canals and gondola-like *moliceiros* passing beneath the small footbridges that span them certainly create a vaguely similar scene. Canal Central is Aveiro's Grand Canal, with others such as the Canal do Coio, the Canal de São Roque and Canal do Paraiso extending from it. These canals are man-made and were built when the town was cut off from the lagoon by shifting sandbanks.

HISTORY

A prosperous seaport in the early 16th century, Aveiro suffered a ferocious storm in the 1570s that blocked the mouth of the Rio Vouga, closing it to ocean-going ships and creating fever-breeding marshes. Over the next two centuries, Aveiro's population shrank by three-quarters. But in 1808 the Barra Canal forged a passage back to the sea, and within a century Aveiro was rich once more, as evidenced by the spate of art nouveau houses that still define the town's old centre. Salt harvested here was taken to Newfoundland to preserve cod that came back as *bacalhau* (dried salt-cod).

 SIGHTS

Museu de Aveiro/
Santa Joana   Museum

(☏234 423 297; www.ipmuseus.pt; Avenida Santa Joana; €4, 10am-2pm Sun free; ☺10am-6pm Tue-Sun) This fine museum in a beautiful space, the former Mosteiro de Jesus, owes its finest treasures to Princesa Joana (later canonised), daughter of Afonso V. In 1472, 11 years after the convent was founded, Joana 'retired' here and, though forbidden to take full vows, she stayed until her death in 1490.

The extraordinary painting collection spans the 10th to 15th centuries. Her tomb, a 17th-century masterpiece of inlaid marble mosaic, takes centre stage in an equally lavish room (the remodelled lower choir stalls). The adjacent gold-leafed chapel is decorated with *azulejos* (hand-painted tiles) depicting Princesa Joana's life. The museum's paintings include a late-15th-century portrait of her, attributed to Nuno Gonçalves.

Reserva Natural das
Dunas de São Jacinto Nature Reserve

(www.rotadabairrada.pt) Stretching north from São Jacinto, between the sea and the lagoon west of Aveiro, is this supremely peaceful 6.7-sq-km wooded nature reserve, well equipped with trails and birdwatching hides. A meandering 7km loop trail runs through the pines and dunes and can be walked at any time (you should register

Museu de Aveiro/Santa Joana

at the interpretative centre). The best birdwatching here is from November to February.

At the trailhead, 1.5km north of the ferry on the N327, is a map, as well as the small, helpful **Dunas de São Jacinto Interpretative Centre** (234 331 282; Estrada Nacional 327; 9am-noon & 1-5pm Mon-Sat).

To get here, take a bus from Aveiro to Forte da Barra (one way/return €2.50/4), where there is a ferry to São Jacinto (passenger/car return €3/5). Schedules for boats are at www.moveaveiro.pt; bus schedules are at www.transdev.pt. Drivers can also circumnavigate the lagoon and arrive from the north via Ovar, but it's a much longer journey.

Museu Marítimo de Ílhavo
Museum

(234 329 990; www.museumaritimo.cm-ilhavo.pt; Avenida Dr Rocha Madahil; €5; 10am-6pm Tue-Sat year-round, 2-6pm Sun Mar-Sep) The wonderful Museu Marítimo de Ílhavo is in a modern, award-winning building in the town of Ílhavo, 8km south of Aveiro. It covers the history of the maritime identity of the Portuguese, from cod fishing (with superb fishing vessels from the 19th and 20th centuries) to oil paintings on the bows of the *moliceiros* (the traditional seaweed-harvesting boats). A highlight is the codfish aquarium, showcasing the Atlantic cod, which the Portuguese have been fishing (and munching on!) for centuries.

Entry costs €6.50 if included with the associated Santo André ship museum.

Mercado do Peixe
Market

(Largo da Praça do Peixe; 7am-1pm Tue-Sat) A fun place to watch the fishmongers sell their daily seafood wares to the restaurateurs and more besides.

Catedral de São Domingos
Cathedral

(www.paroquiagloria.org) Formerly part of a Dominican convent, with the Manueline stone cross of Saint Domingo displayed within. The facade has two pairs of unusual

Where to Stay

Aveiro has a reasonable selection of rooms to cater to all budgets, though very few are high-end. Things can get crowded during summer holidays; in the winter months you might feel like you have Aveiro to yourself. Hotels and guest houses are pretty spread out around the town, though there's a greater concentration north of the town centre than south of the Canal Central. The town's premier digs are at the Hotel Aveiro Palace, an upmarket affair overlooking the main bridge in the very heart of the action and a few steps from the *moliceiros*.

Hotel Aveiro Palace
AGE FOTOSTOCK / ALAMY STOCK PHOTO ©

Doric pilasters. Note the three figures: Faith, Hope and Charity, along with the coat of arms of Infante D Pedro (the King's son).

Beaches
Beach

The surfing venues of **Praia da Barra** and **Costa Nova**, 13km west of Aveiro, are good for a day's outing. Prettier Costa Nova has a beachside street lined with cafes, kitsch gift shops and picturesque candy-striped cottages. Buses (€2.50/4 one way/return, hourly) go from Aveiro's Rua Clube dos Galitos.

Wilder and more remote is **Praia de São Jacinto**, on the northern side of the lagoon. The vast beach of dunes is a 1.5km walk from São Jacinto port, through a residential area at the back of town. Be sure to visit the interpretative centre (p211). Take a

Ovos Moles

Almost every cafe and *confeitaria* in town advertises *ovos moles*, a sticky-sweet egg-yolk-and-sugar blend encased in a crisp white wafer case. They are often sold by the kilo.

Ovos moles
FISCAL / GETTY IMAGES ©

bus from Aveiro to Forte da Barra (one way/return €2.50/4), where there is a ferry to São Jacinto (passenger/car return €3/5). Schedules for boats are at www.move aveiro.pt; bus schedules are at www.trans dev.pt. Drivers can also circumnavigate the lagoon and arrive from the north via Ovar, a much longer trip.

TOURS

Oficina do Doce   Food

(234 098 840; www.oficinadodoce.com; Rua João Mendonça 23; tours €2; 10am-7pm Jun-Sep, 10am-5pm Oct-May) Part living museum, part workshop, Oficina do Doce introduces visitors to Aveiro's proudest culinary tradition – *ovos moles:* eggy, sugary sweets originally developed by local nuns. You can watch as modern-day confectioners work their magic, or learn about the process first-hand by filling your own. Reserve your visit ahead (tours are 45 minutes) by visiting their premises, or via email.

Ecoria   Boating

(www.ecoria.pt; adult/child €8/4) Near the *turismo,* this is one of several canalside

operators offering 45-minute trips daily on *moliceiros* around the Ria, with departures subject to passenger numbers.

Viva a Ria   Boating

(969 008 687; www.vivaaria.com; adult/child €8/4) Offers trips in *moliceiros* on the Ria; also arranges trips to the Oficina do Doce (though you can arrange these directly).

O Cicerone   Walking

(234 094 074; www.o-cicerone-tour.com; from per person €22.50) In summer, O Cicerone leads various (half- and full-day) tours in Aveiro and surrounds.

EATING

A Peixaria   Seafood €€

(234 331 165; www.restauranteapeixaria. pt; Rua Mestre Jorge Pestana, São Jacinto; mains €14-18, fish per kg €30-60; noon-3pm & 7-10pm Tue-Sun) A block back from the waterfront in São Jacinto, this no-frills family restaurant has the best fish in town and, many say, the region. There's always a big variety of Atlantic species, simply and deliciously done – try the eel stew, too.

Tasca Palhuça   Portuguese €

(Rua Antónia Rodrigues 28; daily plate half-portion €7; hours vary Sun & Mon) As '*tasca*-like' and genuine as they come, this place is largely shielded from tourists due to its side-street location. We think it's great – the type of place where clients have stuck to their (regular) seats longer than the tiles have been glued to the walls. The cuisine is meaty, fishy and plentiful. This is the place to try *caldeirada de enguias* (eel stew) for two (€20).

Maré Cheia   Seafood €€

(Rua José Rabumba 8-12; fish per kg €30-60; lunch & dinner Thu-Tue) *Maré cheia* means 'high tide' in Portuguese, but '*cheia*' (full) applies equally to this popular seafood eatery, complete with 'meet your meal' fish tanks. You'll often have to elbow your way through a crowd of locals just

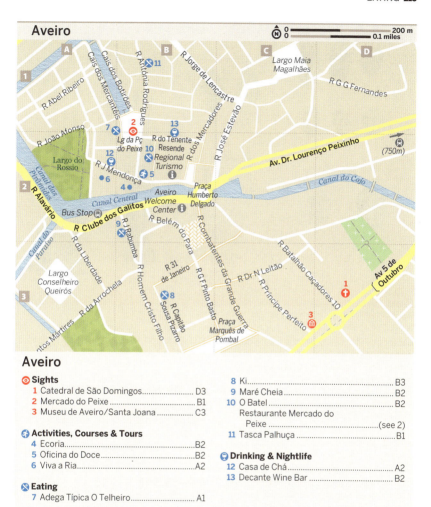

Aveiro

to get your name on the waiting list. It's a great place to try the local *enguias* (eels), served fried, grilled or *caldeiradas* (stewed).

Ki
Vegetarian €

(www.kimacrobiotico.com; Rua Capitão Sousa Pizarro 15; meals €8; ☉10am-6pm Mon-Fri; ☝) Vegetarians, your prayers have been answered. This small, vegan-focused spot tucked away in a street in a quiet part of

town offers a different set plate daily, plus soup and tea. Desserts cost an extra €3. Nothing from animals is used; everything is *vegan-licious*.

Adega Típica O Telheiro
Portuguese €

(☎234 429 473; Largo da Praça do Peixe 20-21; mains €7-9; ☉noon-3.30pm & 7.30-11pm Tue-Sun) A charismatic old-style place with hanging curios and rather nifty stools at the

African art at the Aliança Underground Museum

bar for comfier eating (also a great spot to sit if dining solo). The food is reliably tasty, with cheap daily specials and abundant doses of fish and grilled meat.

O Batel   Portuguese €€
(Travessa Tenente Resende 21; fish per kg €30-60; ⏱lunch & dinner Mon-Sat, lunch Sun) This narrow, nautically themed restaurant in a small alley is worth tracking down. Its good-value daily specials (€7.50) are backed up by a great-quality seafood-heavy menu with some innovative touches. Service is professional and friendly.

Restaurante
Mercado do Peixe   Portuguese €€
(☎234 383 511; http://mercadopeixeaveiro. pt; Largo da Praça do Peixe; mains €12-20; ⏱noon-3pm & 7.30-11pm Tue-Sat, noon-3pm Sun) Perched above the city's homely fish market, this industrial-chic restaurant has large windows overlooking the canal and the adjacent square. The seafood is good, and low-priced lunch specials Monday to Friday include homemade bread, soup and a main course.

🍷 DRINKING & NIGHTLIFE

A big student population and summer holiday crowds make for some raucous nightlife. Action radiates from Largo da Praça do Peixe, with several places clustered on Rua do Tenente Resende.

Casa de Chá   Bar
(www.casadechaartenova.com; Rua Dr Barbosa Magalhães 9; ⏱9.30am-2am Tue-Fri, noon-2am Sat, noon-10pm Sun; 🛜) In the town's most striking art nouveau building, this casual cafe-bar has a fine range of tea and infusions and livens up at night with excellent *caipirinhas*, Friday night DJs and a perky summer scene.

Decante Wine Bar   Wine Bar
(Rua do Tenente Resende 28; ⏱5pm-late) People congregate at the streetside tables to sip wine during the early evening, then move inside for live music most nights, including

everything from Latin rhythms, rock and
blues to jazz and world music.

INFORMATION

TOURIST INFORMATION

Aveiro Welcome Center (☏234 377 761; www.
cm-aveiro.pt; Rua Clube dos Galitos 2; ☺9am-
6pm) Its helpfulness varies, although it can book
some excursions.

Regional Turismo (☏234 420 760; www.turismo
docentro.pt; Rua João Mendonça 8; ☺9am-8pm
Mon-Fri, 9am-6pm Sat & Sun Jun-Sep, 9am-1 &
2-6pm Oct-May) In an art-nouveau gem beside
the Canal Central; has some information on
Portugal's central region.

GETTING THERE & AWAY

Trains run from the modern station. Aveiro is
within Porto's *urbano* network, which means
there are commuter trains there at least every
half hour (€3.40, one hour); much pricier IC/
AP links (€11.70/14.20, 30 to 40 minutes)
are only slightly faster. There are also at least
hourly links to Coimbra (regional/intercity/AP
€5.25/11.70/14.20, 30 to 60 minutes) and several daily IC (€21.45, 2½ hours) and AP (€27.55,
two hours) trains to Lisbon.

Few long-distance buses terminate here –
there isn't even a bus station. Catch buses at the
stop on Rua Clube dos Galitos; many also stop at
the train station.

Rede Expresso (www.rede-expressos.pt)
has five to six daily services to/from Lisbon
(€16, three to four hours) and Coimbra (€6, 45
minutes).

GETTING AROUND

Loja BUGA (Bicicleta de Utilização Gratuita de
Aveiro; www.moveaveiro.pt; Praça do Mercado
2; ☺9am-6pm Mon-Fri, 10am-1pm & 2-6pm Sat
& Sun) provides bikes for use within the town

Worth a Trip

Between Aveiro and Coimbra, in the
village of Sangalhos in the Bairrada
wine-producing region, **Aliança Underground Museum** (☏916 482 226, 234 732
045; www.alianca.pt; Rua do Comércio 444,
Sangalhos; €3; ☺90min visits 10am, 11.30am,
2.30pm, 4pm) is part *adega* (winery), part
repository of an eclectic, enormous and
top-quality art and artefact collection.
Under the winery, vast vaulted chambers hold sparkling wine, barrels of
maturing *aguardente* (a distilled spirit),
and a series of galleries displaying a
huge range of objects.

The highlight is at the beginning: a
superb collection of African sculpture,
ancient ceramics and masks, but you'll
also be taken by the spectacular miner-
al and fossil collection and the beauty
of some of the spaces. Other pieces
include *azulejos* (hand-painted tiles)
and quirky animals by former ceramics
company Bordallo Pinheiro (still an icon
in Portugal), plus an upstairs gallery
devoted to India.

The downside is that you don't have
time to linger at leisure and there's no
information on individual pieces. Phone
ahead to book your visit, which can
be in English and includes a glass of
sparkling wine.

limits, all for free. Bike quality can vary a bit.
Leave an ID such as your driver's licence or
passport.

Catch buses to the coast at the stop on Rua
Clube dos Galitos (€1.90, or €9.40 for a 10-trip
ticket). It's an easy 15-minute walk southwest
from the train station into town.

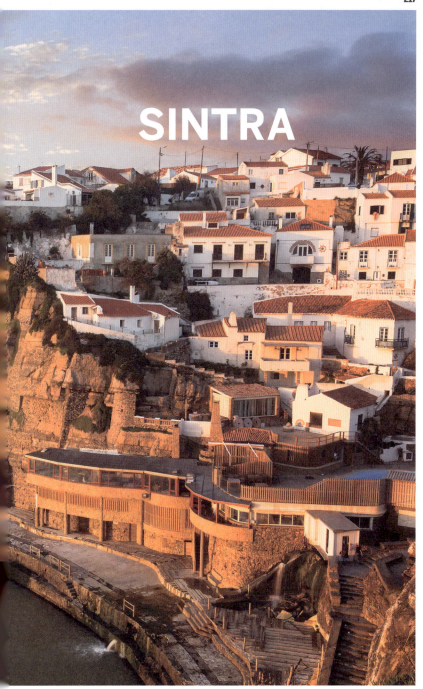

SINTRA

In this Chapter

Sintra at a Glance...

With its rippling mountains, dewy forests thick with ferns and lichen, exotic gardens and glittering palaces, Sintra is like a page torn from a fairy tale. Its Unesco World Heritage–listed centre, Sintra-Vila, is dotted with pastel-hued manors folded into luxuriant hills that roll down to the blue Atlantic.

Celts worshipped their moon god here, the Moors built a precipitous castle and 18th-century Portuguese royals swanned around its dreamy gardens. Even Lord Byron waxed lyrical about Sintra's charms: 'Lo! Cintra's glorious Eden intervenes, in variegated maze of mount and glen', which inspired his epic poem Childe Harold's Pilgrimage.

Sintra in Two Days

Two days in Sintra is just enough to get a taste of its grand buildings. Start with the **Castelo dos Mouros** (p220) on day one, followed by the **Palácio Nacional de Sintra** (p220) on day two, perhaps squeezing in the **Palácio Nacional da Pena** (p221) in between.

Sintra in Four Days

Four days allows you to explore some of the lesser-known attractions of Sintra such as the **Convento dos Capuchos** (p222), the **Museu das Artes de Sintra** (p222) and the **Quinta da Regaleira** (p223).

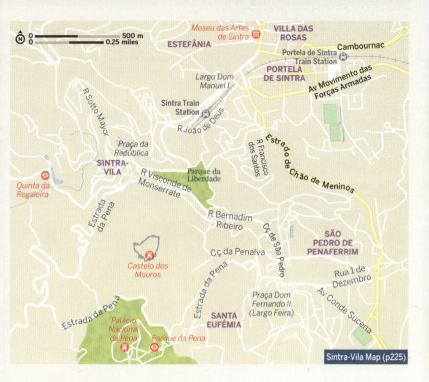

N
0 ____ 500 m
0 ____ 0.25 miles

Museu das Artes de Sintra

VILLA DAS ROSAS

ESTEFÂNIA

Portela de Sintra Train Station

PORTELA DE SINTRA

Cambournac

Av Movimento das Forças Armadas

Largo Dom Manuel I

R Sotto Mayor

Sintra Train Station

R João de Deus

Praça da República

SINTRA-VILA

R Visconde de Monserrate

Parque da Liberdade

R Francisco dos Santos

Estrada de Chão de Meninos

Quinta da Regaleira

Estrada da Pena

R Bernadim Ribeiro

Cç de São Pedro

SÃO PEDRO DE PENAFERRIM

Cç da Penalva

Castelo dos Mouros

Estrada da Pena

Rua 1 de Dezembro

Av Conde Sucena

Praça Dom Fernando II (Largo Feira)

SANTA EUFÉMIA

Estrada da Pena

Palácio Nacional da Pena

Parque da Pena

Sintra-Vila Map (p225)

Arriving in Sintra

Sintra Train Station Both buses and trains arrive here. If arriving by train, go to the last stop – Sintra – from where it's a pleasant 1km walk (or short bus ride) into the village.

Sleeping

It's worth staying overnight, as Sintra has some magical guest houses, from quaint villas to lavish manors. Book ahead in summer.

Anywhere you choose in and around Sintra will be quiet. There's a dense concentration of accommodation in the village itself as well as around the train station. Other options are dotted around the area, with many affording wonderful views of the wooded hills.

Castelo dos Mouros

SAIKO3P / SHUTTERSTOCK ©

Palaces & Castles

There's so much to see in Sintra it can be difficult to know where to start. Here we give you the low-down on the big four sights.

Great For...

☑ Don't Miss

The Chalet da Condessa d'Edla, an often overlooked Alpine-inspired cottage commissioned by King Ferdinand II.

Castelo dos Mouros

Soaring 412m above sea level, this mist-enshrouded ruined **castle** (www.parques desintra.pt; adult/child €8/6.50; ⊙10am-6pm) looms high above the surrounding forest. When the clouds peel away, the vistas over Sintra's palace-dotted hill and dale, across to the glittering Atlantic are – like the climb – breathtaking.

The 10th-century Moorish castle's dizzying ramparts stretch across the mountain ridges and past moss-clad boulders the size of small buses.

Palácio Nacional de Sintra

The star of Sintra-Vila is this **palace** (www. parquesdesintra.pt; Largo Rainha Dona Amélia; adult/child €10/8.50; ⊙9.30am-7pm, shorter hours in low season), with its iconic twin conical chimneys and lavish interior. The interi-

Palácio Nacional da Pena

DANITA DELIMONT / GETTY IMAGES ©

ⓘ Need to Know

Buses run to many of the places of interest. Ask at the tourist office about services.

✕ Take a Break

Casa Piriquita (p224) is a convenient spot for a quick bite near the Palácio Nacional de Sintra.

★ Top Tip

Go early in the day midweek to escape the worst of the crowds.

Palácio Nacional da Pena

Rising from a thickly wooded peak, this **palace** (www.parquesdesintra.pt; combined ticket with Parque Nacional da Pena adult/child €14/12.50; ⊙10am-6pm) is a wacky confection of onion domes, Moorish keyhole gates, writhing stone snakes and crenellated towers in pinks and lemons. It is considered the greatest expression of 19th-century romanticism in Portugal.

Ferdinand of Saxe Coburg-Gotha, the artist husband of Queen Maria II, and later Dom Ferdinand II, commissioned Prussian architect Ludwig von Eschwege in 1840 to build the Moresque-Manueline epic. Inspired by Stolzenfels and Rheinstein castles and Potsdam's Babelsberg Palace, a flourish of imagination and colour commenced.

The eclectic, extravagant interior is equally unusual, brimming with precious Meissen porcelain, Portuguese-style furniture, *trompe l'oeil* murals and Dom Carlos' unfinished nudes of buxom nymphs.

There are daily guided tours at 2.30pm.

or is a mix of Moorish and Manueline styles, with arabesque courtyards, barley-twist columns and 15th- and 16th-century geometric *azulejos* (hand-painted tiles) that figure among Portugal's oldest.

Of Moorish origins, the palace was first expanded by Dom Dinis (1261–1325), enlarged by João I in the 15th century (when the kitchens were built), then given a Manueline twist by Manuel I in the following century.

Highlights include the octagonal Sala dos Cisnes (Swan Room), adorned with frescoes of 27 gold-collared swans; and the Sala das Pegas (Magpie Room), with its ceiling emblazoned with magpies.

Other standouts are the wooden Sala dos Brasões, bearing the shields of 72 leading 16th-century families, the shipshape Galleon Room and the Palatine chapel featuring an Islamic mosaic floor.

⊙ SIGHTS

Convento dos Capuchos Monastery

(Capuchin Monastery; ☏219 237 300; www.
parquesdesintra.pt; adult/child €7/5.50; ⊙10am-
8pm) Hidden in the woods is this bewitch-
ingly hobbit-hole-like convent, which was
originally built in 1560 to house friars who
lived in incredibly cramped conditions, their
tiny cells having low, narrow doors. Byron
mocked the monastery in his poem *Childe
Harold's Pilgrimage*, referring to recluse
Honorius who spent a staggering 36 years
here (before dying at age 95 in 1596).

It's often nicknamed the Cork Convent,
because its minuscule cells are lined with
cork. Visiting here is an *Alice in Wonderland*
experience as you squeeze through to
explore the warren of cells, chapels, kitchen
and cavern. The monks lived a simple,
touchingly well-ordered life in this idyllic yet
spartan place, hiding up until 1834 when
it was abandoned after all religious orders
were abolished.

You can walk here – the monastery is
7.3km from Sintra-Vila (5.1km from the
turn-off to Parque da Pena) along a remote,
wooded road. There is no bus connection
to the convent (taxis charge around €35
return; arrange for a pickup ahead). Well-
worth-it audio guides are available for €3.

Museu das Artes de Sintra Museum

(MU.SA; www.cm-sintra.pt; Av Heliodoro Salgado;
adult/child €1/free; ⊙10am-8pm Tue-Fri, 2-8pm
Sat-Sun) This new museum took over the
former Museu de Arte Moderna space in
2014 and features a small and manageable
collection of contemporary and modern
art, 80% or so of which is dedicated to local
works. The permanent collection features
some of Portugal's best-known artists,
most notably painters Columbano Bordalo
Pinheiro and António Carneiro and sculptor
Dorita de Castel-Branco.

Temporary exhibitions run the gamut
from war photography to abstract art.
Permanent highlights include Carneiro's
Maria Josefina; Maria do Céu Crispim's *Can
You See Me?* (made of nails); and several
paintings from various artists of Sintra's
18th-century glory days.

Parque da Pena

Palácio & Parque de Monserrate
Palace

(www.parquesdesintra.pt; adult/child €8/6.50; ⊙10am-6pm) At the centre of a lush, 30-hectare park, a manicured lawn sweeps up to this whimsical, Moorish-Gothic-Indian *palácio*, the 19th-century romantic folly of English millionaire Sir Francis Cook. The wild and rambling gardens were created in the 18th century by wealthy English merchant Gerard de Visme, then enlarged by landscape painter William Stockdale (with help from London's Kew Gardens).

Its wooded hillsides bristle with exotic foliage, from Chinese weeping cypress to dragon trees and Himalayan rhododendrons. Seek out the Mexican garden nurturing palms, yuccas and agaves, and the bamboo-fringed Japanese garden abloom with camellias.

The park is 3.5km west of Sintra-Vila.

Parque da Pena
Gardens

(☏219 237 300; www.parquesdesintra.pt; adult/child €7.50/6.50, combined ticket with Palácio Nacional da Pena €14/12.50; ⊙10am-6pm) Nearly topped by King Ferdinand II's whimsical Palácio Nacional da Pena (only Cruz Alta, at 528m, is higher), these romantic gardens are filled with tropical plants, huge redwoods and fern trees, camellias, rhododendrons and lakes (note the castle-shaped duck houses for web-footed royalty!). Save by buying a combined ticket if you want to visit Palácio Nacional da Pena (p221) too.

While the crowds descend on the palace, another less-visited but fascinating site within the park is the *Snow White & the Seven Dwarfs*-evoking **Chalet da Condessa d'Edla** (adult/child €9.50/8.50), an Alpine-inspired summer getaway cottage commissioned by King Ferdinand II and his future second wife, Elise Hensler (the Countess of Edla).

Buses to the **park entrance** (www.parquesdesintra.pt) leave from Sintra train station and near Palácio Nacional de Sintra, among other spots around town.

 Quinta da Regaleira

This magical **villa** (www.regaleira.pt; Rua Barbosa du Bocage; adult/child €6/3; ⊙10am-8pm high season, shorter hours in low season) and gardens is a neo-Manueline extravaganza, dreamed up by Italian opera-set designer, Luigi Manini, under the orders of Brazilian coffee tycoon, António Carvalho Monteiro, aka 'Monteiro dos Milhões' ('Moneybags Monteiro'). The villa is surprisingly homely inside, despite its ferociously carved fireplaces, frescoes and Venetian-glass mosaics. Keep an eye out for mythological and Knights Templar symbols.

The playful gardens are fun to explore – footpaths wriggle through the dense foliage to follies, fountains, grottoes, lakes and underground caverns. All routes seem to eventually end at the revolving stone door leading to the initiation well, **Poço Iniciático**, plunging some 27m. You walk down the nine-tiered spiral (three by three – three being the magic number) to mysterious hollowed-out underground galleries, lit by fairy lights.

Poço Iniciático
DALE JOHNSON / 500PX ©

A taxi costs around €10 one-way. The steep, zigzagging walk through pine and eucalyptus woods from Sintra-Vila is around 3km to 4km.

Sweet Sintra

Sintra is famous for its luscious sweeties. **Fábrica das Verdadeiras Queijadas da Sapa** (www.facebook. com/queijadasdasapa; Alameda Volta do Duche 12; pastries from €0.85; ⊘9am-6pm Tue-Fri, 9.30am-6.30pm Sat & Sun) has been fattening up royalty since 1756 with bite-sized *queijadas* – crisp pastry shells filled with a marzipan-like mix of fresh cheese, sugar, flour and cinnamon. Since 1952, **Casa Piriquita** (www. facebook.com/pastelaria.piriquita; Rua das Padarias 1-5; travesseiros €1.30; ⊘9am-9pm Thu-Tue) has been tempting locals with another sweet dream: the *travesseiro* (pillow), light puff pastry turned, rolled and folded seven times, then filled with delicious almond-and-egg-yolk cream and lightly dusted with sugar.

Queijadas
ATLANTICO PRESS / ALAMY STOCK PHOTO ©

😊 ACTIVITIES

Sintra is a terrific place to get out and stride, with waymarked **hiking trails** (look for red and yellow stripes) that corkscrew up into densely wooded hills strewn with giant boulders. Justifiably popular is the gentle 50-minute trek from Sintra-Vila to Castelo dos Mouros. You can continue to Palácio Nacional da Pena (another 15 minutes). From here you can ascend Serra de Sintra's highest point, the 529m Cruz Alta (High Cross), named after its 16th-century cross, with amazing views all over Sintra. It's possible to continue on foot to São

Pedro de Penaferrim and loop back to Sintra-Vila. You can print off maps and info on various hiking trails from the municipality's website under 'Percursos Pedestres' (www. cm-sintra.pt).

Horse riding is available in the Parque da Pena, from 30-minute teasers (€10) to six-hour excursions (€100).

MuitAventura   Adventure

(☑967 021 248; www.muitaventura.com; Rua Marquês Viana 31) This adventure outfitter has a regular schedule of organised activities, including mountain-biking, rappelling, jeep tours, trekking and night-time hikes. It's based in São Pedro.

Ozono Mais   Adventure

(☑219 619 927; www.ozonomais.com) Offers a variety of outdoor excursions, including canoeing, rafting, mountain-biking and jeep tours. Call ahead for times and prices.

🌀 TOURS

Sight Sintra   Vehicle Hire

(☑219 242 856; www.sightsintra.pt; Rua João de Deus; tour €35-45; ⊘10am-7pm) If you have limited time and you'd like to see some of the attractions beyond Sintra-Vila, Sight Sintra rents out tiny two-person buggies that guide you by GPS along one of three different routes. The most popular takes you to Castelo dos Mouros (p220) and Palácio Nacional da Pena (p221), among other places. It's located around the corner from the train station.

You can also create your own itinerary, and hire a buggy for €25 per hour.

Go2Sintra Tours   Cycling

(☑917 855 428; www.go2cintra.com; Av Dr Miguel Bombarda 37; ⊘10.30am-7pm) Offers highly recommended electric-bike tours (from €35) as well as eBike rental (take our word for it – you'll want the motorised option in Sintra!). A full day's rental with support starts at €30. Its office is across from the Sintra train station, inside the SintraCan shop.

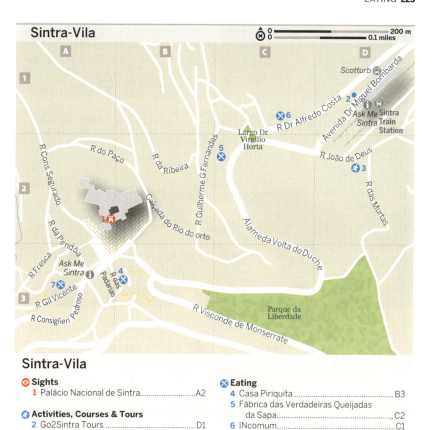

Sintra-Vila

⊗ EATING

Tulhas — Portuguese €€

(Rua Gil Vicente 4; mains €10-18; ⊗noon-11pm, to 10pm winter; ⊛) This converted grain warehouse is dark, tiled and quaint, with wrought-iron chandeliers and a relaxed, cosy atmosphere. It's rightfully renowned for its *bacalhau com natas* (creamy bécha-mel with shredded cod, served au gratin) but the tasty *arroz de pato* (duck rice) is worth your consideration as well.

Nau Palatina — Portuguese €€

(⌂219 240 962; www.facebook.com/barnaupa-latina; Calçada São Pedro 18; tapas €5.50-9.90;

⊗6pm-midnight Wed-Sat, 3-9pm Sun; ⊛) Sintra's friendliest and most-welcoming restaurant is a travel-highlight-reel star-in-the-making. Congenial owner Zé's creative tapas are as slightly off-centre as his location, a well-worth-it 1km walk from the centre. Spice Route undertones are weaved throughout the small but tasty menu of small (€1.50) and medium (from €5.50) tidbits strongly forged from local and regional ingredients.

Paired with an excellent house Setúbal red and Zé's convivial nature, you have yourself an evening to remember.

Cruz Alta (p224)

INcomum   Portuguese €€

(☎219 243 719; www.incomumbyluissantos.pt; Rua Dr Alfredo Costa 22; mains €14.50-15.50; ☺noon-midnight; 🛜) Chef Luis Santos is shaking up the scene in Sintra with his modern upgrades to Portuguese cuisine, served amid the muted greys and greens of his synchronic dining room. INcomum quickly established itself as the anti-traditional choice among serious foodies, first by dangling an unbeatable €9.50, three-course lunch carrot, then by letting the food seal the deal.

The Swiss-trained chef does memorable things with chestnuts (cream of chestnut soup, pumpkin cheesecake with chestnut confit, chestnut puree alongside duck magret), but nothing that emerged from his kitchen was underwhelming. A holiday highlight.

DRINKING & NIGHTLIFE

Saloon Cintra   Bar

(www.facebook.com/barsaloon.cintra; Av do Movimento das Forças Armadas 5, Portela da Sintra; ☺8pm-2am Mon-Fri, from 3pm Sat-Sun; 🛜) Sintra's best bar isn't in the Vila, but that shouldn't stop seasoned drinkers from checking it out. A potpourri of antiques and Portuguese bric-a-brac hovering over numerous mismatched vintage sofas makes for an atmospheric spot to take in the Belgian-heavy beer list (including McChouffe on tap), good cocktails and a cool local crowd. It's 700m east of Sintra station.

✪ ENTERTAINMENT

Taverna dos
Trovadores   Live Music

(☎219 233 548; www.tavernadostrovadores.pt; Praça Dom Fernando II 18; ☺noon-4pm & 7pm-2am Mon-Sat, to 4pm Sun) This atmospheric restaurant and bar features live music (folk and acoustic) on Friday and Saturday nights – an institution that's been around for more than two decades. Concerts run from 11.30pm to 2am. Nearby, the new Sabores de Sintra offers dinner and fado. It's located in São Pedro de Penaferrim.

 INFORMATION

Ask Me Sintra (Turismo; ☎219 231 157; www. askmelisboa.com/sintra; Praça da República 23; ⊙9.30am-6pm) Near the centre of Sintra-Vila, Turismo de Lisboa's helpful multilingual office has expert insight on Sintra and the surrounding areas, as well as the interactive 'Myths & Legends' presentation (€4.50). However, keep in mind this is a member-driven organisation, which only promotes those who pay. There's also a small **train station** (☎211 932 545; www. askmelisboa.com/sintra; Sintra train station; ⊙10am-noon & 2.30-6pm) branch, often overrun by arriving visitors.

 GETTING THERE & AWAY

Scotturb (☎219 230 381; www.scotturb.com; Av Dr Miguel Bombarda 59; ⊙9am-6pm) buses 403 and 417 leave regularly for Cascais (€4.10, one hour). Most services leave from **Sintra train station** (which is *estação* on timetables) and travel via Portela de Sintra. Scotturb's useful information office, open 9am to 1pm and 2pm to 8pm, is opposite the station.

Comboios de Portugal (www.cp.pt) trains (€2.15, 40 minutes) run every 15 minutes between Sintra and Lisbon's Rossio station.

 GETTING AROUND

Various buses run to and around Sintra. Ask at the tourist office for details. Taxis are available at the train station or opposite the Sintra Vila post office.

Festival de Sintra

Usually held in May or June, the three-week-long Festival de Sintra features classical recitals, ballet and modern dance, world music and multimedia events, plus concerts for kids.

Palácio Nacional de Sintra (p220)
SEAN PAVONE / ALAMY STOCK PHOTO ©

Driving can be a challenge on the narrow roads around Sintra. Parking is limited around town and there are very few spaces at Palácio Nacional de Pena, so it's better to avoid driving there in busy times. For parking near town, there's a free car park below Sintra-Vila; follow the signs by the *câmara municipal* (town hall) in Estefânia. Alternatively, park at Portela Interface and take the bus.

On weekends, Sintra's restored electric tram, the **Elétrico de Sintra** (www.cm-sintra. pt; one-way €3; ⊙Fri-Sun 8 May-21 Jun) offers access to the coast, running from Rua Alves Roçadas near Portela de Sintra train station, arriving at Praia das Maçãs 45 minutes later. Trams depart hourly from 10.20am to 5pm from Friday to Sunday (11.55am to 6.45pm Saturday and Sunday). The last tram back leaves the beach at 5.45pm during the week and 6pm on weekends.

ÓBIDOS

Óbidos at a Glance...

Surrounded by a classic crenellated wall, Óbidos' gorgeous historic centre is a labyrinth of cobblestoned streets and flower-bedecked, whitewashed houses livened up with dashes of vivid yellow and blue paint. It's a delightful place to pass an afternoon, but there are plenty of reasons to stay overnight, as there's excellent accommodation including a hilltop castle now converted into one of Portugal's most luxurious pousadas (upmarket hotels).

Hill-town aficionados looking to savour Óbidos' 'lost in time' qualities may find the main street ridiculously touristy, especially on weekends and during festivals. There are pretty bits outside the walls too.

Óbidos in One Day

With just a day to spare in Óbidos, exploring the old centre should be your top priority. The town's top sights are without doubt the Castelo, the walls and the aqueduct but the **Igreja de Santa Maria** (p233), the **Museu Municipal** (p233) and the **Santuário do Senhor da Pedra** (p233) are also worth a visit.

Óbidos in Two Days

With a second day to fill in Óbidos, perhaps head to the coast to catch some rays at Foz do Arelho. Alternatively soak up the atmosphere of this wonderful spot, dipping in and out of the boutiques, bookshops and cafes as you go.

Arriving in Óbidos

Bus stop On the main road just outside Porta da Vila.

Train station Handles trains to Lisbon. The station is located outside the north-eastern section of the castle walls. It's a pretty but uphill walk to town.

Sleeping

Although touristy, Óbidos has an excellent array of accommodations, from an atmospheric *pousada* to cosy guest houses and some cutting-edge boutique hotels.

Santuário do Senhor da Pedra

DAVIDIONUT / GETTY IMAGES ©

Óbidos' Historic Centre

Aimless wandering is a delight in walled Óbidos, but the town does have some very worthwhile attractions. You'll need to be fit as there's a lot of climbing involved.

Great For...

☑ Don't Miss

It's possible to walk the entire circle of the town's walls.

Castelo, Walls and Aqueduct

If you've got the legs for it, you can take a stroll around the unprotected *muro* (wall) for uplifting views over the town and surrounding countryside. The walls date from Moorish times though they have been restored since; the *castelo* (castle) itself is one of Dom Dinis' 13th-century creations. It's a stern edifice, with lots of towers, battlements and big gates. It was converted into a palace in the 16th century (some Manueline touches add levity) but today it serves as a deluxe hotel, the **Pousada do Castelo** (☎262 955 080; www.pousadas.pt; d/ste from €220/350; ✳🛜).

The impressive 3km-long aqueduct, southeast of the main gate, dates from the 16th century. Unlike other aqueducts in Portugal, Óbidos' is fully intact and in

Óbidos town centre

remarkably serviceable condition. It once provided water to the town's fountains as well as drinking water to its residents.

Igreja de Santa Maria

The town's elegant main **church** (Praça de Santa Maria; 9.30am-12.30pm & 2.30-7pm summer, to 5pm winter), near the northern end of Rua Direita, stands out for its interior, with a wonderful painted ceiling and walls done up in beautiful blue-and-white 17th-century *azulejos* (hand-painted tiles). Paintings by the renowned 17th-century painter Josefa de Óbidos are to the right of the altar. There's a fine 16th-century Renaissance tomb on the left, probably carved by French sculptor Nicolas Chanterène. The church is closed on Mondays.

❶ Need to Know

Óbidos' sights do not charge admission.

✕ Take a Break

Ja!mon Ja!mon (p236) is a great place for a bite to eat at lunchtime.

★ Top Tip

Take care with children on the walls as many sections are unprotected.

Museu Municipal

Located in an 18th-century manor house just next to Igreja de Santa Maria, the town's museum (Solar da Praça de Santa Maria; 262 955 500; 10am-1pm & 2-6pm Tue-Sun) houses a small collection of paintings spanning several centuries. The highlight is a haunting portrait by Josefa de Óbidos, *Faustino das Neves* (1670), remarkable for its dramatic use of light and shade.

Santuário do Senhor da Pedra

Below town this imposing, if a little ramshackle, church (Largo do Santuário; 9am-12.30pm & 2.30-7pm Tue-Sun May-Sep, to 5pm Oct-Apr) is an 18th-century baroque gem in need of some tender loving care. It's worth the stroll down here for the unusual hexagonal interior; in the altar is the stone sculpture of Christ crucified that gives the place its name.

HISTORY

When Dom Dinis first showed Óbidos to his wife Dona Isabel in 1228, it must have already been a pretty sight because she fell instantly in love with the place. The king decided to make the town a wedding gift to his queen, initiating a royal tradition that lasted until the 19th century.

Any grace it had in 1228 must be credited to the Moors, who had laid out the streets and had only recently abandoned the strategic heights. The Moors had chased out the Visigoths, who in turn had evicted the Romans, who also had a fortress here.

Until the 15th century Óbidos overlooked the sea; the bay gradually silted up, leaving the town landlocked.

◎ SIGHTS

Buddha Eden   Sculpture, Gardens
(www.buddhaeden.com; Carvalhal; €3; ⊙9am-6pm) What have the Taliban got to do with a rural winery 12km south of Óbidos? Well, when they blew up the Buddhas of Bami-yan in Afghanistan in 2001, the millionaire art collector José Berardo was so incensed at the wanton destruction of culture that he decided to do something to balance it out and created a large sculpture park on the grounds of his winery. The result is an astonishing sight, with monumental Buddhist statues standing proud above the cork trees, a phalanx of terracotta warriors looking down on a duck-filled lake, modern contemporary sculpture among the vines, and a little tourist train (adult/child €3/ free) doing the rounds for the sore-of-foot. It's a great place to relax, and there's a cafe here, as well as a wine shop. To make a day of it, there's an appealing restaurant in the nearby village – **Mãe d'Água** (www.restaurantemaedagua.com; Rua 13 Maio 26, Sobral do Parelhão; mains €11-20; ⊙noon-4pm & 7pm-late Tue-Sun) does confident modern Portuguese fare in a contemporary setting within a noble old building.

To get here, take the A8 motorway south from Óbidos and exit at junction 12, then follow signs for Carvalhal.

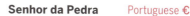

🍴 EATING

After years of catering to tourist crowds, Óbidos is coming into its own. There are a couple of decent eateries, including the contrasting, but equally delightful Ja!mon Ja!mon (p236) and Tasca Torta (p235). The larger hotels, including the Pousada do Castelo (p232), have good, if pricey, dining rooms.

Tasca Torta   International €€

(☎262 958 000; Rua Direita 81; mains €9-15; ⏱12.30-2.30pm & 7-9.30pm Wed-Mon) A pleasant hum, appealing aromas and colourful plates sum up this stylish, contemporary spot. There's a cosy line of tables down one side, a kitchen on the other and black-and-white photos of Portuguese fishermen. As for the cuisine? Everything from delicious salmon lasagne to a trilogy of octopuses. Delicious starters are arranged on a slate plate.

It's very much the 'in' place but with good reason.

Senhor da Pedra   Portuguese €

(Largo do Santuário; mains €6-9; ⏱10am-10pm) Behind the striking church of Senhor da Pedra below town, this simple white-tiled eatery (the one on the right as you look at the row of restaurants) is a recommended place to try low-priced authentic Portuguese cuisine. It's a classic affair with mum in the kitchen and dad on the tables. Don't expect fast service.

The name isn't signed – it just says 'Snack Bar', but if these are snacks, we'd hate to see what they consider a full meal. Serves among the cheapest desserts in Portugal (€1.60 for a chocolate mousse and other sugary standards).

Petrarum Domus   Portuguese €€

(☎262 959 620; www.petrarumdomus.com; Rua Direita; mains €9-19; ⏱noon-3.30pm & 7-9.45pm) Amid age-old stone walls, Petrarum has been churning out the same old menu for a while now. Think hearty dishes such as pork with mushrooms, mixed seafood sautés and several *bacalhau* (dried salt-cod) plates. There are plainer pastas for those wanting a change of Portuguese fare.

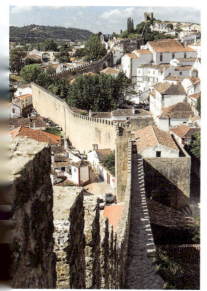

> ### ☆ Literary Óbidos
>
> In recent years Óbidos has been reinventing itself as a literary centre: quirky and very atmospheric, themed bookshops abound and in 2015 it held Folio, its first literary festival, intended to be an annual event.

From left: Igreja de Santa Maria; Óbidos' fortified walls; Bookshop in the old market

Ja!mon Ja!mon   Portuguese €

(☎916 208 162; mains €5; ⏰10am-late Tue-Sun) Just outside Porta da Vila, before the tourism office, is this cute little eatery. Six tables are crammed into a quaint room, a former *padeiria* (bakery) and fresh bread is baked in the woodfired oven (along with other dishes). Each day brings a small selection of daily specials. We suggest just sitting back and letting the experience happen.

With the cheery Andre and his family at the helm, the hospitality is oh-so Portuguese (read happy and generous). Come with time. And for a good time.

Comendador
Silva   Modern Portuguese €€

(☎262 955 360; Rua Padre Nunes Tavares 6; mains €10-20; ⏰12.30-2.30pm & 7.30-10pm Tue-Sun; 🔊) Attached to the Casa das Senhoras Rainhas hotel, this elegant restaurant is named after the Brazilian owner who took over the establishment. Serves up Portuguese dishes with a gourmet touch, including good organic pork dishes

and *polvo a lagareiro* (octopus and potato; €16.50).

Alcaide   Portuguese €€

(☎262 959 220; Rua Direita 60; mains €12-17; ⏰noon-3pm & 7-10pm) Holding a place in history as Óbidos' first restaurant, this upstairs spot has windows overlooking the town and features creative dishes such as *requinte de bacalhau* (cod with cheese, chestnuts and apples). It's better than most of the main-street options.

🍷 DRINKING & NIGHTLIFE

Óbidos has some atmospheric places for a late-night tipple.

Bar Cave Do Vale
(Toupeiro)   Bar

(Rua Dom João de Ornelas; ⏰7pm-2am Mon-Fri, 4pm-2am Sat & Sun) A true medieval drinking den (it's an underground 'cave') with dripping wax and stone walls. A fun bar on this street and as a place for a post-meal snifter. They serve their own '*toupeiro*' (a fruit and wine mix).

Alfresco dining space, Óbidos

Troca Tintos   Bar

(Rua Dom João de Ornelas; ⊙6pm-2am Mon-Sat)
A fado shawl and guitar on the wall sets
the precedent for what's to come in this
intimate space, a former chapel: a warm,
friendly wine bar serving up a good selection of Portuguese wines, *petiscos* (tapas;
€3 to €15) and live music, including fado on
Monday evenings.

At other times, guests can choose what
music plays.

INFORMATION

Turismo (☑262 959 231; www.obidos.pt;
⊙9.30am-7.30pm summer, to 6pm winter) Just
outside Porta da Vila, near the bus stop, with
helpful multilingual staff offering town brochures
and maps in five languages.

GETTING THERE & AWAY

BUS

Buses stop on the main road just outside
Porta da Vila. There are frequent departures for
Peniche (€3.15, 40 minutes) and hourly buses
on weekdays to Lisbon (€8.15, 65 minutes), plus
five buses on Saturday and Sunday.

CAR

There is a fee-charging car park just outside the
gate, while the one just across the road is free.

TRAIN

There are at least six daily trains to Lisbon
(€8.45 to €9.30, 2½ hours) mostly via connections at Mira Sintra-Meleças station on the
suburban Lisbon line.

 **Pousada
do Castelo**

One of Portugal's most unusual *pousadas*, **Pousada do Castelo** (☑262
955 080; www.pousadas.pt; d/ste from
€220/350; ❄☎) occupies the town's
forbidding 13th-century castle. The
rooms are within two sections – the
castle (traditional decor) and the attached building known as 'the cottage'
(more modern interiors). Reserve
ahead for the split-level rooms in the
two castle towers (warning: cosy, and
not for claustrophobes) – especially
the King D Dinis room, popular with
honeymooners.

Pousada do Castelo
NBAY PHOTOS / ALAMY STOCK PHOTO ©

SAGRES & CABO DE SÃO VICENTE

Sagres & Cabo de São Vicente at a Glance...

Overlooking some of the Algarve's most dramatic scenery, the small, elongated village of Sagres has an end-of-the-world feel with its sea-carved cliffs and empty, wind-whipped fortress high above the frothing ocean. Its appeal lies in its sense of isolation, plus access to some fine beaches. The village has a laid-back vibe and simple, cheery cafes and bars; it's become particularly popular in recent years with a surfing crowd.

Outside town, the striking cliffs of Cabo de São Vicente make for an enchanting visit. This is Europe's southwesternmost point, the last land America-bound sailors see as they head out into the Atlantic.

Sagres & Cabo do São Vicente in Two Days

The vast majority of visitors stay in Sagres, a place boasting some fine beaches. Spend your first day lounging around on the beach, heading to a seafood restaurant in the evening. On day two take a trip to Cabo do São Vicente to view one of the edges of the ancient world.

Sagres & Cabo de São Vicente in Four Days

Contact one of the local surfing companies, hire some gear and get out onto those rollers on day three. Day four could be spent exploring Sagres' huge **Fortaleza de Sagres** (p244) and hitting the surfer bars in the evening.

ALGARVE

Carrapateira

Praia do Amado

Bensafrim

Praia do Castelejo

Lagos

Almadena

Budens

Raposeira

Vila do Bispo

Luz

Burgau

Salema

Figueira

Parque Natural do Sudoeste Alentejano e Costa Vicentina

Praia da Figueira

Boca do Rio

Beliche

Praia do Martinhal

Cabo de São Vicente

Sagres

Ponta de Sagres

See Sagres Map (p245)

Caption

Arriving in Sagres

Bus stop The main bus stop for services to Cabo de São Vicente and Lagos is next to the tourist office.

Sleeping

Sagres has a few tourist hotels as well as private rooms and the odd B&B – things fill up here even off-season so booking ahead is often essential. Surfers often camp at special surf camps and campervans parked by the roadside are a common sight. The tourist office may be able to help with bookings.

Sagres fills up in summer, though it's marginally easier to find accommodation here than in the rest of the Algarve during high season, thanks in part to the number of informal 'hostels' and the private houses that advertise rooms or apartments. Doubles cost around €40, flats €45 to €80.

Lighthouse at Cabo de São Vicente

VENTURA / SHUTTERSTOCK ©

Experiencing Portugal's Southwest Tip

There's an end-of-the-world feel at the southwesternmost extremity of the Portuguese mainland. Beyond the high cliffs and pounding surf stretches the vast Atlântico.

Great For...

☑ Don't Miss

It's possible to hike from Sagres to Cabo de São Vicente along a clifftop path.

Sagres

Surfers and tourists pack out tiny Sagres when the sun is shining, the former to catch some of the monster waves tumbling off the seething Atlantic, the latter using the place as a base to explore this far-flung chunk of the Algarve. The beaches around the town are superb and draw big crowds from May to September. Other than that, Sagres has some good eating options and a row of funky surfer cafe-bars, characterful places to hang out in the evenings, even if you've never set foot on a board.

Cabo de São Vicente

Five kilometres from Sagres, Europe's southwesternmost point is a barren headland, the last piece of home that Portuguese sailors once saw as they launched into the unknown. It's a spectacular spot:

Canon, Fortaleza de Sagres (p244)

GKUNA / SHUTTERSTOCK ©

❶ Need to Know

Sagres is 33km west of Lagos. Cabo de São Vicente is 5km west of Sagres.

✕ Take a Break

Sagres has several restaurants and cafes. A Casínha (p247) in Sagres is a traditional spot for lunch.

★ Top Tip

Two buses run from Lagos to Cabo de São Vicente via Sagres.

launched Portugal's expansion into the Atlantic and the New World, is said to have founded a school of navigation, though the exact site is unknown. Many famous sea battles have taken place off the cape.

Surfing

Surfing is the reason many head down to Portugal's far southwest, most hoping to catch some of the curling waves that pound angrily against the beaches and cliffs. There's a great surfer vibe around the village, especially at night when weary, salt-encrusted surfers head out for some food and a few beers after a day riding the tide. There are several surfing schools and equipment hire centres in Sagres offering lessons for beginners and there's even a campsite set up specially for surfers. Other waterborn activities on offer include paddleboarding and off-shore wildlife spotting trips.

at sunset you can almost hear the hissing as the sun hits the sea. A red lighthouse houses the small but excellent Museu dos Faróis (p245).

A kilometre before reaching the lighthouse, you'll pass the **Fortaleza do Beliche**, built in 1632 on the site of an older fortress. The interior, once a hotel, is off limits, but you can descend a pretty pathway down to near the water. The sheltering walls here make for a more appealing picnic spot than the wind-whipped cape.

History of the Cape

The cape – a revered place even in the time of the Phoenicians and known to the Romans as Promontorium Sacrum – takes its present name from a Spanish priest martyred by the Romans. It was here that Henry the Navigator, the monarch who

◎ SIGHTS

Fortaleza de Sagres   Fort

(📞282 620 140; adult/child €3/1.50; ⊙9.30am-
6.30pm Apr, 9am-8pm May, Jun & Sep, 9am-
8.30pm Jul & Aug, 9am-5pm Oct-Mar) Blank,
hulking and forbidding, Sagres' fortress
offers breathtaking views over the sheer
cliffs and all along the coast to Cabo de São
Vicente. According to legend, this is where
Prince Henry the Navigator established
his navigation school and primed the early
Portuguese explorers. It's quite a large site,
so allow at least an hour to see everything.

Inside the gate is a huge, curious stone
pattern that measures 43m in diameter.
Named the **rosa dos ventos** (literally, a
pictorial representation of a compass), this
strange configuration is believed to be a
mariner's compass or a sundial of sorts.
Excavated in 1921, the paving may date
from Prince Henry's time but is more likely
to be from the 16th century.

The precinct's oldest buildings include a
cistern tower to the east, a house, and the
small, whitewashed, 16th-century **Igreja
de Nossa Senhora da Graça**, a simple

barrel-vaulted structure with a gilded
17th-century altarpiece. Take a closer look
at the tiled altar panels, which feature
elephants and antelopes.

Many of the gaps you will see between
buildings are the result of a 1960s spring
clean of 17th- and 18th-century ruins
that was organised to make way for a
reconstruction (later aborted) that was
to coincide with the 500th anniversary of
Henry's death.

It's a great walk around the perimeter
of the promontory, information boards
shedding light on the rich flora and fauna of
the area. Don't miss the limestone crevices
descending to the sea, or the labyrinth art
installation by Portugal's famous sculpture
architect Pancho Guedes. Near the southern end of the promontory is a **lighthouse**.
Death-defying anglers balance on the cliffs
below the walls, hoping to land bream or
sea bass.

At the time of research a huge, new and
incongruously 21st-century visitors centre
was being bolted together opposite the
entrance. This will contain a gift shop, an
exhibition centre and a cafe.

Rosa dos Ventos, Fortaleza de Sagres

Sagres

Museu dos Faróis   Museum

(adult/child €1.50/1; ◉10am-6pm Tue-Sun Apr-Sep, to 5pm Oct-Mar) In the lighthouse complex at Cabo São Vicente, this small but excellent museum gives a good overview of Portugal's maritime-navigation history, displays replica folios of a 1561 atlas and gives information on the history of the lighthouse.

**Statue of
Henry the Navigator**   Statue

(Rua Comandante Matoso) Near the *turismo* stands this statue of Henry the Navigator, map in hand, pointing out to sea as if saying 'What are you waiting for, guys? It's all out there!'

✈ ACTIVITIES

There are four good beaches a short drive or long walk from Sagres: **Praia da Mareta**, just below the town; lovely **Praia do Martinhal** to the east; **Praia do Tonel** on the other side of the Ponta de Sagres, and especially good for surfing; and the isolated **Praia de Beliche**, on the way to Cabo de São Vicente. Surfing is possible at all beaches except Praia do Martinhal and nearby Praia da Baleeira. The best way to choose a reputable surf school is to check the website of the **Surf School Association of Costa Vicentina** (www.algarvesurf-schoolsassociation.com).

Sagres Natura   Surfing

(📱282 624 072; www.sagresnatura.com; Rua São Vicente) This recommended surf school also rents out bodyboards, surfboards, wetsuits and bikes. The same company also runs a surf-equipment shop and hostel.

Wave Sensations   Surfing

(📱282 625 154; www.wavesensations.pt; Rua Comandante Matoso) Offers a range of lessons in surfing and paddleboarding, rents equipment and offers packages including accommodation at the Casa Azul hotel.

DiversCape   Diving

(📱965 559 073; www.diverscape.com; Porto da Baleeira) The PADI-certified DiversCape organises snorkelling expeditions (€25, two hours), plus dives of between 12m and 30m around shipwrecks. A dive and equipment costs €50/240/380 for one/six/10 dives, while the four-day PADI open-water course is €395. Beginners' courses (from €80) are available and there are even sessions for children aged over eight (€60).

✈ TOURS

Walkin'Sagres   Walking

(📱925 545 515; www.walkinsagres.com) 🌿 Multilingual Ana Carla offers recommended guided walks in the Sagres area, explaining the history and other details of the surrounds. The walks head through pine forests to the cape's cliffs and vary from shorter 7.7km options (€25, three hours) to a longer 15km walk (€40, 4½ hours). There's also a weekend walk for parents

with young children (€15, children free). In March and April you can walk among flowers, including orchids. Occasionally Ana takes themed walks, such as stargazing.

Cape Cruiser   Boating
(☏919 751 175; www.capecruiser.org; Porto da Baleeira) Offers a range of boat trips, including dolphin watching (€35, 1½ hours), seabird watching (€45, 2½ hours), trips to Cabo do São Vicente (€25, one hour) and various fishing excursions.

Mar Ilimitado   Boating
(☏916 832 625; www.marilimitado.com; Porto da Baleeira) ☙ This team of marine biologists, offers a variety of highly recommended, ecologically sound boat trips, from dolphin spotting (€35, 1½ hours) and seabird watching (€45, 2½ hours) to excursions up to Cabo de São Vicente (€25, one hour).

Sea Xplorer Sagres   Boating
(☏918 940 128; www.seaxplorersagres.com; Porto da Baleeira) Leaving from the harbour in Sagres, Sea Xplorer boat trips include dolphin watching (€35, two hours), fishing (€45, three hours) and the cliffs of Cabo São Vicente from the sea (1½ hours, €20).

⊗ EATING

Many places close or operate shorter hours during low season (November to April).

There are cafes on Praça de República and restaurants along the way to Cabo de São Vicente. Elsewhere, there are several inviting restaurants on the sands of Praia do Martinhal.

A Eira do Mel   Portuguese €€€
(☏282 639 016; Estrada do Castelejo, Vila do Bispo; mains €16-22; ☺noon-2.30pm & 7.30-10pm Tue-Sat) It's worth driving 10km north of Sagres to Vila do Bispo to enjoy José Pinheiro's creations at this much-lauded

---

Henry, Francis & the Great Earthquake

Somewhere near Sagres once stood Henry the Navigator's semi-monastic school of navigation, a place that specialised in cartography, astronomy and ship design, steering Portugal towards the Age of Discoveries. Nothing remains of this grand institution. English privateer Sir Francis Drake captured and wrecked Sagres in May 1587. The Great Earthquake of 1755 finished off the job.

From left: Praia do Tonel; Atlantic Ocean sailing; Statue of Henry the Navigator

KONSTANTIN KALISHKO / GETTY IMAGES ©

CRO MAGNON / ALAMY STOCK PHOTO ©

Sagres street

slow-food restaurant. The meat leans towards the Algarvian; the seafood has a more contemporary touch. Think rabbit in red-wine sauce (€16), octopus *cataplana* (seafood stew) with sweet potatoes (€35 for two people), curried Atlantic wild shrimps (€22) and *javali* (wild boar; €17). Mouthwatering.

Vila Velha   International €€€
(📞282 624 788; www.vilavelha-sagres.com; Rua Patrão António Faustino; mains €13-30; ⊙6.30pm-midnight Tue-Sun; ✍️) In a stylish old house with a lovely mature garden in front, the upmarket, Dutch-owned Vila Velha offers consistently good seafood mains (go for the catch of the day), plus meat dishes such as rabbit and pork in mango sauce. It's more internationally flavoured than all of Sagres' other restaurants.

A Casínha   Portuguese €€
(📞917 768 917; www.facebook.com/acasinha. restaurantesagres; Rua São Vicente; mains €13-19; ⊙12.30-3pm & 7-10.30pm Tue-Sat, closed Jan & Feb) This cosy terracotta-and-white

spot – built on the site of the owner's grandparents' house – serves up some fabulous Portuguese cuisine, including standout barbecued fish, a good variety of *cataplanas* for two (€34) and *arroz de polvo* (octopus rice). High quality, with a pleasant atmosphere.

A Grelha   Portuguese €€
(Rua Comandante Matoso; mains €8-13; ⊙noon-3pm & 7-10pm Mon-Sat) The nylon tablecloths, concrete floor and generally rough interior aren't that alluring, but the food, mainly grilled chicken and local fish, is tasty, honestly prepared and filling – and fairly cheap. It's popular with cash-strapped locals, always a good sign in these parts.

Mum's   International €€
(📞968 210 411; www.mums-sagres.com; Rua Comandante Matoso; mains €10-18; ⊙7pm-2am Wed-Mon; 🛜✍️) ✍️ This warm and cosy, eclectically decorated and friendly place on the main drag is a popular choice for dinner and drinks. The food – mostly vegetarian with some seafood – is delicious

and wholesome. It has a good wine list and staff members are happy to recommend matches. It stays open for drinks after the kitchen closes at midnight. No cards.

DRINKING & NIGHTLIFE

It's Groundhog Day (albeit a pleasant one) along Rua Comandante Matoso, with several atmospheric, good-value cafe-bars located cheek-to-cheek, the centre of Sagres' post-surfing nightlife scene.

Agua Salgada   Bar

(☎282 624 297; Rua Comandante Matoso; ⊙10am-late; ☎) Situated in a strip of cafe-bars, Agua Salgada has good crêpes and is one of the liveliest places at night, with DJs and a party mood.

Dromedário   Bar

(☎282 624 219; Rua Comandante Matoso; ⊙10am-late; ☎) Sagres' original cafe-bar, Dromedário is still going strong (it's been here for well over 30 years). There's good food (try the burgers), karaoke and 'mixol-ogy', aka creative cocktails. The spacious, mildly Moorish-themed interior is a cool spot to hang out after a day on the waves.

Pau de Pita   Cafe

(Rua Comandante Matoso; ⊙10am-2am; ☎) The funkiest of its neighbours in the bar strip (at least in terms of its design), this place has great salads, crêpes and juices (snacks €4 to €10), all enjoyed to a chilled-out soundtrack. At night, it mixes decent drinks and is as lively as any of the other bars, with a good post-surfing vibe.

INFORMATION

There's a bank and ATM on Rua Comandante Matoso.

Turismo (☎282 624 873; www.cm-vilado bispo.pt; Rua Comandante Matoso; ⊙9am-1pm & 2-6pm Tue-Sat, extended hours summer) is situated on a patch of green lawn, 100m east of Praça da República. Buses stop nearby.

 E9 European Long Distance Path

The Cabo de São Vicente is still the launchpad for journeys of exploration, but unlike the sailors of yore who ploughed the waves towards unknown horizons, modern-day explorers head the opposite direction – the cape is the terminus of the E9 European Long Distance Path, a walking trail that concludes over 5000km later in Estonia! The path follows the coasts of Portugal, Spain, Britain, France and the Low Countries before heading along the Baltic coast. An extension as far as St Petersburg is planned.

SIMON DANNHAUER / SHUTTERSTOCK ©

GETTING THERE & AWAY

The **bus stop** (Rua Comandante Matoso) is by the *turismo*. You can buy tickets on the bus.

Buses come from Lagos via Salema (€3.85, one hour, six daily). On weekends there are fewer services. It's only 10 minutes to Cabo de São Vicente (twice daily on weekdays only; €2).

GETTING AROUND

Handy bike rental is available at **Sagres Natura** (p246) and also at **Maretta Shop** (☎282 624 535; www.marettashop.com; Rua Comandante Matoso; ⊙9.30am-10.30pm).

BATALHA

Batalha at a Glance...

Among the achievements of Manueline architecture, Batalha's monastery transports visitors to another world, where solid rock has been carved into myriad forms. This extraordinary abbey was built to commemorate the 1385 Battle of Aljubarrota. Most of the monument was completed by 1434 in Flamboyant Gothic, but Manueline exuberance steals the show, thanks to additions made in the 15th and 16th centuries.

At the Battle of Aljubarrota, around 6500 Portuguese repulsed a 30,000-strong force of Juan I of Castile, who had come claiming the throne of João d'Avis. João called on the Virgin Mary for help and vowed to build a superb abbey in return for victory.

Batalha in a Day

Take at least half a day to explore Batalha's exquisite abbey (p254), making sure you don't miss the Unfinished Chapels. Also don't forget that a special ticket also covers Alcobaça and the Convento de Cristo in Tomar, all of which you can reach if you have a hire car at your disposal.

Batalha in Two Days

With two days to fill in Batalha, you can explore the rest of the town at your leisure, checking out the **Batalha de Aljubarrota Centro de Interpretação** (p256) and the **MCCB** (p256). End your day with a hearty dinner of Estremadura dishes at **Burro Velho** (p256).

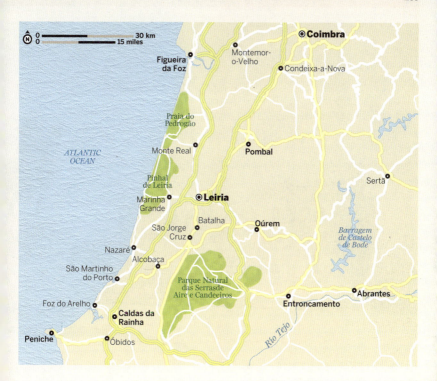

Arriving in Batalha

Bus stop Near the Intermarché super-market, behind the police station, very close to the abbey and *turismo*.

Sleeping

Batalha has several places to stay and there are other good options in surrounding villages. The tourist office is the best place to start if you choose to turn up unannounced, though this is not recommended at the height of summer.

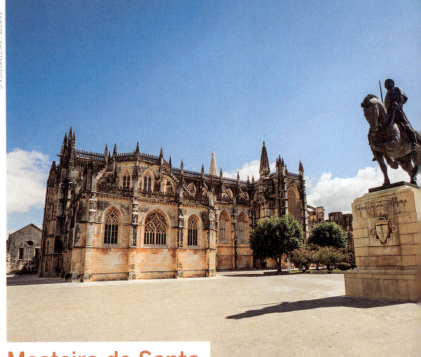

SAIKOSP / SHUTTERSTOCK ©

Mosteiro de Santa Maria da Vitória

Visiting this architecturally rich abbey is one of the highlights of the Estramadura. Allow half a day to do the place justice.

Great For...

☑ Don't Miss

The tomb of Prince Henry the Navigator, Portugal's most important monarch.

Exterior

The glorious limestone exterior bristles with pinnacles and parapets, flying buttresses and balustrades, and late-Gothic carved windows, as well as octagonal chapels and massive columns. The spectacular western doorway's layered arches pack in apostles, angels, saints and prophets, all topped by Christ and the Evangelists.

Interior

The vast, vaulted Gothic interior is plain, long and high (the highest in Portugal), warmed by light from the deep-hued stained-glass windows. Some of the interior was originally painted. To the right as you enter is the intricate Capela do Fundador (Founder's Chapel), an achingly beautiful, lofty, star-vaulted square room lit by an octagonal lantern. In the centre is the

Portal detail

MAURICIO ABREU / SHUTTERSTOCK ©

❶ Need to Know

☎244 765 497; www.mosteirobatalha.pt; adult/child €6/free, church free, with Alcobaça & Tomar €15; ⏰9am-6.30pm Apr-Sep, 9am-6pm Oct-Mar

✗ Take a Break

Burro Velho (p256) is the best place in the village for lunch.

★ Top Tip

A multi-monastery ticket valid for Batalha, Alcobaça and the Convento de Cristo in Tomar costs €15.

Cloisters

Afonso Domingues, master of works during the late 1380s, built the fabulous Claustro Real (Royal Cloister) in a Gothic style, but it's the later Manueline embellishments by the great Mateus Fernandes that really take your breath away. Every arch is a tangle of detailed stone carvings of Manueline symbols, such as armillary spheres and crosses of the Order of Christ, entwined with writhing vegetation, exotic flowers and marine motifs – corn and shells. Three graceful cypresses echo the shape of the Gothic spires atop the adjacent chapter house. (And we challenge you to spot the ancient graffiti on the walls!)

Anything would seem austere after the Claustro Real, but the simple Gothic Claustro de Dom Afonso V is like being plunged into cold water – sobering you up after all that frenzied decadence. Between the two cloisters there is an interpretation centre.

joint tomb (the first pantheon to be built in Portugal) of João I and his English wife, Philippa of Lancaster, whose marriage in 1387 cemented the alliance that still exists between Portugal and England. The tombs of their four youngest sons line the south wall of the chapel, including that of Henry the Navigator (second from the right).

The Unfinished Chapels

The roofless Capelas Imperfeitas are perhaps the most astonishing aspect of Batalha. Only accessible from outside the abbey, the octagonal mausoleum with its seven chapels was commissioned in 1437. However, the later Manueline additions by the architect Mateus Fernandes overshadow everything else. Although Fernandes' plan was never finished, the staggering ornamentation is all the more dramatic for being open to the sky.

⊙ SIGHTS

Batalha de Aljubarrota Centro de Interpretação
Historic Site

(www.fundacao-aljubarrota.pt; adult/student/child/family €7/5/3.50/20; ⊙10am-5.30pm Tue-Sun) For Portuguese people Aljubarrota conjures up a fierce sense of national pride, a 1385 battle where they defeated an odds-on favourite Castilian force and established the foundations for the Portuguese golden age. We thought the entry fee to the modern interpretation centre here, 3km south of Batalha, was steep until we saw the multimedia show, a no-expenses-spared blood-and-thunder half-hour medieval epic (showing at 11.30am, 3pm and 4.30pm, audioguide €3) that brings the whole thing to vivid life.

The display on bones is also fascinating – one skull still has the tip of an arrowhead in it. The battlefield itself is freely accessible and has some English explanations, but to really understand what went on here, you'll want the audioguide from the interpretation centre. It's available in eight languages.

MCCB
Museum

(Museu da Comunidade Concelhia da Batalha; www.museubatalha.com; Largo Goa, Rua Damão e Diu 4; €2.50; ⊙10am-1pm & 2-6pm Wed-Sun) This modern, award-winning municipal museum in the centre of town is well worth the visit, taking you through the prehistory and history of the region, including some well-presented Roman remains and sections on the Battle of Aljubarrota and Mosteiro de Santa Maria da Vitória's construction.

⊗ EATING

Eating options in Batalha are average; not terrible, but not outstanding, either.

Burro Velho
Portuguese €€

(☑244 764 174; www.burrovelho.com; Rua Nossa Sra do Caminho 6A; dishes €10.50-15.50; ⊙noon-3.30pm & 7-10pm Mon-Sat, noon-3.30pm Sun) The pick of Batalha's limited eating options, this bustling place serves up decent dishes.

Plaza adjacent to Mosteiro de Santa Maria da Vitória

DAVID LOPES / GETTY IMAGES ©

It's run by a young guy who not only works the floor but has established the recipe for success: service flair and quality products. Cuisine is full-on Portuguese, from *alheira* (sausage) to octopus rice, and there's plenty of other sea life in the tanks to choose from.

Churrasqueira Vitória Grill House €

(☏244 765 678; Largo da Misericórdia; mains €7-10; ⊙noon-3pm & 7-10pm) Neither outstanding nor terrible, this simple, friendly place serves tasty grilled meat and other Portuguese standards. Grab half a chicken for €7 and go home happy. Good-value lunch menus are only €8.

ℹ INFORMATION

Turismo (☏244 765 180; www.descobrirbatalha. pt; Praça Mouzinho de Albuquerque; ⊙10am-1pm & 2-6pm) The very helpful, enthusiastic Nelia has worked here for years and knows the lot. The *turismo* faces the back side of the monastery.

ℹ GETTING THERE & AWAY

Buses with **Rodotejo** (www.rodotejo.pt) and **Rede Expressos** (www.rede-expressos.pt) leave from the stop on Rua do Moinho da Via, near the Intermarché supermarket, behind the police station, very close to the abbey and *turismo*. Express services go to major cities, including Lisbon (€12, two hours) four to five times daily – buy tickets online or at Cafe Frazão behind the church nearby.

Food of the Estremadura

Seafood dominates the culinary palate in Estremadura; *caldeiradas de peixe* (fish stews) rule the menus, closely followed by *escabeche* (marinated vinegar fish stew) and *sopas de mariscos* (shellfish soups). Carnivores should head to Ribatejo – this is meat and tripe country.

Caldeirada (fish stew)
SIMON REDDY / ALAMY STOCK PHOTO ©

In Focus

Porto (p89)

Portugal Today

*The Portuguese have been through some tough times.
Cuts to pensions and social programs, privatisation of
government industries – all were part of the austerity
package imposed by a conservative government and the
EU powers holding the purse strings. Change, however, is
on the horizon, as a new left-wing government takes the
reins. Economic challenges aside, one of Portugal's biggest
slow-brewing crises is its shrinking population.*

A New Way Forward

After four years of austerity measures under prime minister Pedro Passos Coelho, Portugal
was ready to turn the page. And it did so in rather dramatic fashion. Following an inconclu-
sive election in 2015, Coelho's conservative government failed to gain an overall majority
in parliament. Seizing an opportunity, Socialist Party leader António Costa formed an
anti-austerity coalition with two other left-wing parties and voted down the new centre-
right government in an extraordinary parliamentary move. Kicked to the kerb after just 11
days in power, the centre-right administration would go down as the shortest in Portugal's
history.

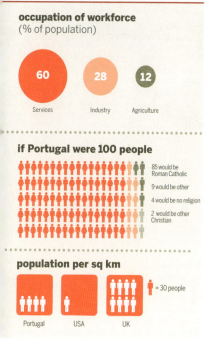

occupation of workforce
(% of population)

60 Services
28 Industry
12 Agriculture

if Portugal were 100 people

85 would be Roman Catholic
9 would be other
4 would be no religion
2 would be other Christian

population per sq km

Portugal USA UK ♦ ≈ 30 people

The rise of António Costa, a former mayor of Lisbon and the son of a communist poet from Goa, suggests a new era in Portuguese politics. In fact, the mere existence of a left-wing coalition is something unusual – unseen since the arrival of democracy at the end of the military dictatorship in the 1970s. The challenges, however, are substantial: unemployment stands at 12% (though markedly down from an all-time high of 17.5% in early 2013). And although the economy showed signs of life (growing 0.9% in 2014, then 1.5% in 2015), it appeared to have stalled in early 2016. And pressure was mounting from the EU for Portugal to rein in its budget deficit.

Most Portuguese, however, have clearly tired of receiving ultimatums from Brussels. In exchange for a €78-billion loan package from 'the Troika' – the International Monetary Fund, the European Central Bank and the European Commission – Portugal went through a draconian period of belt tightening. The conservative government raised taxes, cut wages and pensions, and clipped spending on social welfare. Critics of the measures say the cuts only drove more people into poverty, caused a further erosion of the middle class, and sent job-seeking Portuguese out of the country in droves. Costa's objective now is clear: achieve economic growth and reduce the deficit, while reversing painful austerity measures – a daunting challenge, particularly given the fragile left-wing alliance holding his administration together.

Population Crisis

It's been called a 'perfect demographic storm' that could have catastrophic effects on society and the economy. The population in Portugal has been shrinking – falling year on year since 2010 – and unless things change, demographers estimate that the population could fall to just six million by 2060. The fertility rate has sunk to an all-time low, averaging 1.2 children per woman in 2013, compared to three per woman back in 1970. According to European statistics office Eurostat, Portugal has the lowest fertility rate in the EU.

Meanwhile, the population is greying; lurking in the background is the danger that communities will no longer be self-sustaining. The effect is visible to anyone who travels around the small villages in the interior, where elderly residents are the norm and local children are a rare sight. Toy shops and schools are closing, while more businesses are being transformed into nursing homes.

Former prime minister Pedro Passos Coelho described the situation as one of Portugal's biggest problems. Some municipalities have begun offering incentives of up to €1000 for babies born to local mothers and some business owners are offering financial incentives to their workers to have offspring.

Praça do Comércio, Lisbon (p61)

LUIS BARROS / EYEEM / GETTY IMAGES ©

History

*This small nation on Europe's edge has seen a long line
of conquerors and foreign princes over the last 3000
years. In the 15th century, intrepid explorers transformed
Portugal into the seat of a global empire. The following
centuries witnessed devastation and great changes before
Portugal became a democracy in the 1980s.*

5000 BC
Little-understood Neolithic
peoples build protected
hilltop settlements in the
lower Tejo valley.

700 BC
Celtic peoples, migrating
across the Pyrenees with
their families and flocks,
sweep through the Iberian
Peninsula.

197 BC
After defeating Carthage in
the Second Punic War, the
Romans invade Iberia, ex-
panding their empire west.

Conímbriga Roman Ruins (p199)

IAN CANHAM / ALAMY STOCK PHOTO ©

Early Peoples

One of Europe's earliest places of settlement, the Iberian Peninsula was first inhabited many millennia ago, when hominids wandered across the landscape some time before 200,000 BC. During the Palaeolithic period, early Portuguese ancestors left traces of their time on Earth in fascinating stone carvings in the open air near Vila Nova de Foz Côa in the Alto Douro. These date back some 30,000 years and were only discovered by accident, during a proposed dam-building project in 1992. Other signs of early human artistry lie hidden in the Alentejo, in the Gruta do Escoural, where cave drawings of animals and humans date back to around 15,000 BC.

Homo sapiens weren't the only bipeds on the scene. Neanderthals coexisted alongside modern humans in a few rare places like Portugal for as long as 10,000 years. In fact, some of the last traces of their existence were found in Iberia.

Neanderthals were only the first of a long line of inhabitants to appear (and later disappear) from the Iberian stage. In the 1st millennium BC Celtic people started trickling into

AD 100	800	1147
Romans collect taxes to build roads, bridges and other public works. They cultivate vineyards and teach the natives to preserve fish.	The Umayyad dynasty rules the Iberian Peninsula. The region flourishes under the tolerant caliphate.	The Reconquista is under way as Christians attain decisive victories over the Moors.

The Mystery of the Neanderthals

Scientists have never come to an agreement about the fate of the Neanderthals – stout and robust beings who used stone tools and fire, buried their dead and had brains larger than those of modern humans. The most common theory is that *Homo sapiens* drove Neanderthals to extinction (perhaps in some sort of genocidal warfare). A less-accepted theory is that Neanderthals and humans bred together and produced a hybrid species. This idea gained credence when Portuguese archaeologists found a strange skeleton – the first complete Palaeolithic skeleton ever unearthed in Iberia – just north of Lisbon in 1999. The team, led by João Zilhão, director of the Portuguese Institute of Archaeology, discovered the 25,000-year-old remains of a young boy with traits of both early humans (pronounced chin and teeth) and of Neanderthals (broad limbs). The boy had been interred in what was clearly a ritual burial. Some believe this kind of relationship (lovemaking rather than war making) happened over the span of thousands of years and that some Neanderthal elements entered the modern human gene pool.

the peninsula, settling northern and western Portugal around 700 BC. Dozens of *citânias* (fortified villages) popped up, such as the formidable Citânia de Briteiros. Further south, Phoenician traders, followed by Greeks and Carthaginians, founded coastal stations and mined metals inland.

Roman Settlements

When the Romans swept into southern Portugal in 210 BC, they expected an easy victory. They hadn't reckoned on the Lusitani, a Celtic warrior tribe that settled between the Rio Tejo and Rio Douro and resisted ferociously for half a century. Unable to subjugate the Lusitani, the Romans offered peace instead and began negotiations with Viriato, the Lusitanian leader. Unfortunately for Viriato and his underlings, the peace offer was a ruse, and Roman agents, posing as intermediaries, poisoned him. Resistance collapsed following Viriato's death in 139 BC.

For a vivid glimpse into Roman Portugal, you won't see a better site than Conímbriga, near Coimbra, or the monumental remains of the so-called Temple of Diana, in Évora.

By the 5th century, when the Roman Empire had all but collapsed, Portugal's inhabitants had been under Roman rule for 600 years. So what did the Romans ever do for them? Most usefully, they built roads and bridges. But they also brought wheat, barley, olives and vines; large farming estates called *latifúndios* (still found in the Alentejo); a legal system; and, above all, a Latin-derived language. In fact, no other invader proved so useful.

1297

The boundaries of the Portuguese kingdom are formalised with neighbouring Castile. The kingdom of Portugal has arrived.

1348

The plague reaches Portugal (most likely carried on ships that dock in Porto and Lisbon). The disease devastates, killing one in three.

1411

Newly crowned Dom João builds an elaborate monastery to commemorate his victory at Aljubarrota.

Moors & Christians

The gap left by the Romans was filled by barbarian invaders from beyond the Pyrenees: Vandals, Alans, Visigoths and Suevi, with Arian Christian Visigoths gaining the upper hand in 469.

Internal Visigothic disputes paved the way for Portugal's next great wave of invaders, the Moors – North African Muslims invited in 711 to help a Visigoth faction. They quickly occupied large chunks of Portugal's southern coast.

Southerners enjoyed peace and productivity under the Moors, who established a capital at Shelb (Silves). The new rulers were tolerant of Jews and Christians. Christian smallholding farmers, called Mozarabs, could keep their land and were encouraged to try new methods and crops, especially citrus and rice. Arabic words filtered into the Portuguese language, such as *alface* (lettuce), *arroz* (rice) and dozens of place names (including Fatima, Silves and Algarve). Locals became addicted to Moorish sweets.

Rio Lima or River Lethe

When Roman soldiers reached the Rio Lima in 137 BC, they were convinced they had reached the Lethe, the mythical river of forgetfulness that flowed through Hades and from which no one could return. Unable to persuade his troops to cross waters leading (they thought) to certain oblivion, the Roman general Decimus Junius Brutus Callaicus forded the river alone. Once on the other side he called out to his men, shouting each of their names. Stunned that the general could remember them, they followed him and continued their campaign. Incidentally, Brutus, who led legions to conquer Iberia after Viriato's death, was later named proconsul of Lusitania.

Meanwhile, in the north, Christian forces were gaining strength and reached as far as Porto in 868. But it was in the 11th century that the Reconquista (the Christian reconquest) heated up. In 1064 Coimbra was taken and, in 1085, Alfonso VI thrashed the Moors in their Spanish heartland of Toledo; he is said to have secured Seville by winning a game of chess with its emir. But in the following year, Alfonso's men were driven out by ruthless Moroccan Almoravids who answered the emir's distress call.

Alfonso called for help and European crusaders came running – rallying against the 'infidels'. With the help of Henri of Burgundy, among others, Alfonso made decisive moves towards victory. The struggle continued in successive generations, and by 1139 Afonso Henriques (grandson of Alfonso VI) won such a dramatic victory against the Moors at Ourique (Alentejo) that he named himself Dom – King of Portugal – a title confirmed in 1179 by the Pope (after extra tribute was paid, naturally). Afonso also retook Santarém and Lisbon from the Moors.

By the time he died in 1185, the Portuguese frontier was secure to the Rio Tejo, though it would take another century before the south was torn from the Moors.

1415	**1418**	**1443**
Dom João's third son, Prince Henry the Navigator, joins his father in the conquest of Ceuta in North Africa.	Shipbuilding advances lead to the development of the caravel, a fast, agile ship that changes the face of sailing.	Explorers bring the first African slaves to Portugal, marking the beginning of a long, dark era of slavery in Europe.

Castelo de São Jorge (p52), Lisbon

JOHN KELLERMAN / ALAMY STOCK PHOTO ©

★ **Best Islamic Sites**

Alcáçova (Mértola)

Núcleo Islâmico (p135; Tavira)

Castelo de São Jorge (p52; Lisbon)

Mouraria (Moura)

Museu Municipal de Arqueologia (p131; Silves)

The Burgundian Era

During the Reconquista, people faced more than just war and turmoil: in the wake of Christian victories came new rulers and settlers.

The Church and its wealthy clergy were the greediest landowners, followed by aristocratic fat cats. Though theoretically free, most common people remained subjects of the landowning class, with few rights. The first hint of democratic rule came with the establishment of the *cortes* (parliament). This assembly of nobles and clergy first met in 1211 at Coimbra, the then capital. Six years later, the capital moved to Lisbon.

Afonso III (r 1248–79) deserves credit for standing up to the Church, but it was his son, the 'Poet King' Dinis (r 1279–1325), who really shook Portugal into shape. A far-sighted, cultured man, he took control of the judicial system, started progressive afforestation programs and encouraged internal trade. He suppressed the dangerously powerful military order of the Knights Templar, refounding them as the Order of Christ. He cultivated music, the arts and education, and he founded a university in Lisbon in 1290, which was later transferred to Coimbra.

Dom Dinis' foresight was spot on when it came to defence: he built or rebuilt some 50 fortresses along the eastern frontier with Castile and signed a pact of friendship with England in 1308, the basis for a future long-lasting alliance.

It was none too soon. Within 60 years of Dinis' death, Portugal was at war with Castile. Fernando I helped provoke the clash by playing a game of alliances with both Castile and the English. He dangled promises of marriage to his daughter Beatriz in front of both nations, eventually marrying her off to Juan I of Castile, thus throwing Portugal's future into Castilian hands.

On Fernando's death in 1383, his wife, Leonor Teles, ruled as regent. But she too was entangled with the Spanish, having long had a Galician lover. The merchant classes preferred unsullied Portuguese candidate João, son (albeit illegitimate) of Fernando's father. João assassinated Leonor's lover, Leonor fled to Castile and the Castilians duly invaded.

1494	1497	1519
The race for colonial expansion is on: Spain and Portugal carve up the world, with the Treaty of Tordesillas.	Following Bartolomeu Dias' historic journey around the Cape of Good Hope in 1488, Vasco da Gama sails to India and becomes a legend.	Fernão de Magalhães embarks on his journey to circumnavigate the globe. He is killed in the Philippines.

The showdown came in 1385 when João faced a mighty force of Castilians at Aljubarrota. Even with Nuno Álvares Pereira (the Holy Constable) as his military right-hand man and English archers at the ready, the odds were stacked against him. João vowed to build a monastery if he won – and he did. Nuno Álvares, the brilliant commander-in-chief of the Portuguese troops, deserves much of the credit for the victory. He lured the Spanish cavalry into a trap and, with an uphill advantage, his troops decimated the invaders. Within a few hours the Spanish were retreating in disarray and the battle was won.

The victory clinched independence and João made good his vow by commissioning Batalha's stunning Mosteiro de Santa Maria da Vitória (aka the Mosteiro da Batalha or Battle Abbey). It also sealed Portugal's alliance with England, and João wed John of Gaunt's daughter. Peace was finally concluded in 1411.

Age of Discoveries

João's success had whetted his appetite and, spurred on by his sons, he soon turned his military energies abroad. Morocco was the obvious target, and in 1415 Ceuta fell easily to his forces. It was a turning point in Portuguese history, a first step into its golden age.

It was João's third son, Henry, who focused the spirit of the age – a combination of crusading zeal, love of martial glory and lust for gold – into extraordinary explorations across the seas. These explorations were to transform the small kingdom into a great imperial power.

The biggest breakthrough came in 1497 during the reign of Manuel I, when Vasco da Gama reached southern India. With gold and slaves from Africa and spices from the East, Portugal was soon rolling in riches. Manuel I was so thrilled by the discoveries (and resultant cash injection) that he ordered a frenzied building spree in celebration. Top of his list was the extravagant Mosteiro dos Jerónimos in Belém, later to become his pantheon. Another brief boost to the Portuguese economy at this time came courtesy of an influx of around 150,000 Jews expelled from Spain in 1492.

Spain, however, had also jumped on the exploration bandwagon and was soon disputing Portuguese claims. Christopher Columbus' 1492 'discovery' of America for Spain led to a fresh outburst of jealous conflict. It was resolved by the Pope in the bizarre 1494 Treaty of Tordesillas, by which the world was divided between the two great powers along a line 370 leagues west of the Cape Verde islands. Portugal won the lands east of the line, including Brazil, officially claimed in 1500.

The rivalry spurred the first circumnavigation of the world. In 1519 Portuguese navigator Fernão de Magalhães (Ferdinand Magellan), his allegiance transferred to Spain after a tiff with Manuel I, set off in an effort to prove that the Spice Islands (today's Moluccas) lay in Spanish 'territory'. He reached the Philippines in 1521 but was killed in a skirmish there. One of his five ships, under the Basque navigator Juan Sebastián Elcano, reached the Spice Islands and then sailed home via the Cape of Good Hope, proving the Earth was round.

1572
Luís Vaz de Camões writes *Os Lusíadas*, an epic poem that celebrates da Gama's historic voyage.

1578
King Sebastião raises an army and invades Morocco. The expedition ends at the Battle of Alcácer Quibir.

1622
Portugal's empire is slipping out of Spain's grasp. The English seize Hormoz.

As its explorers reached Timor, China and eventually Japan, Portugal cemented its power with garrison ports and trading posts. The monarchy, taking its 'royal fifth' of profits, became stinking rich – indeed the wealthiest monarchy in Europe, and the lavish Manueline architectural style symbolised the exuberance of the age.

It couldn't last, of course. By the 1570s the huge cost of expeditions and maintaining an empire was taking its toll. The final straw came in 1578. Young, idealistic Sebastião was on the throne and, determined to bring Christianity to Morocco, he rallied a force of 18,000 and set sail from Lagos. He was disastrously defeated at the Battle of Alcácer-Quibir (also known as the Battle of Three Kings): Sebastião and 8000 others were killed, including much of the Portuguese nobility. Sebastião's aged successor, Cardinal Henrique, drained the royal coffers ransoming those captured.

On Henrique's death in 1580, Sebastião's uncle, Felipe II of Spain (Felipe I of Portugal), fought for and won the throne. This marked the end of centuries of independence, Portugal's golden age and its glorious moment at the centre of the world stage.

Spanish Rule & Portuguese Revival

Spanish rule began promisingly, with Felipe vowing to preserve Portugal's autonomy and attend the long-ignored parliament. But commoners resented Spanish rule and held on to the dream that Sebastião was still alive (as he was killed abroad in battle, some citizens were in denial); pretenders continued to pop up until 1600. Though Felipe was honourable, his successors proved to be considerably less so, using Portugal to raise money and soldiers for Spain's wars overseas, and appointing Spaniards to govern Portugal.

An uprising in Catalonia gave fuel to Portugal's independence drive (particularly when the Spanish King Felipe III ordered Portuguese troops to quell the uprising) and finally in 1640 a group of conspirators launched a coup. Nationalists drove the female governor of Portugal and her Spanish garrison from Lisbon. It was then that the duke of Bragança reluctantly stepped forward and was crowned João IV.

With a hostile Spain breathing down its neck, Portugal searched for allies. Two swift treaties with England led to Charles II's marriage to João's daughter, Catherine of Bragança, and the ceding of Tangier and Bombay to England.

In return the English promised arms and soldiers: however, a preoccupied Spain made only half-hearted attempts to recapture Portugal and recognised Portuguese independence in 1668.

João IV's successors pursued largely absolutist policies (particularly under João V, an admirer of French king Louis XIV). The crown hardly bothered with parliament and another era of profligate expenditure followed, giving birth to projects such as the wildly extravagant monastery-palace in Mafra.

Cementing power for the crown was one of Portugal's most revered (and feared) statesmen – the Marquês de Pombal, chief minister to the epicurean Dom José I (the latter

1703
France and Britain are at war. Facing (disastrous!) wine shortages, the English sign a new treaty with Portugal.

1717
Brazilian gold extraction nears its peak, with over 600,000oz imported annually. Dom João V becomes Europe's richest monarch.

1755
Lisbon suffers Europe's biggest natural disaster. On All Saints' Day, three massive earthquakes destroy the city.

more interested in opera than political affairs). Described as an enlightened despot, Pombal dragged Portugal into the modern era, crushing opposition with brutal efficiency.

He set up state monopolies, curbed the power of British merchants and boosted agriculture and industry. He abolished slavery and distinctions between traditional and New Christians (Jews who had converted), and overhauled education.

When Lisbon suffered a devastating earthquake in 1755, Pombal swiftly rebuilt the city. He was by then at the height of his power, and dispensed with his main enemies by implicating them in an attempt on the king's life.

He might have continued had it not been for the accession of the devout Dona Maria I in 1777. The anticlerical Pombal was promptly sacked, tried and charged with various offences, though he was never imprisoned. While his religious legislation was repealed, his economic, agricultural and educational policies were largely maintained, helping the country back towards prosperity.

But turmoil was once again on the horizon, as Napoleon was sweeping through Europe.

A Devastating Earthquake

Lisbon in the 1700s was a thriving city, with gold flowing in from Brazil, a thriving merchant class and grand Manueline architecture. Then, on the morning of 1 November 1755, a devastating earthquake levelled much of the city, which fell like a pack of dominoes, never to regain its former status; palaces, libraries, art galleries, churches and hospitals were razed to the ground. Tens of thousands died, crushed beneath falling masonry, drowned in the tsunami that swept in from the Tejo or killed in the fires that followed.

Enter the formidable, unflappable, geometrically minded Marquês de Pombal. As Dom José I's chief minister, Pombal swiftly set about reconstructing the city, true to his word to 'bury the dead and heal the living'. In the wake of the disaster, the autocratic statesman not only kept the country's head above water as it was plunged into economic chaos but also managed to propel Lisbon into the modern era.

Together with military engineers and architects Eugenio dos Santos and Manuel da Maia, Pombal played a pivotal role in reconstructing the city in a simple, cheap, earthquake-proof way that created today's formal grid; the Pombaline style was born. The antithesis of rococo, Pombaline architecture was functional and restrained: *azulejos* (hand-painted tiles) and decorative elements were used sparingly, building materials were prefabricated and wide streets and broad plazas were preferred.

Dom José I, for his part, escaped the earthquake unscathed. Instead of being in residence at the royal palace, he had ridden out of town to Belém with his extensive retinue. After seeing the devastation, the eccentric José I refused to live in a masonry building ever again, so he set up a wooden residence outside town, in the hills of Ajuda, north of Belém. What was known as the Real Barraca (Royal Tent) became the site of the Palácio Nacional de Ajuda after the king's death.

1807	1815	1822
Napoleon invades Portugal. The Portuguese royal family and several thousand in their retinue pack up and set sail for Brazil.	Having fallen hard for Brazil, Dom João VI declares Rio the capital of the United Kingdom of Portugal and Brazil and the Algarves.	In Brazil, Prince Regent Pedro leads a coup d'état and declares Brazilian independence, with himself the new 'emperor'.

★ **Best Historic Collections**

Museu do Oriente (Lisbon)

Museu Nacional de Machado de Castro (p196; Coimbra)

Casa Museu Passos Canavarro (Santarém)

Museu Nacional de Machado de Castro (p196), Coimbra

The Dawn of a Republic

A French Invasion Unleashes Royal Chaos

In 1793 Portugal found itself at war again when it joined Britain in sending naval forces against revolutionary France. Before long, Napoleon gave Portugal an ultimatum: close your ports to British shipping or be invaded.

There was no way Portugal could turn its back on Britain, upon which it depended for half of its trade and the protection of its sea routes. In 1807 Portugal's royal family fled to Brazil (where it stayed for 14 years), and Napoleon's forces marched into Lisbon, sweeping Portugal into the Peninsular War (France's invasion of Spain and Portugal, which lasted until 1814).

To the rescue came Sir Arthur Wellesley (later Duke of Wellington), Viscount Beresford and their seasoned British troops, who eventually drove the French back across the Spanish border in 1811.

Free but weakened, Portugal was administered by Beresford while the royals dallied in Brazil. In 1810 Portugal lost a profitable intermediary role by giving Britain the right to trade directly with Brazil. The next humiliation was João's 1815 proclamation of Brazil as a kingdom united with Portugal – he did this to bring more wealth and prestige to Brazil (which he was growing to love) and, in turn, to him and the rest of the royal family residing there. With soaring debts and dismal trade, Portugal was at one of the lowest points in its history, reduced to a de facto colony of Brazil and a protectorate of Britain.

Meanwhile, resentment simmered in the army. Rebel officers quietly convened parliament and drew up a new liberal constitution. Based on Enlightenment ideals, it abolished many rights of the nobility and clergy, and instituted a single-chamber parliament.

Faced with this fait accompli, João returned and accepted its terms – though his wife and his son Miguel were bitterly opposed to it. João's elder son, Pedro, had other ideas: left behind to govern Brazil, he snubbed the constitutionalists by declaring Brazil independent in 1822 and himself its emperor. When João died in 1826, the stage was set for civil war.

1865	1890	1900
Portugal enjoys a period of peace and prosperity. Advancements are made in industry, agriculture, health and education.	Portugal takes a renewed interest in its African colonies. Britain wants control of sub-Saharan Africa and threatens Portugal with war.	The republican movement gains force. The humiliating Africa issue is one among many grievances against the crown.

Offered the crown, Pedro dashed out a new, less liberal charter and then abdicated in favour of his seven-year-old daughter, Maria, on the provisos that she marry uncle Miguel and that uncle Miguel accept the new constitution. Miguel took the oath but promptly abolished Pedro's charter and proclaimed himself king. A livid Pedro rallied the equally furious liberals and forced Miguel to surrender at Évoramonte in 1834.

After Pedro's death, his daughter Maria, now queen of Portugal at just 15, kept his flame alive with fanatical support of his 1826 charter. The radical supporters of the liberal 1822 constitution grew vociferous over the next two decades, bringing the country to the brink of civil war. The Duke of Saldanha, however, saved the day, negotiating a peace that toned down Pedro's charter while still radically modernising Portugal's infrastructure.

A Hopeful New Era

The latter half of the 19th century was a remarkable period for Portugal. It became known as one of the most advanced societies in southern Europe. Casual visitors to Lisbon, such as Hans Christian Andersen, were surprised to find tree-lined boulevards with gas street lamps, efficient trams and well-dressed residents. Social advances were less anecdotal. The educational reformer João Arroio dramatically increased the number of schools, doubling the number of boys' schools and quadrupling the number of girls' schools. Women gained the right to own property; slavery was abolished throughout the Portuguese empire, as was the death penalty; even the prison system received an overhaul – prisoners were taught useful trades while in jail so they could integrate into society upon their release.

Professional organisations, such as the Literary Guild, emerged and became a major force for the advancement of ideas in public discourse, inspiring debate in politics, religious life and the art world.

As elsewhere in Europe, this was also a time of great industrial growth, with a dramatic increase in textile production, much of it to be exported. Other significant undertakings included the building of bridges and a nationwide network of roads, as well as the completion of major architectural works such as the Palácio Nacional da Pena above Sintra.

Dark Days & A King's Death

Bby 1900, discontent among workers began to grow. With increased mechanisation, workers began losing their jobs (some factory owners began hiring children to operate the machines) and their demands for fair working conditions went unanswered. Those who went on strike were simply fired and replaced. At the same time, Portugal experienced a dramatic demographic shift: rural areas were increasingly depopulated in favour of cities, and emigration (especially to Brazil) snowballed.

Much was changing; more and more people began to look towards socialism as a cure for the country's inequalities. Nationalist republicanism swept through the lower-middle

1910	**1916**	**1932**
King Carlos' younger son, 18-year-old Manuel, takes the throne but is soon ousted. Portugal is declared a republic.	Despite initial neutrality, Portugal gets drawn into WWI. The war effort is devastating for the economy, creating a long recession.	António de Oliveira Salazar seizes power. The Portuguese economy grows but at enormous human cost.

classes, spurring an attempted coup in 1908. It failed, but the following month King Carlos and Crown Prince Luís Filipe were brutally assassinated in Lisbon.

Carlos' younger son, Manuel II, tried feebly to appease republicans, but it was too little, too late. On 5 October 1910, after an uprising by military officers, a republic was declared. Manuel, dubbed 'the Unfortunate', sailed into exile in Britain, where he died in 1932.

The Rise & Fall of Salazar

After a landslide victory in the 1911 elections, hopes were high among republicans for dramatic changes, but the tide was against them. The economy was in tatters, an issue only exacerbated by a financially disastrous decision to join the Allies in WWI. In the postwar years the chaos deepened: republican factions squabbled, unions led strikes and were repressed and the military grew more powerful.

The new republic soon had a reputation as Europe's most unstable regime. Between 1910 and 1926 there were an astonishing 45 changes of government, often resulting from military intervention. Another coup in 1926 brought forth new names and faces, most significantly António de Oliveira Salazar, a finance minister who would rise through the ranks to become prime minister in 1932 – a post he would hold for the next 36 years.

Salazar hastily enforced his 'New State' – a corporatist republic that was nationalistic, Catholic, authoritarian and essentially repressive. All political parties were banned except for the loyalist National Union, which ran the show, and the National Assembly. Strikes were forbidden and propaganda, censorship and brute force kept society in order. The sinister new Polícia Internacional e de Defesa do Estado (PIDE) secret police inspired terror and suppressed opposition using imprisonment and torture. Various attempted coups during Salazar's rule came to nothing. For a chilling taste of life as a political prisoner under Salazar, you could visit the 16th-century Fortaleza at Peniche – used as a jail by the dictator.

The only good news was the dramatic economic turnaround. Through the 1950s and 1960s Portugal experienced an annual industrial growth rate of 7% to 9%.

Internationally, the wily Salazar played two hands, unofficially supporting Franco's nationalists in the Spanish Civil War and allowing the British to use Azores airfields during WWII despite official neutrality (and illegal sales of tungsten to Germany). It was later discovered that Salazar had also authorised the transfer of Nazi-looted gold to Portugal – 44 tonnes, according to Allied records.

But it was something else that finally brought the Salazarist era to a close – decolonisation. Refusing to relinquish the colonies, he was faced with ever more costly and unpopular military expeditions. In 1961 Goa was occupied by India and nationalists rose up in Angola. Guerrilla movements also appeared in Portuguese Guinea and Mozambique.

Salazar, however, didn't have to face the consequences. In 1968 he had a stroke, and he died two years later.

1935	**1943**	**1961**
The largely unpublished 47-year-old poet Fernando Pessoa dies, leaving a trunk containing a staggering collection of writing.	Portugal, neutral during WWII, becomes a crossroads for the intelligence activities of Allied and Axis operatives.	The last vestiges of Portugal's empire begin to crumble as India seizes Goa.

His successor, Marcelo Caetano, failed to ease unrest. Military officers sympathetic to African freedom fighters grew reluctant to fight colonial wars – the officers had seen the horrible conditions in which the colony lived beneath the Portuguese authorities. Several hundred officers formed the Movimento das Forças Armadas (MFA), which on 25 April 1974 carried out a nearly bloodless coup, later nicknamed the Revolution of the Carnations (after victorious soldiers stuck carnations in their rifle barrels). Carnations are still a national symbol of freedom.

From Revolution to Democracy

Despite the coup's popularity, the following year saw unprecedented chaos. It began where the revolution had begun: in the African colonies. Independence was granted immediately to Guinea-Bissau, followed by the speedy decolonisation of the Cape Verde islands, São Tomé e Príncipe, Mozambique and Angola.

The transition wasn't smooth: civil war racked Angola and East Timor, freshly liberated in 1975, was promptly invaded by Indonesia. Within Portugal, too, times were turbulent, with almost a million refugees from African colonies flooding into the country.

The nation was an economic mess, with widespread strikes and a tangle of political ideas and parties. The communists and a radical wing of the MFA launched a revolutionary movement, nationalising firms and services. Peasant farmers seized land to establish communal farms that failed because of infighting and poor management. While revolutionaries held sway in the south, the conservative north was led by Mário Soares and his Partido Socialista (PS; Socialist Party).

In the early post-Salazar days, radical provisional governments established by the military failed one after the other, as did an attempted coup led by General António de Spínola in 1975. A period of relative calm finally arrived in 1976, when Portugal adopted a new constitution and held its first elections for a new parliament. General António Ramalho Eanes was elected president the same year and helped steer the country toward democracy. He chose as his prime minister Soares, who took the reins with enormous challenges facing Portugal, including soaring inflation, high unemployment and downward-spiraling wages.

The Rocky Road to Stability

Portugal was soon committed to a blend of socialism and democracy, with a powerful president, an elected assembly and a Council of the Revolution to control the armed forces.

Mário Soares' minority government soon faltered, prompting a series of attempts at government by coalitions and non-party candidates, including Portugal's first female prime minister, Maria de Lourdes Pintasilgo. In the 1980 parliamentary elections a new political force took the reins: the conservative Aliança Democrática (AD; Democratic Alliance), led by Francisco de Sá Carneiro.

1974	**1986**	**1998**
Army officers overthrow Salazar's successor in the Revolution of the Carnations. Portugal veers to the left.	Portugal joins the EC along with Spain.	Lisbon hosts Expo 98, showcasing new developments, including Santiago Calatrava's cutting-edge train station.

After Carneiro's almost immediate (and suspicious) death in a plane crash, Francisco Pinto Balsemão stepped into his shoes. He implemented plans to join the European Community (EC).

It was partly to keep the EC and the International Monetary Fund (IMF) happy that a new coalition government under Soares and Balsemão implemented a strict program of economic modernisation. Not surprisingly, the belt-tightening wasn't popular. The loudest critics were Soares' right-wing partners in the Partido Social Democrata (PSD; Social Democrat Party), led by the dynamic Aníbal Cavaco Silva. Communist trade unions organised strikes, and the appearance of urban terrorism by the radical left-wing Forças Populares 25 de Abril (FP-25) deepened unrest.

In 1986, after nine years of negotiations, Portugal joined the EC. Flush with new funds, it raced ahead of its neighbours with unprecedented economic growth. The new cash flow also gave prime minister Cavaco Silva the power to push ahead with radical economic plans. These included labour-law reforms that left many workers disenchanted. The 1980s were crippled by strikes – including one involving 1.5 million workers – though they were to no avail: the controversial legislation was eventually passed.

The economic growth, however, wouldn't last. In 1992 EC trade barriers fell and Portugal suddenly faced new competition. Fortunes dwindled as a recession set in, and disillusionment grew as Europe's single market revealed the backwardness of Portugal's agricultural sector.

Strikes, crippling corruption charges and student demonstrations over rising fees only undermined the PSD further, leading to Cavaco Silva's resignation in 1995. The general elections that year brought new faces to power, with the socialist António Guterres running the show. Despite hopes for a different and less conservative administration, it was business as usual, with Guterres maintaining the budgetary rigour that qualified Portugal for the European Economic & Monetary Union (EMU) in 1998. Indeed, for a while Portugal was a star EMU performer, with steady economic growth that helped Guterres win a second term. But corruption scandals, rising inflation and a faltering economy soon spelt disaster. Portugal had slipped into economic stagnation by the dawn of the 21st century. The next 10 years were ones of hardship for the Portuguese economy, which saw little or negative GDP growth and rising unemployment from 2001 to 2010. As elsewhere in Europe, Portugal took a huge hit during the global financial crisis. Ultimatums from the EU governing body to rein in its debt (to avoid a Greece-style meltdown) brought unpopular austerity measures – pension reform, increased taxes, public-sector hiring freezes – that led to protests and strikes.

1998	1999	2004
José Saramago receives the Nobel Prize in Literature for his darkly humorous tales about ordinary characters facing fantastical obstacles.	Legendary *fadista* (performer of traditional song) Amália Rodrigues dies aged 79. Three days of mourning are declared.	Hosting the UEFA European Championship, Portugal makes it to the final only to suffer an agonising loss to Greece.

Hard Times

Portugal's economy wasn't particularly strong in the years before the economic crisis, making the economic fire all the more destructive. Lumped in with other economically failing euro-zone nations, the group of them collectively known as PIIGS (Portugal, Italy, Ireland, Greece and Spain), Portugal – in dire financial straits – accepted an EU bailout worth €78 billion in 2011. The younger generation has borne the heaviest burden following the crisis, with unemployment above 40% for workers under the age of 25. In addition, there are the underemployed and those scraping by on meagre wages.

The EU bailout came with the stipulation that Portugal improve its budget deficit by reducing spending and increasing tax revenues. Austerity measures followed and the public took to the streets to protest against higher taxes and slashed pensions and benefits, in the context of record-high unemployment. Mass demonstrations and general strikes have grown, with the largest attracting an estimated 1.5 million people nationwide in 2013 – an astounding figure given Portugal's small size. Those in industries most affected by government policy – including education, healthcare and transportation – have joined ranks with the unemployed and pensioners to amass in the largest gatherings since the Revolution of the Carnations in 1974.

Despite the bailout package, Portugal remained in its most severe recession since the 1970s. Every day, Portuguese were confronted with depressing headlines announcing freezes on public spending, cuts in healthcare, removal of free school lunches, curtailing of police patrols, and rising suicides, among other issues. Pensioners living on 200-odd euros a month struggled to feed themselves without family financial support; poverty and hunger affected untold millions; according to TNS Global roughly three out of four people in Portugal struggled to make their money last through the month.

What began as a financial crisis soon turned into a political crisis, as successive government ministers failed to ameliorate the growing problems. With anger mounting on the streets, the public clamoured for the resignation of prime minister Pedro Passos Coelho. Indeed, his time in power would come to an abrupt end in 2015, with a new left-wing government taking control.

2007
Portugal takes over the rotating EU presidency. The Treaty of Lisbon is drafted.

2010
Portugal legalises same-sex marriage, becoming the sixth country in Europe (and the eighth in the world) to do so.

2013
Fed up with rising unemployment, soaring taxes and spending cuts, 1.5 million protestors take to the streets of Portugal.

PHOTOLOCATION 2 / ALAMY STOCK PHOTO ©

Art & Architecture

Portugal has a long and storied art history. Neolithic tribes, Celtic peoples, Romans, Visigoths, Moors and early Christian crusaders have all left their mark on the Iberian nation. The Age of Discoveries – a rich era of grand cathedrals and lavish palaces – began around 1500. In the 500 years that followed, Portugal became a showcase for a dizzying array of architectural styles. Meanwhile, painters, sculptors, poets and novelists all made contributions to Portugal's artistic heritage.

The Palaeolithic Palette

The Cromeleque dos Almendres, a most mysterious group of 95 huge monoliths, forms a strange circle in an isolated clearing among Alentejan olive groves near Évora. It's one of Europe's most impressive prehistoric sites.

All over Portugal, but especially in the Alentejo, you can visit such ancient funerary and religious structures, built during the Neolithic and Mesolithic eras. Most impressive are the dolmens: rectangular, polygonal or round funerary chambers, reached by a corridor of stone slabs and covered with earth to create an artificial mound. King of these is Europe's largest dolmen, the Anta Grande do Zambujeiro, near Évora, with six 6m-high stones forming a huge chamber. Single monoliths, or menhirs, often carved with phallic or religious symbols, also dot the countryside like an army of stone sentinels. Their relationship to promoting fertility seems obvious.

With the arrival of the Celts (800–200 BC) came the first established hilltop settlements, called *castros*. The best-preserved example is the Citânia de Briteiros, in the Minho, where you can step into Portugal's past. Stone dwellings were built on a circular or elliptical plan, and the complex was surrounded by a drystone defensive wall. In the *citânias* (fortified villages) further south, dwellings tended to be rectangular.

The Romans

The Romans left Portugal their typical architectural and engineering feats – roads, bridges, towns complete with forums (marketplaces), villas, public baths and aqueducts. These have now largely disappeared from the surface, though the majority of Portugal's cities are built on Roman foundations. Today you can descend into dank subterranean areas under new buildings in Lisbon and Évora, and see Roman fragments around Braga. At Conímbriga, the country's largest Roman site, an entire town is under excavation. Revealed so far are some spectacular mosaics, along with structural or decorative columns, carved entablatures and classical ornamentation, giving a sense of the Roman high life.

Portugal's most famous and complete Roman ruin is the Templo Romano, the so-called Temple of Diana in Évora, with its flouncy-topped Corinthian columns nowadays echoed by the complementary towers of Évora's cathedral. This is the finest temple of its kind on the Iberian Peninsula, its preservation the result of having been walled up in the Middle Ages and later used as a slaughterhouse.

Architectural Movements

Great Gothic

Cistercians introduced the Gothic trend, which reached its pinnacle in Alcobaça, in one of Portugal's most ethereally beautiful buildings. The austere abbey church and cloister of the Mosteiro de Santa Maria de Alcobaça, begun in 1178, has a lightness and simplicity strongly influenced by Clairvaux Abbey in France. Its hauntingly simple Cloisters of Silence were a model for later cathedral cloisters at Coimbra, Lisbon, Évora and many other places. This was the birth of Portuguese Gothic, which flowered and transmuted over the coming years as the country gained more and more experience of the outside world – for centuries it had been culturally dominated and restricted by Spain and the Moors.

By the 14th century, when the Mosteiro de Santa Maria da Vitória (commonly known as Mosteiro da Batalha or Battle Abbey) was constructed, simplicity was a distant, vague memory. Portuguese, Irish and French architects worked on this breathtaking monument for more than two centuries. The combination of their skills and the changing architectural fashions of the times, from Flamboyant (late) Gothic to Renaissance and then Manueline, turned the abbey into a seething mass of carving, organic decorations, lofty spaces and slanting stained-glass light. A showcase of High Gothic art, it exults in the decorative (especially in its Gothic Royal Cloisters and Chapter House) and its flying buttresses tip their hat to English Perpendicular Gothic.

Secular architecture also enjoyed a Gothic boom, thanks to the need for fortifications against the Moors and to the castle-building fervour of 13th-century ruler Dom Dinis. Some of Portugal's most spectacular, huddled, thick-walled castles – for example, Estremoz, Óbidos and Bragança – date from this time, many featuring massive double-perimeter walls and an inner square tower.

Manueline

Manueline is a uniquely Portuguese style: a specific, crazed flavour of late Gothic architecture. Ferociously decorative, it coincided roughly with the reign of Dom Manuel I (r 1495–1521) and is interesting not just because of its extraordinarily imaginative designs, burbling with life, but also because this dizzyingly creative architecture skipped hand in hand with the era's booming confidence.

During Dom Manuel's reign, Vasco da Gama and fellow explorers claimed new overseas lands and new wealth for Portugal. The Age of Discoveries was expressed in sculptural creations of eccentric inventiveness that drew heavily on nautical themes: twisted ropes, coral and anchors in stone, topped by the ubiquitous armillary sphere (a navigational device that became Dom Manuel's personal symbol) and the cross of the Order of Christ (symbol of the religious military order that largely financed and inspired Portugal's explorations).

Manueline first emerged in Setúbal's Igreja de Jesus, designed in the 1490s by French expatriate Diogo de Boitaca, who gave it columns like trees growing into the ceiling, and ribbed vaulting like twisted ropes. The style quickly caught on and soon decorative carving was creeping, twisting and crawling over everything (aptly described by 19th-century English novelist William Beckford as 'scollops and twistifications').

Outstanding Manueline masterpieces are Belém's Mosteiro dos Jerónimos, masterminded largely by Diogo de Boitaca and João de Castilho; and Batalha's Mosteiro de Santa Maria da Vitória's otherworldly Capelas Imperfeitas (Unfinished Chapels).

Other famous creations include Belém's Torre de Belém, a Manueline-Moorish cake crossed with a chess piece by Francisco de Arruda; his brother Diogo de Arruda's fantastical organic, seemingly barnacle-encrusted window in the Chapter House of Tomar's

---

A Serendipitous Discovery

In 1989 researchers were studying the rugged valley of the Rio Côa, 15km from the Spanish frontier, to understand the environmental impact of a planned hydroelectric dam that was to flood the valley. In the course of their work, they made an extraordinary discovery: a number of petroglyphs (rock engravings) dating back tens of thousands of years.

Yet it wasn't until 1992, after the dam's construction was under way, that the importance of the find began to be understood. Archaeologists came across whole clusters of petroglyphs, mostly dating from the Upper Palaeolithic period (10,000 to 40,000 years ago). Local people joined the search and the inventory of engravings soon grew into the thousands. In 1998 the future of the collection was safeguarded when Unesco designated the valley a World Heritage Site.

Today **Rio Côa** (www.arte-coa.pt; Rua do Museu; park sites each €10, museum €5, park & museum €12; ⏱museum & park 9am-6pm Tue-Sun Mar-Oct, 9am-1pm & 2-6pm Tue-Sun Nov-Feb) holds one of the largest-known collections of open-air Palaeolithic art in the world. Archaeologists are still puzzling over the meaning of the engravings – and why this site was chosen. Most of the petroglyphs depict animals: stylised horses, aurochs (extinct ancestors of domesticated cattle) and long-horned ibex (extinct species of wild goat). Some animals are depicted with multiple heads – as if to indicate the animal in motion – while others are drawn so finely that they require artificial light to be seen. Later petroglyphs begin to depict human figures as well. The most intriguing engravings consist of overlapping layers, with successive artists adding their touches thousands of years after the first strokes were applied – a kind of Palaeolithic palimpsest in which generations of hunters worked and reworked the engravings of their forebears.

Convento de Cristo; and the convent's fanciful 16-sided Charola – the Templar church, resembling an eerie *Star Wars* set. Many other churches sport a Manueline flourish against a plain facade.

The style was enormously resonant in Portugal, and reappeared in the early 20th century in exercises in mystical romanticism, such as Sintra's Quinta da Regaleira and Palácio Nacional da Pena, and Luso's over-the-top and extraordinary neo-Manueline Palace Hotel do Buçaco.

Baroque

With independence from Spain re-established and the influence of the Inquisition on the wane, Portugal burst out in a fever of baroque – an architectural style that was exuberant and theatrical and fired straight at the senses. Nothing could rival the Manueline flourish, but the baroque style – named after the Portuguese word for a rough pearl, *barroco* – cornered the market in flamboyance. At its height during the 18th century (almost a century later than in Italy), it was characterised by curvaceous forms, huge monuments, spatially complex schemes and lots and lots and lots of gold.

Financed by the 17th-century gold and diamond discoveries in Brazil and encouraged by the extravagant Dom João V, local and foreign (particularly Italian) artists created mind-bogglingly opulent masterpieces. Prodigious *talha dourada* (gilded woodwork) adorns church interiors all over the place, but it reached its extreme in Aveiro's Mosteiro de Jesus, Lisbon's Igreja de São Roque and Porto's Igreja de São Francisco.

The baroque of central and southern Portugal was more restrained. Examples include the chancel of Évora's cathedral and the massive Palácio Nacional de Mafra. Designed by the German architect João Frederico Ludovice to rival the palace-monastery of San Lorenzo de El Escorial (near Madrid), the Mafra version is relatively sober, apart from its size – which is such that at one point it had a workforce of 45,000, looked after by a police force of 7000.

Meanwhile, Tuscan painter and architect Nicolau Nasoni (who settled in Porto around 1725) introduced a more ornamental baroque style to the north. Nasoni is responsible for Porto's Torre dos Clérigos and Igreja da Misericórdia, and the whimsical Palácio de Mateus near Vila Real (internationally famous as the image on Mateus rosé wine bottles).

In the mid-18th century a school of architecture evolved in Braga. Local artists such as André Soares built churches and palaces in a very decorative style, heavily influenced by Augsburg engravings from southern Germany. Soares' Casa do Raio in Braga and much of the monumental staircase of the nearby Bom Jesus do Monte are typical examples of this period's ornamentation.

Only when the gold ran out did the baroque fad fade. At the end of the 18th century, architects flirted briefly with rococo (best exemplified by Mateus Vicente's Palácio de Queluz, begun in 1747, or the palace at Estói) before embracing neoclassicism.

The Modern Era

The Salazar years favoured decidedly severe, Soviet-style state commissions (eg Coimbra university's dull faculty buildings, which replaced elegant 18th-century neoclassical ones). Ugly buildings and apartment blocks rose on city outskirts. Notable exceptions dating from the 1960s are Lisbon's Palácio da Justiça in the Campolide district and the gloriously sleek Museu Calouste Gulbenkian. The beautiful wood-panelled Galeto cafe-restaurant is a time capsule from this era.

The tendency towards urban mediocrity continued after the 1974 revolution, although architects such as Fernando Távora and Eduardo Souto de Moura have produced

Two Legendary Architects

Porto is home to not one but two celebrated contemporary architects: Álvaro Siza Vieira (born 1933) and Eduardo Souto de Moura (born 1952). Both remain fairly unknown outside their home country, which is surprising given their loyal following among fellow architects and their long and distinguished careers. Both have earned the acclaimed Pritzker Prize, the Nobel of the architecture world (Siza Vieira in 1992, Souto de Moura in 2011). The two men are quite close and they even have offices in the same building. They have collaborated on a handful of projects (prior to going out on his own, Souto de Moura also worked for Siza Vieira).

On the surface, Siza Vieira's work may seem less than dazzling. Stucco, stone, tile and glass are his building materials of choice. Place means everything in Siza Vieira's work, with geography and climate carefully considered before any plans are laid, regardless of the size or scale of the project. Many of his works are outside the country, although the Serralves Museu de Arte Contemporânea in Porto and the cliffside Boa Nova Casa Chá near Matosinhos are two of his most famous works in Portugal.

Like Siza Vieira, Souto de Moura spurns flashy designs. His works feature minimalist but artful structures that utilise local building materials. The Estádio Municipal de Braga, built for the 2004 European football championship, is set in a former granite quarry (granite from the site was used to make concrete for the stadium). The rock walls of the quarry lie behind one goal; the other side opens to views of the city. Better known is Souto de Moura's design for the Casa das Histórias Paula Rego in Cascais. The red-concrete museum is distinguished by its two pyramid-shaped towers, providing a modern reinterpretation of classic Portuguese shapes (which appear in chimneys, lighthouses, towers, and old palaces such as the Palácio Nacional de Sintra).

impressive schemes. Lisbon's postmodern Amoreiras shopping complex, by Tomás Taveira, is another striking contribution.

Portugal's most prolific contemporary architect is Álvaro Siza Vieira. A believer in clarity and simplicity, he takes an expressionist approach that is reflected in projects such as the Pavilhão de Portugal for Expo 98, Porto's splendid Museu de Arte Contemporânea and the Igreja de Santa Maria at Marco de Canavezes, south of Amarante. He has also restored central Lisbon's historic Chiado shopping district with notable sensitivity, following a major fire in 1988.

Spanish architect Santiago Calatrava designed the lean, organic monster Gare do Oriente for Expo 98, architecture that is complemented by the work of many renowned contemporary artists. The interior is more state-of-the-art spaceship than station. In the same area lies Lisbon's architectural trailblazer the Parque das Nações, with a bevy of unique designs, including a riverfront park and Europe's largest aquarium. The longest bridge in Europe, the Ponte de Vasco da Gama, built in 1998, stalks out across the river from nearby.

Since the turn of the millennium, Portugal has seen a handful of architecturally ambitious projects come to fruition. One of the grander projects is Rem Koolhaas' Casa da Música in Porto (2005). From a distance, the extremely forward-looking design appears to be a solid white block of carefully cut crystal. Both geometric and defiantly asymmetrical, the building mixes elements of tradition – like *azulejos* (hand-painted tiles) hidden in one room – with high modernism, such as the enormous curtains of corrugated glass flanking the concert stage.

Literary Giants

In 2010, Portugal lost one of its greatest writers when José Saramago died at the age of 87. Known for his discursive, cynical and darkly humorous novels, Saramago gained worldwide attention after winning the Nobel Prize in 1998. His best works mine the depths of the human experience and are often set in a uniquely Portuguese landscape. Sometimes his quasi-magical tales revolve around historic events – like the Christian Siege of Lisbon or the building of the Palácio Nacional de Mafra – while at other times he takes on grander topics (writing, for instance, of Jesus' life as a fallible human being) or even creates modern-day fables (in *Blindness*, everyone on earth suddenly goes blind). As a self-described libertarian communist, Saramago had political views that sometimes landed him in trouble. After his name was removed from a list of nominees for a European literary prize, he went into self-imposed exile, spending the last years of his life in the Canary Islands.

In the shadow of Saramago, António Lobo Antunes is Portugal's other literary great – and many of his admirers say the Nobel committee gave the prize to the wrong Portuguese writer. Antunes produces magical, fast-paced prose, often with dark undertones and vast historical sweeps; some critics compare his work to that of William Faulkner. Antunes' writing reflects his harrowing experience as a field doctor in Angola during Portugal's bloody colonial wars, and he often turns a critical gaze on Portuguese history – setting his novels around colonial wars, the dark days of the Salazar dictatorship and the 1974 revolution. Slowly gaining an international following, Antunes is still active today, and many of his earlier novels have finally been translated into English.

Fernando Pessoa

'There's no such man known as Fernando Pessoa,' swore Alberto Caeiro, who, truth be told, didn't really exist himself. He was one of more than a dozen heteronyms (identities) adopted by Fernando Pessoa (1888–1935), Portugal's greatest 20th-century poet.

Heralded by literary critics as one of the icons of modernism, Pessoa was also among the stranger characters to wander the streets of Lisbon. He worked as a translator by day (having learned English while living in South Africa as a young boy) and wrote poetry by night – but not just Pessoa's poetry. He took on numerous personas, writing in entirely different styles, representing different philosophies, backgrounds and levels of mastery. Of Pessoa's four primary heteronyms, Alberto Caeiro was regarded as the great master by other heteronyms Alvaro de Campos and Ricardo Reis. (Fernando Pessoa was the fourth heteronym, but his existence, as alluded to earlier, was denied by the other three.) Any one style would have earned Pessoa renown as a major poet of his time, but considered together, the variety places him among the greats of modern literature.

Pessoa for many is inextricably linked to Lisbon. He spent his nights in cafes, writing, drinking and talking until late into the evening. Many of his works are set in Lisbon's old neighbourhoods. Among Pessoa's phobias: lightning and having his photograph taken. You can see a few of the existing photos of him at the Café Martinho da Arcada, one of his regular haunts.

Despite his quirks and brilliance, Pessoa published very little in his lifetime, with his great work *Livro do Desassossego* (Book of Disquiet) only appearing in 1982, 50 years after it was written. In fact, the great bulk of Pessoa's writing was discovered after his death: thousands of manuscript pages lay hidden away inside a wooden trunk. Scholars are still poring over his elusive works.

Painting

The Early Masters

As Gothic art gave way to more humanistic Renaissance works, Portugal's 15th-century painters developed their own style. Led by the master Nuno Gonçalves, the *escola nacional* (national school) took religious subjects and grounded them against contemporary backgrounds. In Gonçalves' most famous painting, the panels of Santo Antonio (in Lisbon's Museu Nacional de Arte Antiga), he includes a full milieu of Portuguese society – noblemen, Jews, fishermen, sailors, knights, priests, monks and beggars.

Some of Portugal's finest early paintings emerged from the 16th-century Manueline school. These artists, influenced by Flemish painters, developed a style known for its incredible delicacy, realism and luminous colours. The most celebrated painter of his time was Vasco Fernandes, known as Grão Vasco (1480–1543). His richly hued paintings (still striking five centuries later) hang in a museum in Viseu dedicated to his work – as well as that of his Manueline school colleague Gaspar Vaz. Meanwhile, sculptors including Diogo de Boitaca went wild with Portuguese seafaring fantasies and exuberant decoration on some of Portugal's icons.

The Star of Óbidos

The 17th century saw a number of talented Portuguese artists emerge. One of the best was Josefa de Óbidos, who enjoyed success as a female artist – an extreme rarity in those days. Josefa's paintings were unique in their personal, sympathetic interpretations of religious subjects and for their sense of innocence. Although she studied at an Augustine convent as a young girl, she left without taking the vows and settled in Óbidos (where she got her nickname). Still she maintained close ties to the church, which provided many of her commissions, and remained famously chaste until her death in 1684. Josefa left one of the finest legacies of work of any Portuguese painter. She excelled in richly coloured still lifes and detailed religious works, ignoring established iconography.

Naturalism

In the 19th century, naturalism was the dominant trend, with a handful of innovators pushing Portuguese art in new directions. Columbano Bordalo Pinheiro, who hailed from a family of artists, was a seminal figure among the Portuguese artists of his time. He played a prominent role in the Leã d'Ouro, a group of distinguished artists, writers and intellectuals who gathered in the capital and were deeply involved in the aesthetic trends of the day. A prolific artist, Pinheiro painted some of the luminaries of his day, including the novelist Eça de Queirós and Teófilo Braga (a celebrated writer who later became president of the early republic). One of his best-known works is a haunting portrait of the poet Antero de Quental, who later died by suicide.

The 20th Century

Building on the works of the naturalists, Amadeo de Souza-Cardoso lived a short but productive life, experimenting with new techniques emerging in Europe. Raised in a sleepy village outside Amarante, he studied architecture at the Academia de Belas Artes in Lisbon but soon dropped out and moved to Paris. There he found his calling as a painter and mingled with the leading artists and writers of the time, including Amedeo Modigliani, Gertrude Stein, Max Jacob and many others. He experimented with impressionism, and later cubism and futurism, and created a captivating body of work, though he is little known outside Portugal.

Casa das Histórias Paula Rego, Cascais

José Sobral de Almada Negreiros delved even deeper into futurism, inspired by the Italian futurist Filippo Tommaso Marinetti. His work encompassed richly hued portraits with abstract geometrical details – an example is his famous 1954 portrait of Fernando Pessoa – and he was also a sculptor, writer and critic. He managed to walk a fine line during the Salazar regime, creating large-scale murals by public commission as well as socially engaged works critical of Portuguese society.

Paula Rego

The conservative Salazar years of the mid-20th century didn't create the ideal environment to nurture contemporary creativity, so many artists left the country. These include Portugal's best-known living artist, Paula Rego, who was born in Lisbon in 1935 but has been a resident of the UK since 1951. Rego's signature style developed around fairy-tale paintings with a nightmarish twist. Her works deal in ambiguity and psychological and sexual tension, such as The Family (1988), where a seated businessman is either being tortured or smothered with affection by his wife and daughter. Domination, fear, sexuality and grief are all recurring themes in Rego's paintings, and the mysterious and sinister atmosphere, heavy use of chiaroscuro (stark contrasting of light and shade) and strange distortion of scale are reminiscent of the work of surrealists Max Ernst and Giorgio de Chirico.

Rego is considered one of the great early champions of painting from a female perspective and she continues to add to a substantial volume of work. Her acclaim is growing, particularly with the opening of the Casa das Histórias Paula Rego, in Cascais, which showcases her work.

The Unfinished Chapels, Mosteiro de Santa Maria da Vitória (p255)

Religion

Christianity has been a powerful force in shaping Portugal's history, and religion still plays an important role in the lives of its people. Churches and cathedrals are sprinkled across the country, and Portugal's biggest celebrations revolve around religious events. Portugal is also home to a number of pilgrimage sites, the most important of which, Fátima, attracts several million pilgrims each year.

Church & State

Portugal has a deep connection to the church. Even during the long rule of the Moors, Christianity flourished in the north – which provided a strategic base for Christian crusaders to retake the kingdom. Cleric and king walked hand in hand, from the earliest papal alliances of the 11th century through to the 17th century, when the church played a role both at home and in Portugal's expanding empire.

Things ran smoothly until the 18th century, when the Marquês de Pombal, a man of the Enlightenment, wanted to curtail the power of the church – specifically that of the Jesuits, whom he expelled in 1759. He also sought to modernise the Portuguese state (overseeing one of the world's first urban 'grid' systems) and brought education under the state's control. State–church relations see-sawed over the next 150 years, with power struggles

Basilica relief detail, Fátima

DANITA DELIMONT / GETTY IMAGES ©

including the outright ban of religious orders in 1821 and the seizing by the state of many church properties.

The separation of church and state was formally recognised during the First Republic (1910–26). But in practice the church remained intimately linked to many aspects of people's lives. Health and education were largely under religious auspices, with Catholic schools and hospitals the norm. Social outlets for those in rural areas were mostly church related. And the completion of any public-works project always included a blessing by the local bishop.

In 1932 António de Oliveira Salazar swept into power, establishing a Mussolini-like Estado Novo (New State) that lasted until the 1974 Revolution of the Carnations. Salazar had strong ties to the Catholic church – he spent eight years studying for the priesthood before switching to law. His college roommate was a priest who later became the Cardinal Patriarch of Lisbon. Salazar was a ferocious anticommunist and he used Roman Catholic references to appeal to people's sense of authority, order and discipline. He described the family, the parish and the larger institution of Christianity as the foundations of the state. Church officials who spoke out against him were silenced or forced into exile.

Following the 1974 revolution, the church found itself out of favour with many Portuguese; its support of the Salazar regime spelt its undoing in the topsy-turvy days following the government's collapse. The new constitution, ratified in 1976, again emphasised the formal separation of church and state, although this time the law had teeth, and Portugal quickly transitioned into a more secular society. Today, only about half of all weddings happen inside a church. Divorce is legal, as is abortion (up to 10 weeks; the law went into effect following a 2007 referendum). In 2010 same-sex marriage was legalised, making Portugal the sixth European nation to permit it (with several other nations joining the ranks in recent years).

Life Under Muslim Rule

The Moors ruled southern Portugal for almost 400 years; some scholars describe that time as a golden age. The Arabs introduced irrigation, previously unknown in Europe. The Moors opened schools and set about campaigns to achieve mass literacy (in Arabic, of course), as well as the teaching of mathematics, geography and history. Medicine reached new levels of sophistication. There was also a degree of religious tolerance, but this evaporated when Christian crusaders came to power. Much to the chagrin of Christian slave owners, slavery was not permitted in the Islamic kingdom – making it a refuge for runaway slaves. Muslims, Christians and Jews all peacefully co-existed and at times even collaborated, creating one of the most scientifically and artistically advanced societies the world had ever known.

The Inquisition

'After the earthquake, which had destroyed three-quarters of the city of Lisbon, the wise men of that country could think of no means more effectual to preserve the kingdom from utter ruin than to entertain the people with an *auto-da-fé...*'
  – Voltaire, *Candide*

One of the darkest episodes in Portugal's history, the Inquisition was a campaign of church-sanctioned terror and execution that began in 1536 and lasted for 200 years, though it was not officially banned until 1821. It was initially aimed at Jews, who were either expelled from Portugal or forced to renounce their faith. Those who didn't embrace Catholicism risked facing the *auto-da-fé* (act of faith), a church ceremony consisting of a Mass, a procession of the guilty, the reading of their sentences and, later, their burning at the stake.

'Trials' took place in public squares in Lisbon, Porto, Évora and Coimbra in front of crowds sometimes numbering in the thousands. At the centre, atop a large canopied platform, sat the Grand Inquisitor, surrounded by his staff of aristocrats, priests, bailiffs, torturers and scribes, who meticulously recorded the proceedings.

The victims usually spent years in prison, often undergoing crippling torture, before seeing the light of day. They stood accused of a wide variety of crimes – such as skipping meals on Jewish fast days (signs of 'unreformed' Jews), leaving pork uneaten on the plate, failing to attend Mass or observe the Sabbath, as well as blasphemy, witchcraft and homosexuality. No matter how flimsy the 'evidence' – often delivered to the tribunal by a grudge-bearing neighbour – very few were found not guilty and released. After a decade or so in prison, the condemned were finally brought to their *auto-da-fé*. Before meeting their judgement, they were dressed in a *san benito* (yellow penitential gown painted with flames) and a *coroza* (high conical cap) and brought before the tribunal.

After the sentence was pronounced, judgement was carried out in a different venue. By dawn the next morning, for instance, executioners would lead the condemned to a killing field outside town. Those who repented were strangled before being burnt at the stake. The unrepentant were simply burnt alive.

During the years of the Inquisition, the church executed over 2000 victims and tortured or exiled tens of thousands more. The Portuguese even exported the *auto-da-fé* to the colonies, burning Hindus at the stake in Goa, for instance.

As Voltaire sardonically suggested, superstition played no small part in the *auto-da-fé*. Some believers thought that the earthquake of 1755 was the wrath of God upon them, and that they were being punished – not for their bloody *auto-da-fés* but because the Holy Office hadn't done quite enough to punish the heretics.

The Apparitions at Fátima

For many Portuguese Catholics, Fátima represents one of the most momentous religious events of the 20th century. It transformed a tiny village into a major pilgrimage site for Catholics across the globe. On 13 May 1917, 10-year-old Lúcia Santos and her two younger cousins, Jacinta and Francisco Marto, were out tending their parents' flocks in the fields outside the village of Fátima. Suddenly a bolt of lightning struck the earth, and a woman 'brighter than the sun' appeared before them. According to Santos, she came to them with a message exhorting people to pray and do penance to save sinners. She asked the children to pray the rosary every day, which she said was key to bringing peace to one's own life and to the world. At the time, peace was certainly on the minds of many Portuguese, who were already deeply enmeshed in WWI. She then told the children to come again on the 13th of each month, at the same time and place, and that in October she would reveal herself to them.

Word of the alleged apparition spread, although most who heard the tale of the shepherd children reacted with scepticism. Only a handful of observers came to the

Crypto Jews

When Manuel I banned Judaism, most Jews fled or converted. Some, however, simply hid their faith from public view and wore the facade of being a New Christian (the name given to Jewish converts). Religious ceremonies were held behind closed doors, with the Sabbath lamp placed at the bottom of a clay jar so that it could not be seen from outside. Within their Catholic prayer books Jews composed Jewish prayers, and they even overlaid Jewish prayers atop Catholic rituals (like the making of the sign of the cross).

One Crypto-Jewish community in Belmonte managed to maintain its faith in hiding for over 400 years and was only revealed in 1917. No longer underground (Belmonte now has its own synagogue and Jewish cemetery), members of the community remain quite secretive about the practices they maintained in hiding.

field for the 13 June appearance, but the following month several thousand showed up. That's when the apparition apparently entrusted the children with three secrets. In the weeks that followed, a media storm raged, with the government accusing the church of fabricating an elaborate hoax to revive its flagging popularity. The church, for its part, didn't know how to react. The children were even arrested and interrogated at one point, but the three refused to change their story.

On 13 October 1917, some 70,000 people gathered for what was to be the final appearance of the apparition. Many witnesses there experienced the so-called Miracle of the Sun, where the sun seemed to grow in size and dance in the sky, becoming a whirling disc of fire, shooting out multicoloured rays. Some spoke of being miraculously healed; others were frightened by the experience; still others claimed they saw nothing at all. The three children claimed they saw Mary, Jesus and Joseph in the sky. Newspapers across the country reported on the event and soon a growing hysteria surrounded it.

Only Lúcia made it into adulthood. Jacinta and Francisco, both beatified by the church in 2000, were two of the more than 20 million killed during the 1918 influenza epidemic. Lúcia later became a Carmelite nun and died at the age of 97 on 13 February 2007.

★ Religious Events

Semana Santa (Braga)

Festa de São João (Porto & Braga)

Festa de Santo António (Lisbon)

Fátima Romaris (Fátima)

Romaria de Nossa Senhora d'Agonia
(Viana do Castelo)

Farricoco (hooded man), Semana Santa procession

EMANUELE SIRACUSA / GETTY IMAGES ©

Faith on the Decline

The percentage of Portuguese who consider themselves Catholics (around 85%) ranks among the highest in Western Europe. The number of the faithful, however, has been on a steady decline since the 1970s, when over 95% of the nation was Catholic. Today nearly half a million residents describe themselves as agnostic and less than 20% of the population are practising Catholics.

Regional differences reveal a more complicated portrait: around half of northern Portugal's population still attend Sunday Mass, as do more than a quarter in Lisbon – with noticeably fewer churchgoers on the southern coast.

O Fado by José Malhoa (1910), Museu do Fado

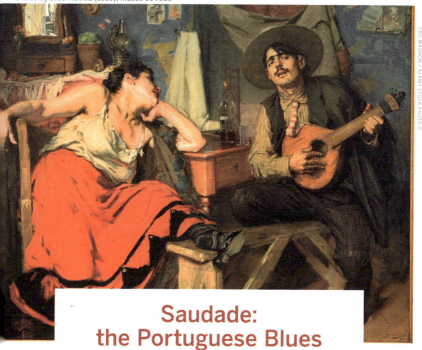

CRO MAGNON / ALAMY STOCK PHOTO ©

Saudade:
the Portuguese Blues

The Portuguese psyche is a complicated thing, particularly when it comes to elusive concepts like saudade. In its purest form, saudade is the nostalgic, often deeply melancholic longing for something: a person, a place or just about anything that's no longer obtainable. Saudade is profoundly connected to the seafaring nation's history and remains deeply intertwined with Portuguese identity.

Roots of Saudade

Scholars are unable to pinpoint exactly when the term *'saudade'* first arose. Some trace it back to the grand voyages during the Age of Discoveries, when sailors, captains and explorers spent many months at sea and gave voice to the longing for the lives they left behind. Yet even before the epic voyages across the ocean, Portugal was a nation of seafarers, and *saudade* probably arose from those on *terra firma* – the women who longed for the men who spent endless days out at sea, some of whom never returned.

Naturally, emigration is also deeply linked to *saudade*. Long one of Europe's poorest peoples, the Portuguese were often driven by hardship to seek better lives abroad. Until recently, this usually meant the men leaving behind their families to travel to northern Europe or America to find work. Families sometimes waited years before being reunited, with emigrants experiencing years of painful longing for their homeland – for the familiar faces and foods, and village life. Many did eventually return, but of course things had changed and so *saudade* reappeared, this time in the form of longing for the way things were in the past.

A Nation of Emigrants

The great discoveries of Portuguese seafarers had profound effects on the country's demographics. With the birth and expansion of an empire, Portuguese settled in trading posts in Africa and Asia, but the colony of Brazil drew the biggest numbers of early Portuguese emigrants. They cleared the land (harvesting the Brazil wood that gave the colony its name), set up farms and set about the slow, steady task of nation-building – with help, of course, from the millions of slaves brought forcibly from Africa. Numbers vary widely, but an estimated half a million Portuguese settled in Brazil during the colonial period, prior to independence in 1822, and over 400,000 flooded in during the second half of the 19th century.

By the 1900s, Portuguese began emigrating in large numbers to other parts of the world. The US and Canada received over half a million immigrants, with huge numbers heading to France, Germany, Venezuela and Argentina. The 1960s saw another surge of emigrants, as young men fled the country in order to avoid the draft that would send them to fight bloody colonial wars in Africa. The 1974 revolution also preceded a big exodus, as those associated with the Salazar regime went abroad rather than face reprisals.

What all these emigrants had in common was the deep sadness of leaving their homeland to struggle in foreign lands. Those left behind were also in a world of heartache – wives left to raise children alone, villages deserted of young men, families torn apart. The numbers are staggering: over three million emigrants between 1890 and 1990; no other European country apart from Ireland lost as many people to emigration.

Saudade in Literature

One of the first great Portuguese works of literature that explores the theme of *saudade* is *Os Lusíadas* (The Lusiads; The Portuguese). Luís Vaz de Camões mixes mythology with historical events in his verse epic about the Age of Discoveries of the 15th and 16th centuries. The heroic adventurer Vasco da Gama and other explorers strive for glory, but many never return, facing hardship (sea monsters, treacherous kings) along the way. First-hand experience informed Camões' work: he served in the overseas militia, lost an eye in Ceuta in a battle with the Moors, served prison time in Portugal and survived a shipwreck in the Mekong (swimming ashore with his unfinished manuscript held aloft, according to legend).

The great 19th-century Portuguese writer Almeida Garrett wrote an even more compelling take on the Age of Discoveries. In his book *Camões*, a biography of the poet, he describes the longing Camões felt for Portugal while in exile. He also captured the greater sense of *saudade* that so many experienced as Portugal's empire crumbled in the century following the great explorations.

More recent writers also explore the notion of *saudade*, though they take radically different approaches from their predecessors. Contemporary writer António Lobo Antunes deconstructs *saudade* in cynical tales that expose the nostalgic longing for something as a form of neurotic self-delusion. In *As Naus* (The Return of the Caravels; 1988), he turns the discovery myth on its head when, four centuries after da Gama's voyage, the great explorers, through some strange time warp, become entangled with the *retornados* (who returned to Portugal in the 1970s, after the loss of the country's African empire) as Renaissance-era achievements collapse in the poor, grubby, lower-class neighbourhoods of Lisbon.

Saudade in Film

Portugal's most prolific film-maker, Manoel de Oliveira (1908–2015), was making films well past his 100th birthday. In a career that spanned 75 years, he became known for carefully crafted, if slow-moving, films that delve deep into the world of *saudade* – of growing old, unrequited loves and longing for things that no longer exist. In *Viagem ao Princípio do Mundo* (Voyage to the Beginning of the World; 1997), several companions make a nostalgic tour of the rugged landscapes and traditional villages of the north – one in search of a past that he knows only in his dreams (having heard of his ancestral land from his Portuguese-born father), another haunted by a world that no longer exists (the places of his childhood having been uprooted). Past and present, nostalgia and reality collide in this quiet, meditative film. It stars a frail, 72-year-old Marcello Mastroianni as Oliveira's alter ego; this was the actor's final film before he died.

One of the finest love letters to the capital is the sweet, meandering *Lisbon Story* (1994), directed by German film-maker Wim Wenders. The story follows a sound engineer who goes in search of a missing director, discovering the city through the footage his friend left behind. Carefully crafted scenes conjure up the mystery and forlorn beauty of Lisbon (and other parts of Portugal, including a wistful sequence on the dramatic cliffs of Cabo Espichel). *Saudade* here explores many different realms, inspired in large part by the ethereal soundtrack by Madredeus – band members also play supporting roles in the film.

Fado

'I don't sing fado. It sings me.' – Amália Rodrigues.

Portugal's most famous style of music, fado (Portuguese for 'fate'), couldn't really exist without *saudade*. These melancholic songs are dripping with emotion – and revel in stories of the painful twists and turns of fate, of unreachable distant lovers, fathomless yearning

 Saudade of the Jews

Until the end of the 15th century, Jews enjoyed a prominent place in Portuguese society. The treasurer of King Afonso V (1432–81) was Jewish, as were others who occupied diplomatic posts and worked as trade merchants, physicians and cartographers. Jews from other countries were welcomed in Portugal, including those expelled from Spain in 1492. Eventually, pressure from the church and from Spain forced the king's hand, and in 1497 Manuel I decreed that all Jews convert to Christianity or leave the country. A catalogue of horrors followed, including the massacre of thousands of Jews in 1506 by mobs run riot and two centuries of the bloody Inquisition that kicked off in 1536.

Aside from a secretive Crypto-Jewish group in Belmonte that managed to preserve their faith, the Judaic community slowly withered and perished. Those who converted felt the heart-rending *saudade* of deep loss – essentially the loss of their identity. Once flourishing Jewish neighbourhoods died as residents went into exile or perhaps suffered arrest, torture and even execution. The personal losses paralleled the end of a flourishing and tolerant period in Portugal's history and effectively ended the Jewish presence in Portugal.

for one's homeland and wondrous days that have come and gone. The emotional quality of the singing plays just as important a role as technical skill, helping fado to reach across linguistic boundaries. Listening to fado is perhaps the easiest way of understanding *saudade*, in all its evocative variety.

A style born in the capital in the 19th century, fado is Portugal's greatest contribution to world music. In 2011 Unesco recognised fado's significance by adding the genre to its list of the World's Intangible Cultural Heritage. Its origins are unclear – it may have been influenced by the rhythms and chants from around Portugal's empire. However, it's known that it emerged from the working-class neighbourhoods of Mouraria and Alfama in the late 19th century, only to be taken up by the upper classes. Coimbra has its own, quite different style of fado, heard around the university and performed by men only.

Fados are traditionally sung by one performer accompanied by a 12-string Portuguese *guitarra* (pear-shaped guitar). When two fadistas perform, they sometimes engage in *desgarrada*, a bit of improvisational one-upmanship where the singers challenge and play off one another. At fado houses there are usually a number of singers, each one traditionally singing three songs.

Amália Rodrigues (1920–99) remains the most famous fado performer, reaching her zenith in the 1940s and '50s.

Ponta da Piedade (p141), Lagos

M SWET PRODUCTIONS / GETTY IMAGES ©

Survival Guide

Directory A–Z

Accommodation

Although you can usually show up in any town and find a room on the spot, it's worthwhile booking ahead, especially for July and August.

Accommodation Types

○ **Guest houses** Small, often family-run places, some set in historic buildings; amenities range from simple to luxurious.

○ **Hostels** Portugal has a growing network of hostels around the country, with many choices in Lisbon and Porto.

○ **Turihab Properties** Options to stay in characterful manor houses, restored farmhouses or self-contained stone cottages.

○ **Pousadas** Unique accommodation inside former castles, monasteries and estates; nearly three dozen *pousadas* are spread across the country.

○ **Private rooms and apartments** Loads of online listings throughout Portugal.

Seasons

In popular tourist destinations prices rise and fall with the seasons. Mid-June to mid-September are firmly high season (book well ahead); May to mid-June

and mid-September to October are midseason; and other times are low season, when you can get some really good deals. Outside the resorts, prices don't vary much between seasons.

In the Algarve, you'll pay the highest premium for rooms from mid-July to the end of August, with slightly lower prices from June to mid-July and in September, and substantially less (as much as 50%) if you travel between November and April. Note that a handful of places in the Algarve close in winter.

Price Ranges

The following price ranges refer to a double room with bathroom in high season. Unless otherwise stated breakfast is included in the price.

Category	Cost
€	less than €60
€€	€60–€120
€€€	more than €120

Book Your Stay Online

For more accommodation reviews by Lonely Planet authors, check out http://hotels.lonelyplanet.com/portugal. You'll find independent reviews, as well as recommendations on the best places to stay. Best of all, you can book online.

Turihab Properties

These charming properties are part of a government scheme, through which you can stay in a farmhouse, manor house, country estate or rustic cottage as the owner's guest.

High-season rates for two people, either in a double room or a cottage, range from €70 to €140. Some properties have swimming pools, and most include breakfast (often with fresh local produce).

There are three types of Turihab lodgings:

Aldeias de Portugal (www.aldeiasdeportugal.pt) Lodging in rural villages in the north, often in beautifully converted stone cottages.

Casas no Campo (www.casasnocampo.net) Country houses, cottages and luxury villas.

Solares de Portugal (www.solaresdeportugal.pt) Grand manor houses, some of which date from the 17th or 18th century.

Climate

Lisbon

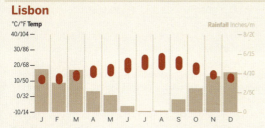

Porto

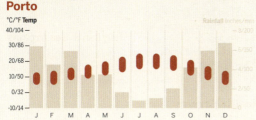

Lagos

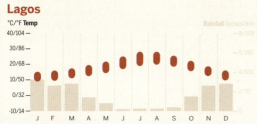

Electricity

220V/50Hz

230V/50Hz

Bargaining

Gentle haggling is common in markets (less so in produce markets); in all other instances you're expected to pay the stated price.

Customs Regulations

You can bring as much currency as you like into Portugal, though €10,000 or more must be declared.

The duty-free allowance for travellers more than 17 years old from non-EU countries:

◉ 200 cigarettes or the equivalent in tobacco.

◉ 1L of alcohol that's more than 22% alcohol, or 2L of wine or beer.
Allowance for nationals of EU countries:

◉ 800 cigarettes or the equivalent.

◉ 10L of spirits, 20L of fortified wine, 60L of sparkling wine or a mind-boggling 90L of still wine or 110L of beer.

Etiquette

◉ **Greetings** When greeting females or mixed company, an air kiss on both cheeks is common courtesy. Men give each other a handshake.

○ **Visiting churches** It is considered disrespectful to visit churches as a tourist during Mass. Taking photos at such a time is definitely inappropriate.

○ **'Free' appetisers** Whatever you eat, you must pay for, whether or not you ordered it. It's common practice for restaurants to bring bread, olives, cheese and other goodies to the table, but these are never free and will be added to your bill at the end. If you don't want them, a polite 'No, thank you' will see them returned to the kitchen.

Food

The following price ranges refer to a standard main dish:

€	less than €10
€€	€10–€20
€€€	more than €20

Health

Portugal has a high-quality healthcare system, with pharmacies and doctors readily available countrywide. Most pharmacists speak some English. They can also advise when more specialised help is required.

Citizens of the EU are eligible for free emergency medical treatment if they have a European Health Insurance Card (EHIC). Citizens from other countries should find out if there is a reciprocal arrangement for free medical care between their country and Portugal.

Tap water is generally safe to drink in Portugal.

Health Hazards

Heat Exhaustion & Heat Stroke

Be mindful of heat exhaustion, particularly on hot summer days in the Algarve, and when engaging in vigorous outdoor activities anywhere in the country during the hottest months. Heat exhaustion occurs following excessive fluid loss with inadequate replacement of fluids and salt. Symptoms include headache, dizziness and tiredness. To treat heat exhaustion, replace lost fluids by drinking water and/or fruit juice or an oral rehydration solution, such as Dioralyte; cool the body with cold water and fans.

Heat stroke is much more serious, resulting in irrational and hyperactive behaviour and eventually loss of consciousness and death. Rapid cooling by spraying the body with water and fanning is ideal. Emergency fluid and electrolyte replacement by intravenous drip is recommended.

Jellyfish & Sea Urchins

In general, jellyfish aren't a major problem in Portuguese waters, though there are rare sightings along the southern beaches. Stings from jellyfish are painful but not dangerous. Douse the wound in vinegar to deactivate any stingers that haven't 'fired'. Applying calamine lotion, antihistamines or analgesics may reduce the reaction and relieve the pain.

Watch for sea urchins around rocky beaches. If you get their needles embedded in your skin, immerse the limb in hot water to relieve the pain. To avoid infection visit a doctor and have the needles removed.

Insurance

Don't leave home without a travel-insurance policy to cover theft, loss and medical problems. You should get insurance for the worst-case scenario; for example, an accident or illness requiring hospitalisation and a flight home.

Travel Health Websites

It's a good idea to consult your government's travel-health website before departure, if one is available:

○ **Australia** (www.smartraveller.gov.au)

○ **Canada** (www.travel.gc.ca)

○ **UK** (www.fitfortravel.nhs.uk)

○ **USA** (http://wwwnc.cdc.gov/travel)

Some policies specifically exclude 'dangerous activities' such as scuba diving, motorcycling or even trekking. If these activities are in your sights, either find another policy or ask about an amendment (usually available for an extra premium) that includes them.

Make sure you keep all documentation for any claims later on. Some policies ask you to call back (reverse charges) to a centre in your home country, where an immediate assessment of your problem is made.

Worldwide travel insurance is available at www. lonelyplanet.com/travel-insurance. You can buy, extend and claim online any time – even if you're already on the road.

Internet Access

Wi-fi access is widespread in Portugal and most hotels, hostels and midrange guest houses offer free wireless access. Many cafes and some restaurants also offer free wi-fi. Cybercafes are now rare.

We use the icon @ to indicate places that have a physical computer where guests can access the internet; the wi-fi icon indicates where wireless access is available.

Other options:

○ Bibliotecas municipais Municipal libraries.

○ Rede de Espaços Internet (www.redeespacos internet.pt) Municipally run spaces where you can get online for free.

Legal Matters

○ Fines for illegal parking are common. If you're parked illegally you'll be towed and will have to pay around €100 to get your car back. Be aware of local road rules, as fines for other transgressions will also be enforced.

○ It's illegal in Portugal to drive while talking on a mobile phone.

○ Narcotic drugs were decriminalised in 2001 in an attempt to clear up the public-health problems among drug users and to address the issue as a social rather than a criminal one. You may be brought before a commission and subject to fines or treatment if you are caught with up to 10 doses of a drug.

○ Drug dealing is still a serious offence and suspects may be held for up to 18 months before coming to trial. Bail is at the court's discretion.

LGBTIQ Travellers

In 2010 Portugal legalised gay marriage, becoming the sixth European country to do so. Most Portuguese profess a laissez-faire attitude about same-sex couples, although how out you can be depends on where you are in Portugal. In Lisbon, Porto and the Algarve, acceptance has increased, whereas in most other areas, same-sex couples would be met with incomprehension. In this conservative Catholic country, homosexuality is still outside the norm. And while homophobic violence is extremely rare, discrimination has been reported in schools and workplaces.

Lisbon has the country's best gay and lesbian network and nightlife. Lisbon and Porto hold Gay Pride marches, but outside these events the gay community keeps a discreet profile.

Maps

National and natural park offices usually have simple park maps, though these are of little use for trekking or cycling. The following offer a good range of maps:
Omni Resources (www.omni-imap.com) US company that sells excellent maps, including 1:25,000 topographic maps.
Stanfords (www.stanfords.co.uk) Good selection of Portugal maps and travel products in the UK.

Money

Portugal uses the euro, along with most other European nations.

ATMs

ATMs are the easiest way to get cash in Portugal and they are easy to find in most cities and towns. Tiny rural villages probably won't have ATMs, so it's wise to get cash in advance. Most banks have a Multibanco ATM, with menus in English (and other languages), that accept Visa, Access, MasterCard, Cirrus and so on. You just need your card and PIN. Keep in mind that the ATM limit is €200 per withdrawal and many banks charge a foreign transaction fee (typically around 2% to 3%).

Changing Money

Note that banks and *bureaux de change* are free to set their own rates and commissions, so a low commission might mean a skewed exchange rate.

Credit Cards

Most hotels and smarter restaurants accept credit cards; smaller guest houses, budget hotels and smaller restaurants might not, so it's wise to have cash with you.

Exchange Rates

Australia	A$1	€0.66
Canada	C$1	€0.70
Japan	¥100	€0.83
New Zealand	NZ$1	€0.63
UK	£1	€1.17
USA	US$1	€0.89

For current exchange rates see www.xe.com.

Tipping

o **Bars** Not expected unless table service is provided, then around 10%.

o **Hotels** One euro per bag is standard; gratuity for cleaning staff is at your discretion.

o **Restaurants** 10% on average, up to 15% in pricier places.

o **Snack bars** It's courteous to leave a bit of spare change.

o **Taxis** Not expected, but it's polite to round up to the nearest euro.

Opening Hours

Opening hours vary throughout the year. We provide high-season opening hours; hours will generally decrease in the shoulder and low seasons.

Banks 8.30am to 3pm Monday to Friday

Bars 7pm to 2am

Cafes 9am to 7pm

Clubs 11pm to 4am Thursday to Saturday

Restaurants noon to 3pm and 7pm to 10pm

Shopping malls 10am to 10pm

Shops 9.30am to noon and 2pm to 7pm Monday to Friday, 10am to 1pm Saturday

Post

Post offices are called CTT (www.ctt.pt). *Correio normal* (ordinary mail) goes in the red letterboxes; *correio azul* (airmail) goes in the blue boxes. Automated red postal stands dispense stamps, saving you the hassle of waiting in line at the post office. Post to Europe takes up to five working days, and to the rest of the world up to seven. Economy mail (or surface airlift) is about a third cheaper, but takes a week or so longer.

Public Holidays

Banks, offices, department stores and some shops close on the public holidays listed here. On New Year's Day, Easter Sunday, Labour Day and Christmas Day, even *turismos* close.

New Year's Day 1 January

Carnaval Tuesday February/March – the day before Ash Wednesday

Good Friday March/April

Liberty Day 25 April

Labour Day 1 May

Corpus Christi May/June – ninth Thursday after Easter

Portugal Day 10 June – also known as Camões and Communities Day

Feast of the Assumption 15 August

Republic Day 5 October

All Saints' Day 1 November

Independence Day 1 December

Feast of the Immaculate Conception 8 December

Christmas Day 25 December

Safe Travel

○ Once behind the wheel of a car, the otherwise mild-mannered Portuguese change personality. Macho driving, such as tailgating at high speeds and overtaking on blind corners, is all too common. Portugal has one of the highest road accident rates in Europe. Police have responded by aggressively patrolling certain dangerous routes, such as on the cheerfully named 'highway of death' from Salamanca in Spain.

○ Compared with other European countries, Portugal's crime rate remains low, but some types of crime – including car theft – are on the rise. Crime against foreigners is of the usual rush-hour-pickpocketing, bag-snatching and theft-from-rental-cars variety. Take the usual precautions: don't flash your cash; keep valuables in a safe place; and, if you're challenged, hand it over – it's not worth taking the risk.

○ Take care in the water; the surf can be strong, with dangerous ocean currents.

Taxes & Refunds

Prices in Portugal almost always include 23% VAT (some basic food stuffs and services carry reduced rates of 6% and 13%, respectively). Non-EU passport holders can claim back the VAT on goods from participating retailers – be sure to ask for the tax back forms and get them stamped by customs. Refunds are processed at the airport or via post.

Telephone

To call Portugal from abroad, dial the international access code (📞00), then Portugal's country code (📞351), then the number. All domestic numbers have nine digits, and there are no area codes. Most public phones accept phone cards only – available at most news stands – though a few coin-operated phones are still around. You can also make calls from booths in Portugal Telecom offices and some post offices – pay when your call is finished.

Long-distance and international calls are cheaper from 9pm to 9am weekdays, all weekend and on holidays.

Government Travel Advice

The following government websites offer travel advisories and information on current hot spots.

○ **Australian Department of Foreign Affairs** (www.smarttraveller.gov.au)

○ **British Foreign Office** (www.gov.uk/foreign-travel-advice)

○ **Canadian Department of Foreign Affairs** (www.travel.gc.ca)

○ **US State Department** (http://travel.state.gov)

The cheapest way to call within Portugal is with a Portugal Telecom *cartão telefónico* (phone card). These are available for €3, €5 and €10 from post and telephone offices and many newsagents. A youth or student card should get you a 10% discount.

Local calls cost around €0.10 per minute to land lines and €0.30 per minute to mobile phones. Numbers starting with 800 (*linha verde*: green line) are toll free. Those starting with 808 (*linha azul*: blue line) are charged at local rates from anywhere in the country.

Mobile phones

Local SIM cards can be used in unlocked European, Australian and quad-band US mobiles. Portugal uses the GSM 900/1800 frequency, the same as found in Australia, the UK and the rest of the EU. Mobile-phone usage is widespread in Portugal, with extensive coverage provided in all but the most rural areas. The main domestic operators are Vodafone, Optimus and TMN. All of them sell pre-paid SIM cards that you can insert into a GSM mobile phone and use as long as the phone is not locked by the company providing you service. If you need a phone, you can buy one at the airport and shops throughout the country with a package of minutes for under €20. This is generally cheaper than renting a phone.

Toilets

Finding public toilets in major cities such as Lisbon and Porto can be difficult. Most towns and villages that draw tourists usually have free public toilets. The *mercado municipal* (municipal market) often has free toilets. These are generally fairly clean and adequately maintained. In more built-up areas, your best bet is to look for a toilet in a shopping centre, or simply duck into a cafe.

Tourist Information

● Turismo de Portugal, the country's national tourist board, operates a handy website: www.visitportugal.com.

● Locally managed *postos de turismo* (tourist offices, usually signposted '*turismo*') are everywhere, offering brochures and varying degrees of help with sights and accommodation.

Travellers with Disabilities

● The term *deficientes* (Portuguese for 'disabled') gives some indication of the limited awareness of disabled needs. Although public offices and agencies are required to provide access and facilities for people with disabilities, private businesses are not.

● Lisbon airport is wheelchair accessible, while Porto and Faro airports have accessible toilets.

● Parking spaces are allotted in many places, but are frequently occupied. The EU parking card entitles visitors to the same street-parking concessions given to disabled residents. If you're in the UK, contact the **Department for Transport** (☑020-7944 8300; www.gov.uk/browse/disabilities).

● Newer and larger hotels tend to have some adapted rooms, though the facilities may not be up to scratch; ask at the local *turismo*. Most campgrounds have accessible toilets and some hostels have facilities for people with disabilities.

● Lisbon, with its cobbled streets and hills, may be difficult for some travellers with disabilities, but not impossible. The Baixa's flat grid and Belém are fine, and all the sights at Parque das Nações are accessible. Download Lonely Planet's free Accessible Travel guide from http://lptravel.to/AccessibleTravel, or for more information, contact:

Accessible Portugal (☑926 910 989; www.accessibleportugal.com; Rua Jorge Barradas 50, 4th fl) This Lisbon-based tour agency offers a wide range of itineraries and can arrange accommodation, transfers, overnight trips and outdoor activities such as tandem skydiving and hot-air balloon trips.

Cooperativa Nacional de Apoio Deficientes (☑218 595 332; www.facebook.com/cooperativa.deficientes; Praça Dr Fernando Amado, Lote 566-E, Lisbon) This is a private organisation that can help with travel needs.

Secretaria do Nacional de Reabilitação (☑217 929 500; www.inr.pt; Av Conde de Valbom 63, Lisbon) The national governmental organisation representing people with disabilities supplies information, provides links to useful operations and publishes guides (in Portuguese) that advise on barrier-free accommodation, transport, shops, restaurants and sights.

Visas

Nationals of EU countries don't need a visa for any length of stay in Portugal. Those from Canada, New Zealand, the USA and (by temporary agreement)

Australia can stay for up to 90 days in any six-month period without a visa. Others, including nationals of South Africa, need a visa unless they're the spouse or child of an EU citizen.

The general requirements for entry into Portugal also apply to citizens of other signatories of the 1990 Schengen Convention (Austria, Belgium, Denmark, Finland, France, Germany, Greece, Iceland, Italy, Luxembourg, the Netherlands, Norway, Spain and Sweden). A visa issued by one Schengen country is generally valid for travel in all the others, but unless you're a citizen of the UK, Ireland or a Schengen country, you should check visa regulations with the consulate of each Schengen country you plan to visit. You must apply for any Schengen visa while you are still in your country of residence.

Women Travellers

○ Women travelling alone in Portugal report few serious problems. As when travelling anywhere, women should take care – be cautious where you walk after dark and don't hitch.

○ If you're travelling with a male partner, people will expect him to do all the talking and ordering and to pay the bill. In some conservative pockets of the north, unmarried couples will save hassle by saying they're married.

○ If you're a victim of violence or rape while you're in Portugal, you can contact the **Associação Portuguesa de Apoio à Vítima** (APAV | Portuguese Association for Victim Support; ☎213 587 900; www.apav.pt; Rua José Estêvão 135, Lisbon), which offers assistance for rape victims. Visit the website for office locations nationwide.

Transport

An increasingly popular destination, Portugal is well connected to North America and European countries by air. There are also handy overland links by bus and train to and from Spain, from where you can continue on to other destinations on the continent.

Flights, cars and tours can be booked online at lonelyplanet.com/bookings.

Getting There & Away

Air

Most international flights arrive in Lisbon, though Porto and Faro also receive some. For more information see www.ana.pt.

TAP (www.flytap.com) is Portugal's international flag carrier as well as its main domestic airline. The three

main airports in Portugal are **Aeroporto de Lisboa** (Lisbon Airport; ☎218 413 700; www.ana.pt; Alameda das Comunidades Portuguesas), **Porto Airport** (OPO; ☎229 432 400; www.ana.pt) and **Faro Airport** (FAO; ☎289 800 800; www.ana.pt;).

Land

Portugal shares a land border only with Spain, but there is both bus and train service linking the two countries, with onward connections to the rest of mainland Europe.

Bus

The major long-distance carriers that serve European destinations are Busabout (www.busabout.com) and Eurolines (www.eurolines.com); though these carriers serve Portugal, it is not currently included in the multicity travel passes of either company.

For some European routes, Eurolines is affiliated with the big Portuguese operators **Internorte** (☎707 200 512; www.internorte.pt) and **Eva Transportes** (☎289 899 760; www.eva-bus.com).

Car & Motorcycle

If you're driving your own car or motorcycle into Portugal, you need the following:

○ vehicle registration (proof of ownership)

○ insurance documents

○ motor vehicle insurance with at least third-party cover

Climate Change & Travel

Every form of transport that relies on carbon-based fuel generates CO_2, the main cause of human-induced climate change. Modern travel is dependent on aeroplanes, which might use less fuel per kilometre per person than most cars but travel much greater distances. The altitude at which aircraft emit gases (including CO_2) and particles also contributes to their climate change impact. Many websites offer 'carbon calculators' that allow people to estimate the carbon emissions generated by their journey and, for those who wish to do so, to offset the impact of the greenhouse gases emitted with contributions to portfolios of climate-friendly initiatives throughout the world. Lonely Planet offsets the carbon footprint of all staff and author travel.

Train

Trains are a popular way to get around Europe – comfortable, frequent and generally on time. But unless you have a rail pass the cost can be higher than flying.

You will have few problems buying long-distance tickets as little as a day or two ahead, even in the summer. For those intending to do a lot of European rail travel, the European Rail Timetable (www.europeanrailtimetable.co.uk) is updated monthly and is available for sale as a digital download on the website. Another excellent resource for train travel around Europe (and beyond) is the Man in Seat Sixty-One website (www.seat61.com).

The Portugal–Spain rail pass (www.raileurope.com) is available only to non-European residents and is valid for a specified period of travel in Spain and Portugal during a two-month period, from four days (US$294)

to 10 days (US$480). First-class tickets cost about 25% more.

River

Transporte Fluvial del Guadiana (www.rioguadiana.net) operates car ferries across the Rio Guadiana between Ayamonte in Spain and Vila Real de Santo António in the Algarve every hour (half-hourly in the summer) from 8.30am to 7pm Monday to Saturday and from 9.30am to 6pm on Sunday. Buy tickets from the waterfront office (€1.80/5.50/1.15 per person/car/bike).

Sea

There are no scheduled seagoing ferries to Portugal, but there are many to Spain. The closest North African ferry connections are from Morocco to Spain; contact Trasmediterranea (www.trasmediterranea.es) for details. Car ferries also run from Tangier to Gibraltar. There

have been rumblings recently that the ferry from Portimão to Madeira and the Canary Islands may be reinstated.

Getting Around

Transport in Portugal is reasonably priced, quick and efficient. Most journeys are taken by bus as the rail network doesn't reach everywhere.

Air

Flights within mainland Portugal are expensive and, for the short distances involved, not really worth considering. Nonetheless, TAP (www.flytap.com) has multiple daily Lisbon–Porto and Lisbon–Faro flights (taking less than one hour) year-round. For Porto to Faro, change in Lisbon.

Bicycle

Cycling is popular in Portugal, even though there are few dedicated bicycle paths. Possible itineraries are numerous in the mountainous national/natural parks of the north (especially Parque Nacional da Peneda-Gerês), along the coast or across the Alentejo plains. Coastal trips are easiest from north to south, with the prevailing winds. More demanding is the Serra da Estrela (which serves as the Tour de Portugal's 'mountain run'). You could also try the Serra do Marão between Amarante and Vila Real.

Local bike clubs organise regular Passeio BTT trips; check their flyers at rental agencies, bike shops and *turismos*. Guided trips are often available in popular tourist destinations.

Cobbled roads in some old-town centres may jar your teeth loose if your tyres aren't fat enough; they should be at least 38mm in diameter.

There are numerous places to rent bikes, especially in the Algarve and other touristy areas. Prices range from €8 to €25 per day.

Boxed or bagged-up bicycles can be taken free on all regional and interregional trains as accompanied baggage. They can also go unboxed on a few suburban services on weekends or for a small charge outside the rush hour. Most domestic bus lines won't accept bikes on board.

Boat

Other than river cruises along the Rio Douro from Porto and the Rio Tejo from Lisbon, Portugal's only remaining waterborne transport are cross-river ferries. Commuter ferries include those across the Rio Tejo to/from Lisbon, and across the mouth of the Rio Sado between Setúbal and Tróia.

Bus

A host of small private bus operators, most amalgamated into regional companies, run a dense network of services across the country. Among the largest are

Rede Expressos (☎707 223 344; www.rede-expressos.pt), **Rodonorte** (☎259 340 710; www.rodonorte.pt) and the Algarve-line Eva Transportes (www.eva-bus.com).

Bus services are of four general types:
Alta Qualidade A fast deluxe category offered by some companies.
Carreiras Marked 'CR'; slow, stopping at every crossroad.
Expressos Comfortable, fast buses between major cities.
Rápidas Quick regional buses.

Even in summer you'll have little problem booking an *expresso* ticket for the same or next day. A Lisbon–Faro express bus takes about four hours and costs €18.50; Lisbon–Porto takes about 3½ hours for around €19. By contrast, local services can thin out to almost nothing on weekends, especially in summer when school is out.

Don't rely on *turismos* for accurate timetable information. Most bus-station ticket desks will give you a little computer printout of fares and services.

Except in Lisbon or Porto, there's little reason to take municipal buses, as most attractions are within walking distance.

Car & Motorcycle

Portugal's modest network of *estradas* (highways) is gradually spreading across the country. Main roads are sealed and generally in good condition. The downside is your fellow drivers: the country's per-capita death

rate from road accidents has long been one of Europe's highest, and drinking, driving and dying are hot political potatoes. The good news is that recent years have seen a steady decline in the road toll, thanks to a zero-tolerance police crackdown on accident-prone routes and alcohol limits.

Driving can be tricky in Portugal's small walled towns, where roads may taper to donkey-cart size before you know it and fiendish one-way systems can force you out of your way.

A common occurrence in larger towns is down-and-outers, who lurk around squares and car parks, waving you into the parking space you've just found for yourself and asking for payment for this service. It's wise to do as Portuguese do, and hand over some coins (€0.50) to keep your car out of 'trouble' (scratches, broken windows, etc).

Automobile Associations

Automóvel Club de Portugal (ACP; ☎213 180 100, 24hr emergency assistance 808 222 222; www.acp.pt), Portugal's national auto club, provides medical, legal and breakdown assistance for its members. Road information and maps are available to anyone at ACP offices, including the head office in Lisbon and branches in Aveiro, Braga, Bragança, Coimbra, Évora, Faro, Porto and elsewhere.

If your national auto club belongs to the Fédération

Internationale de l'Automobile or the Alliance Internationale de Tourisme, you can also use ACP's emergency services and get discounts on maps and other products. Among clubs that qualify are the AA and RAC in the UK, and the Australian, New Zealand, Canadian and US automobile associations.

Driving Licences

Nationals of EU countries, the USA and Brazil need only their home driving licence to operate a car or motorcycle in Portugal. Others should get an International Driving Permit (IDP) through an automobile licencing department or automobile club in their home country.

Fuel

Fuel is expensive – about €1.50 for a litre of *sem chumbo* (unleaded petrol) at the time of writing. There are plenty of self-service stations, and credit cards are accepted at most. If you're near the border, you can save money by filling up in Spain, where it's around 20% cheaper.

Motorways & Tolls

Top of the range roads are *auto-estradas* (motorways), all of them *portagens* (toll roads); the longest of these are Lisbon–Porto and Lisbon–Algarve. Toll roads charge cars and motorcycles a little over €0.06 per kilometre (around €20 from

Lisbon to Porto and €19 from Lisbon to Faro).

Nomenclature can be baffling. Motorway prefixes indicate the following:
A Portugal's toll roads.
E Europe-wide designations.
N Main two-lane *estradas nacionais* (national roads); prefix letter used on some road maps only.
IC (itinerário complementar) Subsidiary highways.
IP (itinerário principal) Main highways.

Note that Portugal's main toll roads now have automated toll booths, meaning you won't be able to simply drive through and pay an attendant. You'll need to hire an electronic tag to pay for the tolls. Many car-rental agencies hire out the small electronic devices (for around €6 per week, less on subsequent weeks) and it's worth inquiring if one is available before renting a car. If you don't use the device, and go through a toll, you may receive a fine (via your car-hire agency) after your trip. The other option is simply to avoid the *auto-estradas*, which isn't always easy to do, especially when travelling across the Algarve.

For more information, including locations where you can hire electronic tag devices throughout the country (useful if your car hire doesn't have them or you're driving your own vehicle), contact government-run **Via Verde** (☎707 500 900; www.viaverde.pt).

Hire

○ To rent a car in Portugal you should be at least 25 years old and have held your driving licence for more than a year (some companies allow younger drivers at higher rates). The widest choice of car-hire companies is at Lisbon, Porto and Faro airports. Competition has driven Algarve rates lower than elsewhere.

○ Some of the best advance-booking rates are offered by internet-based brokers such as Holiday Autos (www.holidayautos. com). Other bargains come as part of 'fly/drive' packages. The worst deals tend to be those done with international firms on arrival, though their prepaid promotional rates are competitive. Book at least a few days ahead in high season. For on-the-spot rental, domestic firms such as Auto Jardim (www.auto-jardim. com) have some of the best rates.

○ The average price for renting the smallest and cheapest available car for a week in high season is around €300 (with tax, insurance and unlimited mileage) if booked from abroad and a similar amount through a Portuguese firm.

○ For an additional fee you can get personal insurance through the rental company, unless you're covered by your home policy. A minimum of third-party coverage is compulsory in the EU.

• Rental cars are especially at risk of break-ins or petty theft in larger towns, so don't leave anything of value visible in the car.

• Motorcycles and scooters can be rented in larger cities, and all over coastal Algarve. Expect to pay from €30/60 per day for a scooter/motorcycle.

Insurance

Your home insurance policy may or may not be extendable to Portugal, and the coverage of some comprehensive policies automatically drops to third party outside your home country unless the insurer is notified.

If you hire a car, the rental firm will provide you with registration and insurance papers, plus a rental contract.

If you are involved in a minor 'fender bender' with no injuries, the easiest way for drivers to sort things out with their insurance companies is to fill out a Constat Aimable (the English version is called a European Accident Statement). There's no risk in signing this: it's just a way to exchange the relevant information and there's usually one included in rental-car documents. Make sure it includes any details that may help you prove that the accident was not your fault. To alert the police, dial 112.

Parking

Parking is often metered within city centres, but is free on Saturday evening and Sunday. Lisbon has car parks, but these can get expensive (upwards of €20 per day).

Road Rules

• Despite the sometimes chaotic relations between drivers, there are rules. To begin with, driving is on the right, overtaking is on the left and most signs use international symbols. An important rule to remember is that traffic from the right usually has priority. Portugal has lots of ambiguously marked intersections, so this is more important than you might think.

• Except when marked otherwise, speed limits for cars (without a trailer) and motorcycles (without a sidecar) are 50km/h in towns and villages, 90km/h outside built-up areas and 120km/h on motorways. By law, car safety belts must be worn in the front and back seats, and children under 12 years may not ride in the front. Motorcyclists and their passengers must wear helmets, and motorcycles must have their headlights on day and night.

• The police can impose steep on-the-spot fines for speeding and parking offences, so save yourself a big hassle and remember to toe the line.

• The legal blood-alcohol limit is 0.5g/L and there are fines of up to €2500 for drink-driving. It's also illegal in Portugal to drive while talking on a mobile phone.

Hitching

Hitching is never entirely safe and we don't recommend it. Travellers who hitch should understand that they are taking a small but potentially serious risk. In any case it isn't an easy option in Portugal. Almost nobody stops on major highways. On smaller roads drivers tend to be going short distances so you might only advance from one field to the next.

Local Transport

Almost all of Portugal's larger towns have a city bus service linking the city centre with outlying suburbs and villages. Fares are low, but services fall away on Saturday afternoons and Sundays. Lisbon has a famous tram system with vintage cars climbing the steep streets of the city centre. Lisbon and Porto also have a metro. Portugal loves cable cars – using them can save you a lot of walking but they are expensive relative to the rest of the public transport system.

Taxi & Rideshare Services

• Taxis offer fair value over short distances, and are plentiful in large towns and cities. Ordinary taxis are usually marked with an 'A' (which stands for *aluguer*, for hire) on the door, number plate or elsewhere. They use meters and are available on the street and at taxi ranks, or by telephone for a surcharge of €0.80.

° The fare on weekdays during daylight hours is about €3.25 *bandeirada* (flag fall) plus around €0.80 per kilometre and a bit more for periods spent idling in traffic. A fare of €6 will usually get you across bigger towns. It's best to insist on the meter, although it's possible to negotiate a flat fare. If you have a sizeable load of luggage you'll pay a further €1.60.

° Rates are about 20% higher at night (9pm to 6am) and on weekends and holidays. Once a taxi leaves the city limits you also pay a surcharge or higher rate.

° In larger cities, including Lisbon and Porto, meterless taxis marked with a T (for *turismo*) can be hired from private companies for excursions. Rates for these are higher but standardised; drivers are honest and polite, and speak foreign languages.

° Uber is available in Lisbon and Porto.

Train

Portugal has an extensive railroad network, making for a scenic way of travelling between destinations; see the Comboios de Portugal website, www.cp.pt.

Discounts

° Children aged under five travel free; those aged five to 12 go for half price.

° A youth card issued by Euro26 member countries gets you a 20% discount on *regional* and *interregional* services on any day. For distances above 100km, you can also get a 20% discount on *intercidade* (express) services and a 10% discount on Alfa Pendular (AP) trains – though the latter applies only from Tuesday to Thursday.

° Travellers aged 65 and over can get 50% off any service by showing some ID.

Information & Reservations

° You can get hold of timetable and fare information at all stations and from www.cp.pt.

° You can book *intercidade* and Alfa Pendular tickets up to 30 days ahead, though you'll have little trouble booking for the next or even the same day. Other services can only be booked 24 hours in advance.

° A seat reservation is mandatory on most *intercidade* and Alfa trains; the booking fee is included in the price.

Train Passes

The One Country Portugal Pass from InterRail (www.interrail.eu) gives you unlimited travel on any three, four, six or eight days over a month (2nd class costs €78/95/125/148; 1st class costs about 35% more). It's available to all travellers who hail from outside of Portugal and can be purchased from many travel agents in Portugal or in advance from the website.

Types & Classes of Service

There are four main types of long-distance service. Note that international services are marked IN on timetables.

Regional (R) Slow, stop everywhere.

Interregional (IR) Reasonably fast.

Intercidade (IC) *Rápido* or express trains.

Alfa Pendular Deluxe This service is marginally faster than express and much pricier.

Only the Faro–Porto Comboio Azul and international trains such as Sud-Expresso and Talgo Lusitânia have restaurant cars, though all IC and Alfa trains have aisle service and most have bars.

Lisbon and Porto have their own *urbano* (suburban) train networks. Lisbon's network extends to Sintra, Cascais and Setúbal, and up the lower Tejo valley. Porto's network takes the definition of 'suburban' to new lengths, running all the way to Braga, Guimarães and Aveiro. *Urbano* services also travel between Coimbra and Figueira da Foz. The distinction matters where long-distance services parallel the more convenient, plentiful and considerably cheaper *urbanos*.

Language

Portuguese pronunciation is not difficult because most sounds are also found in English. The exceptions are the nasal vowels (represented in our pronunciation guides by 'ng' after the vowel), which are pronounced as if you're trying to make the sound through your nose; and the strongly rolled 'r' (represented by 'rr' in our pronunciation guides). Also note that the symbol 'zh' sounds like the 's' in 'pleasure'. The stress generally falls on the second-last syllable of a word. In our pronunciation guides stressed syllables are indicated with italics. Portuguese has masculine and feminine forms of nouns and adjectives. Both forms are given where necessary, indicated with 'm' and 'f' respectively.

To enhance your trip with a phrasebook, visit **lonelyplanet.com**.

Basics

Hello.
Olá.   o·*laa*

Goodbye.
Adeus.   a·de·*oosh*

How are you?
Como está?   *ko*·moo shtaa

Fine, and you?
Bem, e você?   beng e vo·*se*

Yes.
Sim.   seeng

No.
Não.   nowng

Please.
Por favor.   poor fa·*vor*

Thank you.
Obrigado.   o·bree·*gaa*·doo (m)
Obrigada.   o·bree·*gaa*·da (f)

You're welcome.
De nada.   de *naa*·da

Excuse me.
Faz favor.   faash fa·*vor*

Sorry.
Desculpe.   desh·*kool*·pe

Do you speak English?
Fala inglês?   *faa*·la eeng·*glesh*

I don't understand.
Não entendo.   nowng eng·*teng*·doo

Accommodation

Do you have a single/double room?
Tem um quarto de   teng oong *kwaar*·too de
solteiro/casal?   sol·*tay*·roo/ka·*zal*

How much is it per night/person?
Quanto custa   *kwang*·too *koosh*·ta
por noite/pessoa?   poor *noy*·te/pe·*so*·a

Eating

What would you recommend?
O que é que   oo ke e ke
recomenda?   rre·koo·*meng*·da

I don't eat ...
Eu não como ...   e·oo nowng *ko*·moo ...
   meat   *carne*   *kar*·ne
   chicken   *frango*   *frang*·goo
   fish   *peixe*   *pay*·she

Bring the bill/check, please.
Pode-me trazer   po·de·me tra·*zer*
a conta.   a *kong*·ta

Emergencies

Help!
Socorro!   soo·*ko*·rroo

Go away!
Vá-se embora!   *vaa*·se eng·*bo*·ra

Call ...!
Chame ...!   *shaa*·me ...
   a doctor   *um médico* oong me·dee·koo
   the police *a polícia* a poo·lee·sya

I'm lost.
Estou perdido.   shtoh per·*dee*·doo (m)
Estou perdida.   shtoh per·*dee*·da (f)

I'm ill.
Estou doente.   shtoh doo·*eng*·te

Directions

Where's (the station)?
Onde é (a estação)?   ong·de e (a shta·*sowng*)

What's the address?
Qual é o endereço?   kwaal e oo eng·de·*re*·soo

Can you show me (on the map)?
Pode-me mostrar   po·de·me moosh·*traar*
(no mapa)?   (noo *maa*·pa)

Behind the Scenes

Acknowledgements

Climate map data adapted from Peel MC, Finlayson BL & McMahon TA (2007) 'Updated World Map of the Köppen-Geiger Climate Classification', *Hydrology and Earth System Sciences*, 11, 163344.

This Book

This guidebook was curated by Marc Di Duca, who also researched and wrote it, along with Kate Armstrong, Kerry Christiani, Anja Mutić, Kevin Raub and Regis St Louis.

This guidebook was produced by the following:

Destination Editor Tom Stainer

Product Editor Anne Mason

Senior Cartographer Anthony Phelan

Book Designer Lauren Egan

Cartographer Julie Dodkins

Assisting Editors Imogen Bannister, Carolyn Boicos, Kate Chapman, Katie Connolly, Vic Harrison, Kate James, Susan Paterson, Tracy Whitmey

Cover Researcher Naomi Parker

Thanks to Cam Ashley, Brendan Dempsey-Spencer, Liz Heynes, Kat Marsh, Clara Monitto, Jess Rose, Wibowo Rusli

Send Us Your Feedback

We love to hear from travellers – your comments keep us on our toes and help make our books better. Our well-travelled team reads every word on what you loved or loathed about this book. Although we cannot reply individually to postal submissions, we always guarantee that your feedback goes straight to the appropriate authors, in time for the next edition. Each person who sends us information is thanked in the next edition, the most useful submissions are rewarded with a selection of digital PDF chapters.

Visit lonelyplanet.com/contact to submit your updates and suggestions or to ask for help. Our award-winning website also features inspirational travel stories, news and discussions.

Note: We may edit, reproduce and incorporate your comments in Lonely Planet products such as guidebooks, websites and digital products, so let us know if you don't want your comments reproduced or your name acknowledged. For a copy of our privacy policy visit lonelyplanet.com/privacy.

A – Z
Index

Symbols & Map Key

Look for these symbols to quickly identify listings:

- ◉ Sights
- ✪ Activities
- ✿ Courses
- ✪ Tours
- ✿ Festivals & Events
- ✪ Eating
- ☺ Drinking
- ✪ Entertainment
- ✪ Shopping
- ❶ Information & Transport

These symbols and abbreviations give vital information for each listing:

- 🌿 Sustainable or green recommendation
- **FREE** No payment required

- ☎ Telephone number
- ⏱ Opening hours
- Ⓟ Parking
- ⊘ Nonsmoking
- ❄ Air-conditioning
- @ Internet access
- 🛜 Wi-fi access
- ⛑ Swimming pool
- 🚌 Bus
- ⛴ Ferry
- 🚊 Tram
- 🚆 Train
- 📖 English-language menu
- 🍴 Vegetarian selection
- 👪 Family-friendly

Find your best experiences with these Great For... icons.

 Budget
 Short Trip

 Food & Drink
Detour

 Drinking
 Walking

Cycling
 Local Life

 Shopping
History

 Sport
Entertainment

 Art & Culture
 Beaches

 Events
 Winter Travel

Photo Op
 Cafe/Coffee

Scenery
 Nature & Wildlife

 Family Travel

Sights

- Beach
- Bird Sanctuary
- Buddhist
- Castle/Palace
- Christian
- Confucian
- Hindu
- Islamic
- Jain
- Jewish
- Monument
- Museum/Gallery/ Historic Building
- Ruin
- Shinto
- Sikh
- Taoist
- Winery/Vineyard
- Zoo/Wildlife Sanctuary
- Other Sight

Points of Interest

- Bodysurfing
- Camping
- Cafe
- Canoeing/Kayaking
- Course/Tour
- Diving
- Drinking & Nightlife
- Eating
- Entertainment
- Sento Hot Baths/ Onsen
- Shopping
- Skiing
- Sleeping
- Snorkelling
- Surfing
- Swimming/Pool
- Walking
- Windsurfing
- Other Activity

Information

- Bank
- Embassy/Consulate
- Hospital/Medical
- Internet
- Police
- Post Office
- Telephone
- Toilet
- Tourist Information
- Other Information

Geographic

- Beach
- Gate
- Hut/Shelter
- Lighthouse
- Lookout
- Mountain/Volcano
- Oasis
- Park
- Pass
- Picnic Area
- Waterfall

Transport

- Airport
- BART station
- Border crossing
- Boston T station
- Bus
- Cable car/Funicular
- Cycling
- Ferry
- Metro/MRT station
- Monorail
- Parking
- Petrol station
- Subway/S-Bahn/ Skytrain station
- Taxi
- Train station/Railway
- Tram
- Tube Station
- Underground/ U-Bahn station
- Other Transport

Anja Mutić

Born and raised in Zagreb, Croatia, Anja has travelled the globe as a professional wanderer for decades. Her travel writing career has taken her to 60+ countries, taught her several languages (she is fluent in Croatian, English, Spanish and can get by with Portuguese) and won her articles several awards. She has lived, worked and travelled on all the continents (except Antarctica), which included 'mini lives' (stints of several months) in Buenos Aires and Lisbon. Anja's writing has been published in print and online publications such as *The Washington Post*, *New York Magazine*, *National Geographic Traveler*, *AFAR* and *BBC Travel*. Follow her on Instagram @everthenomad.

Kevin Raub

Atlanta native Kevin Raub started his career as a music journalist in New York, working for *Men's Journal* and *Rolling Stone* magazines. He ditched the rock 'n' roll lifestyle for travel writing and has written more than 40 Lonely Planet guides, focused mainly on Brazil, Chile, Colombia, USA, India, the Caribbean and Portugal. Kevin also contributes to a variety of travel magazines in both the USA and UK. Along the way, the self-confessed hophead is in constant search of wildly high IBUs in local beers. Follow him on Twitter and Instagram (@ RaubOnTheRoad).

Regis St Louis

Regis grew up in a small town in the American Midwest—the kind of place that fuels big dreams of travel—and he developed an early fascination with foreign dialects and world cultures. He spent his formative years learning Russian and a handful of Romance languages, which served him well on journeys across much of the globe. Regis has contributed to more than 50 Lonely Planet titles, covering destinations across six continents. His travels have taken him from the mountains of Kamchatka to remote island villages in Melanesia, and to many grand urban landscapes. When not on the road, he lives in New Orleans.

Our Story

A beat-up old car, a few dollars in the pocket and a sense of adventure. In 1972 that's all Tony and Maureen Wheeler needed for the trip of a lifetime – across Europe and Asia overland to Australia. It took several months, and at the end – broke but inspired – they sat at their kitchen table writing and stapling together their first travel guide, *Across Asia on the Cheap*. Within a week they'd sold 1500 copies. Lonely Planet was born. Today, Lonely Planet has offices in Franklin, London, Melbourne, Oakland, Dublin, Beijing, and Delhi, with more than 600 staff and writers. We share Tony's belief that 'a great guidebook should do three things: inform, educate and amuse'.

Our Writers

Marc Di Duca

A travel author for the last decade, Marc has worked for Lonely Planet in Siberia, Slovakia, Bavaria, England, Ukraine, Austria, Poland, Croatia, Portugal, Madeira and on the Trans-Siberian Railway, as well as writing and updating tens of other guides for other publishers. When not on the road, Marc lives between Sandwich, Kent and Mariánské Lázně in the Czech Republic with his wife and two sons.

Kate Armstrong

Kate Armstrong has spent much of her adult life travelling and living around the world. A full-time freelance travel journalist, she has contributed to around 40 Lonely Planet guides and trade publications and is regularly published in Australian and worldwide publications. She is the author of several books and children's educational titles. Over the years, Kate has worked in Mozambique, picked grapes in France and danced in a Bolivian folkloric troupe. You can read more about her on www.katearmstrongtravelwriter.com and @nomaditis.

Kerry Christiani

Kerry is an award-winning travel writer, photographer and Lonely Planet author, specialising in central and southern Europe. Based in Wales, she has authored/co-authored more than a dozen Lonely Planet titles. An adventure addict, she loves mountains, cold places and true wilderness. She features her latest work at https://its-a-small-world.com and tweets @kerrychristiani.

More Writers

STAY IN TOUCH
lonelyplanet.com/contact

AUSTRALIA Levels 2 & 3, 551 Swanston St, Carlton, Victoria 3053
☎ 03 8379 8000,
fax 03 8379 8111

USA 150 Linden Street, Oakland, CA 94607
☎ 510 250 6400,
toll free 800 275 8555,
fax 510 893 8572

UK 240 Blackfriars Road, London SE1 8NW
☎ 020 3771 5100,
fax 020 3771 5101

 twitter.com/ lonelyplanet

 facebook.com/ lonelyplanet

 instagram.com/ lonelyplanet

 youtube.com/ lonelyplanet

 lonelyplanet.com/ newsletter